Spangles, Glam,
Gaywaves & Tubes

Spangles, Glam, Gaywaves & Tubes

An autobiography

Gary James

The Book Guild Ltd

First published in Great Britain in 2019 by
The Book Guild Ltd
9 Priory Business Park
Wistow Road, Kibworth
Leicestershire, LE8 0RX
Freephone: 0800 999 2982
www.bookguild.co.uk
Email: info@bookguild.co.uk
Twitter: @bookguild

Typeset in Adobe Garamond

Printed and bound in Great Britain by CPI Group (UK) Ltd, Croydon, CR0 4YY

ISBN 978 1912575 817

British Library Cataloguing in Publication Data.
A catalogue record for this book is available from the British Library.

MIX
Paper from
responsible sources
FSC® C013604

For Phil

Bits of the book

	Overture	ix
1	Elemental Child – 1958 to 1969	1
2	Get It On & School's Out – 1969 to 1975	23
3	Young Hearts Run Free & I Feel Love – 1975 to 1980	52
4	Smalltown Boy – 1980 to 1982	91
5	The Tubes – 1982 to 1985	105
6	New York, Sydney & Neasden – 1985 onwards	183
	Acknowledgements	197
	About the Author	198

Overture

Do you know what? I wasn't going to write an opening bit to this book at all. But when I finished writing it at the beginning of June 2018 I was faced with the task of giving the bloody thing a title; something that would enthrall and grab the prospective reader and drag them in like Pennywise the clown through a storm drain. But could I think of one? Could I buggery. All the suggestions I came up with referred only to 'The Tube' in some way, because after all that's the only reason most of you will have picked this up? Eh? Be honest. Hey, but that's OK, I get that. You want to read all about the inside story of the most influential TV music show of the 1980s; what went on behind the scenes? What Paula Yates was really like? What Simon Le Bon used to stuff down the front of his jeans before a show? What the Weather Girls thought about Michael Jackson's willy? Why Eartha Kitt looked drunk when miming to 'I Love Men?' Why Divine never got to beat me up on screen? Why Mickey Finn of T.Rex almost failed to appear on the show and what Ringo Starr let me play with at his house? All that type of affair…

And yet, there's so much more to my story than that. This story is also for those of us who grew up as children in the 1960s, the decade when everything changed from black and white to colour, when sweets were Spangles, Flying Saucers, Bazooka Joes and Sherbert Dip-Dabs; for those of us who became teenagers in the 1970s through the Glam and glitter of Bolan, Bowie & Slade to the throbbing beats of Punk and Disco. It's a story driven by a time when music and fashion changed society, moved it on and enraged the establishment.

It is also a story of growing up gay at a time when we were instantly criminals just for existing as such; of how we fought that system using music and fashion to shape a new subculture. How we communicated and promoted in the age before mass media, social networking and where the status quo ruled everything with an oppressive iron fist of ignorance and bigotry, and of how we took that and threw it back in their faces with the first radio broadcasts in history to be made by and for gay people. Whilst the same old famous names always grab the headlines through this time it's also about the people who did amazing, astonishing things who history might have forgotten.

This story spreads through radio and television via groundbreaking theatre productions which so enraged the press that they invented lies and misdirection to try and stop it.

In all cases they failed.

We triumphed.

And after all of that, when our world had to deal with a new threat to our very lives through the early 1980s, the music didn't die. And nor did the fun, contrary to what many will have you believe.

So you see, this was a real toughie. The Spangles led to the Glam, the Gaywaves and The Tube. I know it's a bloody mouthful and that it rolls off the tongue like a brick, but it's much more than just a biog of a TV show. I hope it will make you laugh and maybe even raise an eyebrow or two Roger Moore-style. Don't expect a tough read; I write as I think and speak. This is no work of literary genius; Joan Bakewell and Melvyn Bragg will hate it.

Above all enjoy it. I did and I wrote it.

Love and Peace
Gary
June 10th 2018

1

Elemental Child – 1958 to 1969

When most people think of Royal Tunbridge Wells they'll no doubt conjure up images of the sort of England that only really exists in Agatha Christie novels. A world of half-timbered buildings and cars, cream teas and elegant socialites dressed in Norman Hartnell frocks 'taking the waters' at the Chalybeate Spring at the end of the Georgian arcade called 'The Pantiles', and which gives the town its Spa status. Hey, not only that but even local residents benefitted from the properties of this amazing, iron-rich local water supply. I know this because my mum told me; so it has to be true. When turning on the taps in our house the water always ran a dirty orange colour for a short while. 'Make sure you run that bath tap for a few minutes first,' she'd yell up the stairs as what shot out of the faucet looked like condemned Tizer. This water was hard. So hard it came out with lumps in it. It was the Arthur Mullard of Aqua. I like to think it made us Tunbridge Wellians what we are today: tough, critical and just ever so slightly orange.

Sadly the spring, which had been trickling its weird metallic-tasting natural water for over five hundred years, dried up a few years ago when workmen starting sodding about building a new basement area in a nearby hotel. Therefore for a while the town was probably breaking the Trade Descriptions Act by claiming to be a Spa when what was left of it was no more than a dried-up, orange-tinted hole in the ground full of dog ends and empty crisp packets. Weirdly, and very suddenly, the spring recently started gushing crystal clear water of a clarity the original never had and at a phenomenal flow rate completely at odds with its former trickle. I suspect that in a panic the town council simply connected it up to the mains and turned on a tap somewhere in the town hall. It all seems most underhand, and just the sort of mystery that Enid Blyton's Famous Five should investigate.

The rest of the town has stayed doggedly lodged in a sort of post-war stupor. Its stuffiness was perpetuated by its stagnant political affinity with the Conservative Party and a popular media image of its population being disgusted by almost everything; which if you read the letters page of the local paper it is apparent that they most definitely do.

I'm only droning on about this because Tunbridge Wells is my home town. I was born there in the hot summer of 1958 and awarded three names, Gary Edward James. My hard-up parents lived in a flat above an electrical shop in a small community to the east of the main town. Trust me, the Wells may have its elite, refined and wealthy status, illustrated by the huge houses of Mount Ephraim, Hungershall Park and Forest Road, but it also has what I call its service area.

Travel further east towards its crappier neighbour Tonbridge and you'll happen upon High Brooms, Sherwood and Southborough. High Brooms is famous for its gas and brick works. It is made up of working class houses and estates scattered up and down steep hills exclusively designed to give local youths the perfect bike and scooter runs and the elderly a heart attack trying to navigate up them with heavy shopping. Like most British towns in the 1950s it had a vibrant local economy serviced by small shops and businesses. One such location, which still exists today, is a glorious row of Victorian brick-built shops in Silverdale Road. This was my home for the first years of my life and a place that has stuck in my psyche ever since.

Being the 1950s of course everything was in black and white; nobody could afford anything in colour where we lived. The weather always seemed to be extremes of everything; either baking hot, torrential rain, thick fog or deep snow. The winter of 1962–63 in particular sticks in my mind as it seemed to go for forever. To a five-year-old boy it was utterly magical. My friend Robert and I made slides down the nearby hill which gave our shoes an almost magical amount of skiddage. We built snowmen taller than the Empire State Building and lobbed snowballs the size of cannonballs at anything or anyone who had the temerity to invade the twitten* (*local Kent/Sussex term for a narrow path or thoroughfare between houses) which was our territory and of paramount national security interest. Probably.

Silverdale Road had a fabulous array of shops and was a community all of its own. I loved it. There was a Post Office at one end, then electrical shop, hardware store, sweetshop, newsagent's, hairdresser's, greengrocer, fish shop, butcher's, barber's, shoe repairer, bakery and then a rather odd mini-mart at the far end with a phone box outside it. The pavements were wide and made completely of the familiar red bricks made at the local brickworks. Brick pavements could be found all over the town and their unevenness was a major cause of injury to the elderly and/or pissed staggering out of the pubs after closing time onto streets where the lights went off at 11pm. This being 1950s Britain meant the post-pub closing time darkness had the intensity of deep space, where Fireball XL5 went.

My mum and dad both came from south-east London; my mum from Welling and my dad from Bexleyheath. My maternal grandmother was the link to Tunbridge Wells, although I never found out why my mum and dad decided to move out of London to there, especially since there would have been far better job opportunities in the city (and certainly much more to do entertainment wise). But move they did to a tiny rented flat above the electrical shop at 159a Silverdale Road. The shop was run by a thin, well-spoken man called Keith. He wore little wire-rimmed glasses and had a smiley and happy disposition as he wandered amongst his radios, record players and television sets. He was almost a Richard Attenborough film character, though to the best of my knowledge he never murdered anyone or went down on a ship with any. In a small corner of the shop there was a listening booth for the records he sold. I loved being in there, taking great lung bucketfuls of the weird electrical aroma of glowing warm valves such places had. He would pick me up and plonk me on a high stool in the listening booth and play me Connie Francis discs on the beautiful bright yellow MGM label. I'm convinced it was this that kicked off my lifelong love of music and vinyl records, which are my obsession to this day.

The local school was St. Luke's situated just a few yards away and where I would eventually develop my thirst for books and acting. But more of that later. For now, I was still under two years old and still in black and white. At the time I was born my dad had a job at a local Rowntrees chocolate factory. It was great that he would bring home bags of chocolate misshapes but less great that on my birth certificate under 'Father's Occupation' it says 'Machine Man in Chocolate Biscuit Factory'. Hardly the stuff of Royal Tunbridge Wells is it?

I was lucky to have fantastic parents; my mum was beautiful and very tough, whilst my dad was kind, creative and bursting with imagination. Sadly, the two of them didn't really get on. They rowed and argued frequently and with a ferocity that I found distressing to witness. They were just not meant to be together and though they soldiered on for a wee while it inevitably began to crumble and in the next chapter my dad eventually moved out.

It's amusing to me that the number one song in the hit parade at the time I was born was 'Who's Sorry Now?' By Connie Francis (I know this because it was one of the records that Keith used to play in the shop downstairs). In later years (much later) I'd frequently hear this record being mimed to by ropey drag acts looking over their shoulders whilst pulling grotesque faces to heighten the comic effect of a heavy pregnancy (with a cushion). The biggest laugh always coming when she mouths 'You've had your way, now you must pay'. Somehow, I doubt Connie Francis had this in mind as she warbled into her microphone in early October 1957; even less so that this was probably around the time I was conceived. I don't think either of my parents were sorry though as I was loved and looked after always. Being the first born (and actually within that marriage the only born) also gave me the benefit of especially doting grandparents. I was the golden child. My maternal grandparents became especially close and I was happier spending time with them in their house in Welling, South London more than anywhere. It's good to be doted upon.

People say all babies are beautiful, though to me they all look the same: ugly. In my case though Mum told me that when I was born the midwife told her I was the most beautiful baby she'd ever seen. Goodness me she was right. I was a bouncing round-faced happy smiling cherub with the biggest brown eyes and soft dark hair. Well, I'm not going to sit here and tell you I was pug ugly am I? I might be now, yes, but sixty years ago I was gorgeous. You'll just have to take my word for it. Everyone in my family had dark brown eyes – even though we all existed in shades of grey until 1967 when everything finally burst into colour.

Although I popped out in the local maternity hospital, my brothers and sister were born at home. The local midwife, Sister Chapman, rather unfortunately (for her) reminded me of the witch from the Wizard of Oz as she cruised around the neighbourhood on her bicycle with a basket on the front. A strange science lab antiseptic type of smell used to accompany her visits, shortly followed by another baby. I don't ever recall my father (or subsequently stepfather) being there. She was so fierce that the entire area would be cleared out in advance of any woman giving birth, including fathers. Men obviously had no place at birthings in those days. When my youngest brother was born I remember making the mistake of walking into my mum's bedroom whilst she was in the advanced stages of labour and being ordered out in a manner resembling a North Korean treason trial. I'm assured that actually she was a kind and deeply committed midwife who had the utmost respect from all of the women in her care. 'She really loved all of you,' my mother assured me when we spoke about this years later. Despite this I was still glad we didn't have a dog for her to snatch, although I wouldn't have wished a house to have fallen on her. Round our way everything was built of brick and would have been more than a match for any witch.

You know it's not true that Northerners have a monopoly on monochrome streets, tiny backyards and grubby kids. We had that even in the Royal town. The row of shops where we lived all had small concreted rear yards linked by an access path at the rear which we referred to as 'out the back'. My closest friend Robert's parents ran the greengrocer's a few doors up from us. Robert and I spent our entire early childhood playing out the back and putting on shows in their garage, which led off of it. I can't imagine why they had a garage as the access path was barely wide enough for my sister's pram let alone a car. But who cares? It was big enough to put on a show and that was all that mattered. Our shows were legendary in the area too. Well, within a radius of about 100 yards of the shops and amongst kids under the age of 6 they were. Of course, I was the star (I'd decided). Robert had a wind-up gramophone and some 78s his aunt had given him. For some odd reason I recall dancing to a recording of 'Buttons & Bows' to a bemused audience of about 12 rather snotty kids who we'd conned into paying a penny to get in. With the proceeds Robert and I would go round to Carrie's newsagent's and purchase boxes of flare matches. These lethal items, when struck, would burn either brilliant green or a sort of purple colour. But what young yobbo wants to simply strike a match? No, no, we desired something far more impressive. Robert would purloin a potato from his parents' shop and we would stick large numbers of these flares into it until it resembled a sort of explosive hedgehog. To crown it all we'd stick in a couple of sparklers to fashion a sort of rigid fuse. With great excitement we'd light them and watch the weapon of mass destruction burn down until it reached the tip of the first flare match. With a great waft of phosphorescent smoke the entire concoction would explode lighting up the backyard and our enraptured little faces.

The very thought of anyone doing this these days, barring ISIS trainees, is horrifying. But then let's be honest, even adults back then had little apparent concept of health and safety. Bonfire Night would see virtually every house setting fire to towering heaps of wooden boxes, washing on lines, trees, shrubs and occasionally each other's houses in celebration of Guy Fawkes and his failed gunpowder plot. With fireworks being sold in large cardboard boxes which would routinely explode into premature life on receipt of an errant spark it seems to me that we could have given Guy Fawkes a run for his money. Some of the explosives sold openly at the time seem positively terrifying by today's standards. Surely the worst of these were fireworks called 'Jumping Jacks'. These consisted of a tube of something lethal scrunched up into a sort of concertina and held together with thin twine. After lighting the blue fuse paper it would fizzle into life and leap about with a loud bang every time a section of twine burnt through. How we laughed and screamed as this explosive object hurtled about with abandon into the crowds of enthralled onlookers. I imagine hospitals being crammed full of burns victims as a result of these extraordinary devices, yet somehow it all seemed a perfectly acceptable form of celebratory entertainment at the time.

Bonfire Night was second only to Christmas as far as we were concerned. The air would be so full of smoke by the end of the evening that even as the last Catherine Wheel set fire to the last fence surviving we would have no idea that we were probably inhaling enough chemicals to rival a 60-a-day heavy smoker; not to mention the environmental damage we were inflicting upon the planet. If it was foggy, which it frequently is at that time of year in the UK, the combination of mist, smoke from coal fires, cordite from explosives and cars spewing out leaded petrol exhaust was surely enough to have sent us all to an early grave. Yet, this was our entertainment. Mass public firework displays organised to keep excited children a safe distance away from the conflagrations were unheard of. Who needs that when you can explode weapons of mass destruction in your own backyard? Every Bonfire Night could be like the opening sequence to ITV's *Sunday Night At the London Palladium*.

As children of the late 50s and 60s the main entertainment was still outside and cathode ray tube addiction was reserved to little more than ninety minutes a day. This was mainly because there was so little stuff being broadcast for kids that it was far more interesting to us to go out and put on shows, break the sound barrier on a scooter and make backyard bomb devices than to sit and watch the TV.

Watch With Mother was required viewing, especially Bill & Ben (the flowerpot men heroes of every small boy of the time) and Rag, Tag & Bobtail, the rather deranged hand puppets who appeared to live in a velvet woodland swamp and none of whom apparently had any feet. This was a lunchtime programme and usually followed, rather inexplicably it seems upon reflection, by programmes for the Welsh or the deaf. The test card would then show until around 4.30pm from whence we'd get an hour or so of stuff for kids before the news, tedious documentaries about the war and then Coronation Street. Me and Robert had no time for any of that nonsense until they started showing something called Space Patrol. This early black and white (as was everything then remember) science fiction puppet series filled us with wonder and excitement, even though the robots who strutted about rather jerkily utterly terrified me. It was the same with the robot in Fireball XL5. For some reason these mechanical men reached a part of my developing psyche that resulted in nightmares and waking visions which haunt me to this day.

I was rather a strange little boy to be honest. I had vivid waking dreams, strange detached feelings of retracting vision which manifested itself like a camera tracking shot. This is very hard to describe, but I'll have a go; imagine sitting in a chair and then feeling yourself moving backwards and everything around you moving away into the distance. No? Well, it was like that. I had strange recurring dreams, many of which were deeply unsettling and frightened me to the point where I was scared to fall asleep. Two of them come to mind readily, although I haven't had them now in years. In the first I am in a long, grey, bare featureless room. In front of me is a door. I walk forward, open it and walk through. I then fall and fall through darkness until I land with a soft thump into the same room I have just left. The whole nightmare then repeats – over and over again until I wake up. The second dream is bizarre. It isn't of anything at all except texture (bear with me here, this is as difficult for me to describe as it will be for you to get what I'm on about). I visualise a rough, coarse unpleasant texture and it is as if my mind is forced to brush and scrape against it until eventually it smooths out to a soft and smooth sensation. The images are in stark black and white; imagine white noise on an old badly tuned TV set, which then starts to gradually tune into a plain screen. This dream frightened me more than any of the others. That fear is still with me even as I approach 60 years of age, so powerful was its effect.

I did also have nice dreams though. I'm not completely hatstand you know. I had a dream friend who was a flying elf. We would soar around the brick paved streets of Royal Tunbridge Wells, swooping down through the trees, parks and alleyways and then perching ourselves on the chimneystacks to recover before taking off again. I do wish I could remember his name. I'd so like him to visit me again, take me by the hand and fly with me. But alas, like Peter Pan I fear he only visits the young; although I have never lost my belief that he was and still is utterly real. Coupled with all this weirdness, was a sensation of being able to levitate and walk above the ground at will. No idea where that came from or why. I think I can still do it, at least I feel I ought to be able to and yet for some reason I don't. It would be most handy and save me a lot of money on season tickets if only I could muster the ability again and put it to some practical use?

I can sense some of you now wanting to back away. Don't be concerned. I really was a beautiful little boy. Polite, well spoken and happy. I just did strange things that's all. What's wrong with that? My parents were indulgent of all this for reasons I can't fathom. I used to like getting reels of cotton and creating huge, elaborate webs in the living room by winding it round every object I could find until the whole room was like a scene from a Bond movie bank vault filled with laser alarm traps. I can't recall how this was all disassembled or either parent acknowledging it. One thing was important to me though and that was that they both protected me against ghosts. I loved snuggling up to them in their bed – with me in the middle and then sitting up and shouting to the spectres that were everywhere in the flat, 'You can't get me, my mum and dad are here!', before burying myself deep under the warm, safe bedclothes next to my mum and dad.

Thinking back I almost feel this was my happiest ever childhood memory. My parents were growing apart fast and within a couple of years would split for good. But I loved them both dearly, especially my dad; I utterly worshipped him. He was a kind, gentle and imaginative man, where my mum was loving, strong and forthright. I can easily see which parts of me are from what parent, like most people can I guess. I'm proud of having my father's creativity and kind-heartedness, and my mother's strength, resolve and temper.

I was lucky enough to live just a few yards from St Luke's C of E Infants school, a pretty little Victorian brick edifice with a tarmac playground and iron railings facing the street. We had no playing fields or other greenery, but it didn't matter to us. In our minds we could create whatever landscape we wanted in our heads and act them out between the painted tramlines of the school playground. At playtime small groups would stomp around shouting, 'Who wants to play *whatever it was we wanted to play*?' Most popular with the boys was undoubtedly 'Who wants to play WAR?' It was easy to gather a posse with that cry, slightly less so with my one: 'Who wants to play TRAINS?' I'd become obsessed with trains after my dad took me for trips out on them whenever he could (though I suspect much of this was motivated by a desire to get away from spending time in the flat arguing with my mother). When I'd gathered enough followers to pretend to be carriages in my imaginary train, I would extend both hands forward and flat to create buffers and then we'd run around in a strictly formed line, occasionally stopping at stations which I would proudly announce to the entire neighbourhood. I have no idea what the kids who followed behind me got out of it but I was the engine at the front and I thought it was bloody brilliant. So that's really all that mattered.

I am not quite sure how my parents managed to get me into St. Luke's school as neither I nor any of my brothers and sister were ever christened. None of my family on either side were churchgoers. Indeed my father's side were atheists to a person. I consider myself incredibly lucky that I grew up in a godless family. I firmly believe it was this that made my eventual coming out so relatively easy. I think the only time any of us ever went near a church was for weddings. But then being British these were curiously detached from nonsensical religious ravings. Our respective family sides gathered, sang and went along with all the other bollocks without any spiritual relationship to any of it. I'm so proud of their stance to this repulsive death cult (you'll have gathered by now that I'm not a fan).

Though I was not encouraged by my parents to believe in any of the C of E nonsense, I am convinced I would have come to the same conclusion pretty rapidly regardless. One incident at this school having been my proverbial conversion on the way out of Damascus, so to speak. My bestest friend was the daughter of one of my mother's bestest friends, June. Her name was Jackie (and happily it still is). More of June in a moment, but for this story place yourself looking into the school assembly. About sixty to seventy little boys and girls all sitting in neat lines, dressed in their sweet navy blue and grey uniforms awaiting the arrival of the Reverend White of the school's parent church up the road. He used to rock up once a week to lecture to us about how fantastic it was going to be after we were dead, along with a few daft stories about donkeys, execution and being nice to old ladies. Jackie was, and indeed still is, the funniest person I have ever met. Nobody can make me laugh quite like she does. She possesses a gift for language and situation in truly beautiful expression. She can take a corny gag and make the punchline a catalyst for helpless laughter. I'll relay one of her better jokes later – bear with me, you'll love it. On this fateful day she had been making me laugh as usual and I had become fairly incapacitated for a 5-year-old. The Reverend White sweeping in majestically in his robes became a trigger I could not control. He looked and sounded ridiculous and Jackie's whispered comments only made it worse. I duly collapsed into fits of laughter and we were both unceremoniously yanked out of the assembly and told to wait in the headmistress's office. The headmistress of St Luke's was a ghastly old bag called Miss Cork. She had the warmth and generosity of a Dickensian workhouse matron. We were all terrified of her. Jackie and I were duly rebuked and caned on our hands for daring to 'laugh at the vicar'. When I went home and told my mother what happened she marched up to the school, demanded to see Cork immediately and then told her that if she ever touched one of her children again she would come back and do the same to her. At least that's the story I have chosen to believe all these years. It seems plausible to me. I'm fairly sure that's what I was told happened many years later when we were reminiscing.

Happily the rest of my school days there were idyllic. I loved learning, my other teachers were superb and loved by us all. My favourite was my second year teacher Miss McGill. She looked just like Julie Andrews in Mary Poppins and I'm convinced she was magical and lived on a cloud in the sky. One Christmas we put on a school pantomime *Cinderella* in which I was cast as one of the ugly sisters (how on earth did they know?). I became paranoid about learning my lines. So much so that I learned everybody's lines and got terribly muddled when faced with only having to say my own. When Dandini, or whoever it was, minces in with a fist full of invites to the Prince's ball I simply had to say, 'And one for me!'. To the frustration of our director I refused to stop at that line and carried on with everyone else's. It was my big moment and I wasn't going to stop at one measly line. I might only have been 5, but I was a star and not being shoved off as easily as all that. In my mind I have a picture of being dragged off stage by a shepherd's crook, no doubt appropriated from the year's nativity play (in which I seem to recall being a king for some reason). Learning lines has been the bane of my acting career ever since. I hate it. In order to learn mine I have to also to learn all the other parts around me. This doubles or even trebles the time it takes me to come 'off the book'. I've lost count of the number of times I've been rebuked for this, but I look upon it in a positive fashion. If anyone else dries or cocks up their lines I can usually be relied upon to get them out of it very quickly as I know their parts as well as they do. Now I'm old and cranky it's harder to learn than ever, but my method hasn't changed since those infant school days.

My first crushes were way back then too. I was hopelessly infatuated with Graham and Jonathan, my two fellow school friends. Jonathan and I were inseparable, even though I actually preferred the humour and wit of my female friends far more. I was on the same wavelength as them and that only grew as my loathing of sport and 'playing war' increased.

The long snowy winter of 1962/3 was a child's dream, especially in a town like Tunbridge Wells, which has steep hills and wonderfully slippery brick pavements. That winter seemed to go on forever. Despite the chaos the weather had brought to the country we had the time of our lives creating deadly slides that iced over and then got snowed on. Although there is no official council data available on the subject I suspect our pavement slides probably caused more broken bones than the snow would have if it had just been left freshly fallen. I've loved snow and cold ever since. I don't like hot weather very much. It's a much nicer sensation to get warm in front of a roaring fire than it is trying to fan yourself off in a heatwave. I feel. You see.

Talking of fires, of course high pressure was something of a bonus if you were trying to get one lit in a grate. My mother used to do that weird thing where you build the fire up with newspaper and kindling sticks, light it with a match and then hold a big sheet of newspaper over the front of the fireplace hole to force the flames to take and roar up the chimney. It sounds every bit as dangerous as it actually was, but women back then knew nothing of fear and this was what was done whether anyone else liked it or not. The newspaper used to glow and seemingly come alive as the fire roared into life upwards, sometimes catching poorly maintained chimneys alight in the process. Such fires were commonplace back then, although luckily my mum was a dab hand at the technique and thankfully ours never burnt the house down. On days with low air pressure it was a bugger though as the fire would keep going out no matter how long you held the newspaper in front of the hole or yelled encouraging expletives at it. Such occasions usually called for Zip firefighters to help develop the conflagration. They were whiteish, waxy blocks of indeterminate 'stuff' that smelled strongly of paraffin. It's a wonder that any of us survived those days with the amount of lethal chemicals hiding behind every cupboard and leaking from deformed tin cans. Next door to our terraced flat was a hardware shop that had an Esso Blue paraffin pump outside it on the pavement. People would come and fill jerry cans full of the stuff to put into scary-looking free-standing household heaters. These contraptions had a steampunk look to them which jarred horribly with the transition to modernity of the early 1960s. Usually black or dark grey in colour they looked like small Victorian free-standing nuclear weapons with a carrying handle on the top, and they stank. Paraffin smells bad enough as it is, but when burned in these heaters it gave off a noxious odour that probably asphyxiated millions. Thankfully for our household my mother hated the smell, which would infuse everything around it. You could tell if someone came from a household that used the things as their clothes would reek of it. We were a resolutely coal fire and electric bar heater type of a family. Much nicer smells if no less lethal.

Although my parents' marriage was in its death throes my childhood was about as happy as any child could have wished for. For all the kids in the street the greatest thrill was when the ice cream van drove up, its clunky amplified chimes announcing its arrival from miles away. Ours was made by an Italian man called Demashio (I think that's how it was spelt) and his black, blue and white striped vehicle was actually a converted 1930s Ford hearse. It had huge wheels with massive black mudguards and seemed to us to be at least 50 feet high. Queues of jostling children would form round the large glass covered serving hatch in the side. Mashie (as we called him) was a large, happy man with a striped apron, balding head and a huge bushy grey moustache. He made all the ice cream himself and served it from huge tubs with a sort of spatula. His confections weren't whirled into a cone like the modern operators did; Mashie smeared it and scraunched it into a sort of vanillary clump. It was heaven. We all adored him. He was the acceptable face of capitalism from our perspective. Unlike Mabel and Dolly who ran the sweetshop a few doors up from us. They were sisters straight from an Ealing film. Both rather stout and apparently stuck at the age of 70. I don't ever recall seeing them in their shop without their hats on. Always the same type too; Those odd looking round shaped pillowy things that most women wear to weddings thinking it makes them look glamorous when it actually makes them look like they're wearing a sleeping cat. They were both chain-smokers too. The air in the shop was heavy with sickly sweet face powder and fag smoke.

'Mabel's' was impossibly packed from floor to ceiling with sweet jars, shelves and sloping racks. Every spare inch of space was covered in something or other. All you could see from our angle of attack were their hats moving around in the air, closely followed by clouds of nicotine. Mabel was the nicer of the two with fractionally more patience than her sister. Dolly would be irritated by the time we took to select the Black Jack and Fruit Salad chews, Bazooka Joe bubblegum, sweet cigarettes, sherbet flying saucers and other glorious items which would ensure our milk teeth fell out well before they were supposed to. We couldn't reach the rearmost items on the huge wide sloping rack which faced the door and who knows what fabulous creations existed way back there? Impatient to get rid of us, which now strikes me as rather a strange concept for a shopkeeper, she'd say, 'Buck up love,' and encourage us to complete our transaction by offering tubes of Settlers indigestion tablets. What on earth they sold them for I cannot imagine, but they were cheap and tasted sort of sweet and minty so it seemed fair enough to us. I certainly never had heartburn as a child anyway. People from Royal Tunbridge Wells don't fart or burp of course; now you know why.

My best pal was Robert. His parents ran a greengrocer's shop five or six doors up from us. We were largely inseparable as children and played happily together building the miniature nuclear explosive devices I mentioned earlier. One big advantage of his parents having a shop that sold food was that we could bake cakes in the kitchen at the back of the shop with ingredients that his kindly mother Jane provided. Robert's dad suffered badly from migraines and would often be hidden away in a darkened room upstairs meaning we were forbidden to make any noise. Making cakes didn't involve making noise, just a mess. So that's what we did. We made cakes. Huge ones. Covered in buttercream and chocolate buttons. Zena Skinner and Fanny Cradock would've been proud of us.

In my house food was not exactly plentiful. My mother hated cooking and it showed. So any opportunity to eat elsewhere was to be encouraged. Robert's much older sister Janet didn't like me. She used to call me Gary Guts-ache, which may have been accurate but it wasn't very nice. Not that it bothered me as I didn't like her anyway. She was a always moaning and seemed to have issues with just about everything me and Robert did. Happily for us his mum was fantastic. They were a generous family too to all the children in the street. Every summer they'd use their fabric-covered lorry to take kids on days out to the seaside giving the other hard-up mums some respite. In the winter they'd use it to take us to the fair or the circus when it was in town. Fairs kept us supplied with goldfish in plastic bags, an essential ingredient to a happy home in the 1960s. Unfortunately for me my mum could not bear circuses as she thought it was cruel to animals. Those particular trips became off limits to me and to this day her love for animals and the respect for them she taught me has never subsided.

Robert and I stayed close friends right up until the mid 1970s when we sort of drifted apart like people do when they develop differing interests. I'm not sure Robert was that impressed the first time he saw me with spit-applied glitter under each eye after I'd seen The Sweet doing 'Blockbuster' on *Top Of The Pops*. It kind of accelerated the friendship drift.

My mum's three best friends back then were two Junes and a Vera. June One was Jackie's mum, June Two lived a few doors away with Welsh Vera across the road. Mum had always loved cats and consequently they have always ruled every house we ever lived in. The first I can remember was a tabby called Tibby. He was extremely old and at least twenty before mum appropriated him from my uncle Frank. Tibby was my best friend and a champion mouser. He'd be lent out willingly to any neighbour with rodent issues. Such was the camaraderie of the time. These four women supported each other through pregnancies, births, failed marriages, hard times, chimney fires, rodent infestations and happiness for more than thirty years. They may have had relatively little money and all with large families to support, but their devotion to each other is both humbling and heartwarming. I'm only rambling on about all this because I truly believe that these retained experiences established the values of a solid working class upbringing; we may have lived in black and white but our minds were in glorious Technicolor.

Meanwhile my mum and dad's arguments increased in frequency and volume. Their rowing terrified me and I used to plead with them to stop as the insults reverberated off every wall in that tiny flat. There was never any physical violence, that I recall anyway; everything was vocal. To escape the atmosphere my dad would take me out on the soon to be Beeching decimated Southern railway system. We'd travel around the leafy countryside together on old trains, looking for rabbits in the fields (the going rate was sixpence a rabbit if spotted) and marvelling at the wheeltappers clanging the engine wheels in Tunbridge Wells West station siding (now Sainsbury's). Most of those lines closed shortly afterwards, a bit like my parents' marriage. Dad eventually moved out and our relationship changed into one fractured by time if not by distance. He stayed in Tunbridge Wells but on the other side of town. He'd pick me up on his moped and take me to the Wimpy bar for a Bender Brunch once a week. I also increased the amount of time I spent with my maternal grandparents in Welling in South London. Weirdly, both my paternal and maternal grandparents got on very well together, living only about a mile away from each other. As time went by I began to see more of them than I did my own father.

While all this was going on my mum had met and formed a relationship with a young man fresh out of the Navy. Lo and behold an apparently smooth transition from Dad 1 to Dad 2 tooketh place. During the 'change' I still spent many happy times with my 'real' dad. One such occasion had a profound effect upon me. It was my first trip into central London. I can date this very accurately to the end of December 1964 as he took me to see the newly released *Mary*

Poppins film at a cinema the size of an aircraft hangar in Leicester Square. The screen was so wide that it stretched from one side of the city to the other. We sat together in the front stalls and spent the entire 139 minutes with our necks cricked upwards. I laughed hysterically at Michael's failing attempts to click his fingers as their toys marched around the nursery and cried at the sadness of the old lady feeding the birds on the steps of St. Paul's. When Mary eventually left I cried even more. It all seemed an allegory of what was happening in my own life. The person I loved more than anyone in the world had also left me. To this day I cannot watch that film without welling up. Thank Christ I turned out to be gay, I can't imagine what sort of psychological trauma that would have caused in a straight man.

Trips to London became more frequent with Dad 1. He was a hugely imaginative and creative man and a joy to be with for a child with an enquiring mind and a thirst for knowledge. We would marvel at the stars in the London Planetarium and thrill at the dinosaurs in the Natural History Museum. I was proud of being able to recite the correct order of all planets in our solar system and that the biggest dinosaur was a Diplodocus. What a repulsive little shit I could have turned out to be. But I don't think I was. I was just different. I had nothing in common at all with Dad 2. He was strict and had an angry temper, although it was obvious that my mum loved him very much. He was the father to my two stepbrothers and stepsister. Together we continued and grew as a tight-knit family unit despite the rather awkward background presence of Dad 1.

Shortly after the marital split became permanent we moved from the shitty little over-shop flat to a beautiful newish end-of-terrace council house about a mile away. It had a front and back garden and a shed and an apple tree. It was impossibly luxurious. We even had Indian neighbours, quite possibly the only ethnically different family in the entire county (and certainly in Tunbridge Wells – even though I think I saw a black girl once at Silverdale Road, but she vanished after a while, so it could have been a dream). We couldn't have wished for lovelier neighbours. They were kind, friendly and their food looked, smelt and tasted totally different to the stuff my mother churned out. As children we blended together naturally and without any hint of racial tension whatsoever. We spent our entire childhood playing together quite happily and without a second thought. I am certain though that their parents will have found living in a backward, repressed, stuck-up town like Tunbridge Wells quite a challenge. If this was the case they certainly never showed it. I'm proud that my parents never, ever expressed any negativity throughout the entire time we lived there. They remained close friends for over thirty years and once again adding to my life experience in subtle ways.

In the new house I had my own bedroom for the first time, although the stress levels were building in me. I was continuing to have waking nightmares. I developed a nervous twitch and some mildly obsessional behaviour. I became convinced there were creatures living in the ceiling of my new bedroom. Dad 2, probably more out of desperation than analysis, wallpapered the ceiling to try and distract me away from creating visions out of its original brilliant whiteness. It didn't help because the wallpaper he put up had a thin line starburst motif which was even more disturbing than the monsters I was creating in my mind. Come to think of it most of the wallpaper my mother had plastered all over the house might have suggested heavy drug use had it not been for the fashions of the 60s and 70s. Some of the patterns were so mind-blowing that it was a relief to get to my nan's house and some good old fashioned flowers and pastel stripes.

Even though Dad 2 was an excellent father, I just didn't click with him. I became closer to Mum and wary of my stepfather's moods and manner. I missed Dad 1 terribly. My developing mind simply couldn't cope with the difference between them. At the family court following my parents' divorce I was asked to choose which surname I wanted. I chose Dad 1's probably as an attempt to strengthen the link which had been slowly drifting away from me. But hey ho, as a family unit we were safe, well looked after and happy.

But I still missed my dad. Before I drift into the more stable post-Dad 1 bits and the looming glory of the 1970s I must mention a couple of other significant events. The first involved a big bag of 7" single records that Dad 1 had brought back from the Rowntree factory where he worked. A bloke there had persuaded him to divvy up for a load of ex-jukebox discs, most of which had the middles pushed out (oldies please explain to the youngies what this means, thank you).

Amongst these were such classics as 'Cathy's Clown' by the Everly Brothers, 'Baby Love' by the Supremes, 'Good Timin' by Jimmy Jones and 'You Don't Have To Be A Baby To Cry' by The Caravelles. Like many families back then we had a radiogram. These were enormous sideboardy-looking affairs on legs, with a radio, inset record player and cut-out slot for storing a few LPs. To me it represented the glamour of modernity; it even had a modern smell to it when you opened the lid. I became Prince Regent of the Radiogram and guarded its luxurious machinery with a passion. Suddenly being able to fill it with a million discs was an event of such joy to me that the urge for collecting vinyl records has never left me. I still have those battered old singles now over fifty years later. They're upstairs in a box. Wanna come up and see them? OK, pop round later and I'll show them to you. Just ring the doorbell three times and I'll know it's you.

The other thing I have mention is my first foray into the theatre. The annual Pantomime in Tunbridge Wells used to be at the Opera House, now a dodgy Wetherspoons pub guarded by drunks smoking fags on the door. But back then it was the town's most famed family entertainment spot. It presented films and stage shows with its crowning glory the Grand Annual Christmas Pantomime presented every year by Alan Gale and his wife Patricia Kay. The first one I ever went to was *Mother Goose* in December 1962. To a wide-eyed four-year-old boy this experience was both terrifying and wondrous. We laughed at the antics in Mother Goose's kitchen and screamed both at the baddie and the strange woman with the big nose who appeared on an organ which arose up out of the floor during the interval. I was one of the children dragged up onto the stage to sing 'Why does a brown cow give white milk when it only eats green grass?' and then be teased by Alan Gale's character 'Miffins'. As the older children were given their Trebor sweets and ushered off the stage I was left there with a young girl who had buck teeth. Miffins asked me if I had a girlfriend and playfully attempted to get me paired off with her. But all the while I was transfixed by the wonders of the lighting rigs, scenery, actors and dancers in the wings, sight of the orchestra pit and the smell of the stage from the business side of things. I paid so little attention to either of them that I imagine Miffins was glad to see the back of me. I'd been bitten by the bug. Utterly intoxicated by the whole experience I almost had to be dragged off the stage. I would quite happily have stayed there for the rest of the show and joined in if I could have. Alan Gale was a true master of the genre and we attended his shows religiously throughout my childhood. Over twenty years later whilst I was doing *The Tube* and living in South West London I often used to see Blue Peter presenter Peter Duncan at the Fulham Pools where I used to swim. During the course of our conversations I was stunned to discover that Alan Gale and Patricia Kay were his parents. Sadly he'd lost his dad by that time, but his mother was still alive and appearing in productions locally. It gave me so much joy to be able to tell him just how much those shows had meant to me and how they had inspired me to work in theatre. Thank you Miffins! I wonder whatever happened to the girl with buck teeth?

After the move to the new house I also moved to my primary school in nearby High Brooms. I was billeted into the red coloured 'Caxton House'. I was pleased about this as red is my favourite colour and I'd been in the red house at St. Luke's too. Result! High Brooms Big Boys School (as we referred to it) was very strictly run by the headmaster Mr King and his posse of teachers, a nit lady and a janitor who smelled of Jeyes Fluid. This school also introduced me to a new level of discipline. If you were naughty you'd first be made to stand in the middle of the small assembly hall, around which the classrooms were situated, as fellow pupils filed in from the playground. It was a masterclass in ritual humiliation, although there was worse to follow punishment wise. After the head hanging shame in the hall you would get sent to the headmaster's office to meet 'The Stinger'. This was a small cricket bat which would be smacked onto the child's bum area to inflict a maximum of pain. I am not sure if I was ever subjected to this, but as I tended to hang around with the naughty boys I heard vivid descriptions of its effect often enough. With hindsight I can see that it was a pointless punishment as the naughty boys simply carried on being naughty and being on the receiving end of The Stinger became more of a badge of honour than it ever did a deterrent. However I was utterly terrified of it. I don't think it made me a good boy per se as my parents' home discipline was quite enough to see to that. My mother only had to utter the phrase 'Wait until your father gets home!', and I would be paralysed with fear even though we were rarely ever smacked by either of them.

The nit lady was far scarier than Mr King. She looked like Winston Churchill in drag and armed with killer knitting needles steeping in a glass holder full of noxious smelling antiseptic fluid. We'd be marched in to get our head areas prodded and poked with the meticulous precision of a brain surgeon. As none of my family ever had nits I actually had no idea what she was doing. It's quite probable that the brown knitted balaclavas my mother forced us to wear in the winter months were enough to frighten off head lice. We loathed wearing those knitted monstrosities. They made us look like trainee terrorists.

As my time there drifted past I grew to adore Mr King. He was a kindly and learned man with a passion for educating and inspiring young minds. I'd seen the words 'A-level trigonometry' in a Bash Street Kids strip in *The Beano* comic and recall asking him what this was. He went through an explanation in great detail which went in one ear and out the other. But I was transported by fascination and for minutes afterwards had determined that this is what I wanted to be when I grew up; a mathematician doing A-level trigonometry.

Mr King taught the top class which I entered in the late summer of 1968 for my final year there. That year the school had organised a trip to Paris, which back then was at least hundred thousand miles and several different time zones away. I have no idea how my parents cobbled together the fee for me to go on this as it was insanely expensive, but cobble it they did and off I went *à la belle France pour le premier fois*.

We were billeted at a vacated girls' school in the suburb of Marie Des Lilas. After discovering the Eiffel Tower and the magnificence of Versailles I firmly decided to become French. Well why not? It smelt different there and their bread was long and not called Mother's Pride. They ate cheese with holes in it and their Metro trains looked like something from a Jules Verne novel, with doors that slammed so hard they'd take your arm off if you were too slow to board. During our day trip to the Palace of Versailles our group noticed a familiar figure drifting in and out of the ornate garden features. This was the actor Patrick Newell who was well known at the time for playing Mother in *The Avengers* TV series. As this was the first famous person any of us had ever seen we felt duty bound to follow him around like children following the Pied Piper. How unfortunate for him and the young blonde woman he had in tow to find their day out ruined by a load of pen proffering, snotty kids from High Brooms Boy's School in Kent. In my mind I wanted him to disappear into a water feature, as Mother's HQs were always located in bizarre places. To his credit he was charming and kindly to us, although to be honest he had every right to tell us to piss off.

By the time we got back to Blighty I was of course fluent in French and struggling to speak English again. Well, in my mind I was. Paris has had a special place in my head and heart ever since. I just wish they'd sort out their grammar because it's beflathered and beflummoxed me for years.

During that year Dad 1 had met his new girlfriend Julie and they were living together in a huge flat in a very posh part of Tunbridge Wells. I loved going there. It felt like a haven away from my brothers and sister and the hurly-burly of the family home. Julie was much younger than my dad. Also, unlike my mother who had rarely ventured further than Eastbourne, Julie had travelled the world and had even lived in America for a while (Washington State if you please!). She was (and still is) great fun and I loved spending time with them both there. I slept in a made-up bed on the sofa in the cavernous lounge with ceilings 50 feet high and windows that overlooked fields with real cows in.

Here I could have the TV on whenever I wanted – and as late as I cared. Although my waking nightmares were exacerbated by the vastness of the room, its darkness enveloping me like a shroud until it stifled me to sleep. One episode of the aforementioned *Avengers* still sticks in my mind; 'The Living Dead'. I recall watching it there and being almost paralysed with terror. Having watched it many times since then one can't fail to be amused by its kitsch campy humour, but for me there will always be the memory of watching the Duke's ghost rise up out of the grave, whilst I cowered behind a pillow on that vast sofa in that even vaster lounge room.

And so I approach one of the most significant events in my entire life. One that really defined who I was to become and who I am now. I had gone to the mansion (for that's how I thought of it) for my weekend with Dad 1 and Julie. We had finished our Sunday lunch and were sitting together on the 30-foot-wide sofa (sic) when out came a large map of Australia, which Dad 1 then spread on the coffee table in front of us. 'Look, isn't this amazing?', he said, as I marvelled at the vastness of the detail presented to me, 'This is where we are going.' I'm not certain I quite grasped what he meant as I had school to go to and I knew that we'd never get there and back by Monday morning. It took me a while to realise that he was talking about him and Julie and not the three of us. They were to be married and then emigrate to Australia as 'ten pound POMs' – without me. I was devastated. How could the person who I loved more than anyone else in the world even think of leaving me behind? What's more this was to happen more quickly than I had bargained for.

They married soon afterwards and at their wedding I duly appeared trussed up in a little dark short-trousered suit with bronze-coloured flecks which my mother had bought for me out of her Burlington Catalogue. I even had a carnation in my buttonhole to prove my authenticity. To reflect the joy of the occasion Julie had her hair beehived up several feet higher than I'd ever seen it before whilst sporting a beautiful short white mouse pelt coat (well, that's what it looked like to me). Dad 1, handsome as he was, proudly worked the reception room and all the relatives I was soon to lose almost all contact with.

Shortly afterwards and with their departure for the wide brown continent imminent, a final party was held at my paternal grandmother's house in Bexleyheath, south-east London.

Bear with me here, I need to get this cathartic stuff all out and done with. It might be a bit tedious to read about but I'll try and make it as interesting as I can. My father's side of the family was much bigger than my mother's was as he had many siblings and I therefore cousins. It was to be the last time he would ever see his mother (my nan) and obviously it was tough for him to say goodbye.

I stayed at Nan's that night and went over to my maternal grandparents' house in nearby Welling the next day before returning home to my Mum, Dad 2 and my half siblings in Tunbridge Wells.

And with that Dad 1 was gone. I didn't see him or Julie again for 27 years – until the postscript of my story in fact, where I will tell you what happened when we met again in Sydney. For now though my sense of loss completely overwhelmed me. My nervous tics and waking nightmares became worse and I was put on some sort of medication to calm me down. Unbeknownst to my mother I had also been going back to the flat where Dad 1 and Julie had lived. Somehow I got in and used used to sit alone in the empty flat for hours. When she found out where I had been going she was mortified and warned me that I would get into terrible trouble if I was ever discovered there, with probably a 20 year jail sentence (actually she didn't say that, but it makes it all a bit more dramatic).

As I approached my eleven-plus exams I was frankly not focused on much at all. Dad 1 was gone and I struggled to connect with Dad 2 who frequently argued with my mother, bringing back powerful memories for me of what had gone before. It took me a while to figure that actually the common denominator in all that was my mum; it was she who was fiery and argumentative, not Dad 1 or Dad 2. At this point I feel I have probably been painting too bleak a picture of my home life, which was actually very happy. I adored my brothers and sister and both Dad 2 and my mother were amazing parents. When I realised that if I passed my eleven-plus exams it was likely that I would be sent to The Skinners School in Tunbridge Wells I felt a sense of creeping terror. The pupils there wore short trousers in the first year and straw boater hats throughout the 5 years. Fearing for my life on the council estate where we lived I resolved to flunk the tests and make sure I went to the secondary modern up the road with all my friends. I flunked with aplomb and my wishes were granted. Skinners was duly deprived of my talents to the benefit of Ridgewaye School in nearby Southborough. A place that was to become as magical to me as Hogwarts was to Master Potter.

In September 1969 I ambled up the road to my new secondary modern school for boys and girls, resplendent in my grey and red uniform (the hues of which I thoroughly approved fashion wise). Hell, I even got placed in the red-colour school house to boot. Even better was that my best friend Jackie was also there. The glory days of the 1970s were about to be launched with excitement, laughter, music, drama and my erupting sexuality. I wasn't sorry to see the back of the 1960s. I didn't want to dwell on any of its black and whiteness. The seventies were about to explode in a shower of glitter, satin and crushed velvet. This was to be MY decade in more ways than I could ever possibly have imagined.

2

Get It On & School's Out – 1969 to 1975

Let it hereby be known that the start of this chapter is accompanied with the theme music to Alan Freeman's 'Pick Of the Pops'. Go and find it and put it on. I won't start until you're ready don't worry.

drums fingers on table

Ready?

Then here we go Pop Pickers! Not 'Arf!

The five years I spent at my secondary school were quite possibly the happiest days of my life. I know for many those places were quite the opposite. Certainly Ridgewaye School in Southborough had its share of bullies, rough types and criminals in training, but for me it was a sort of council estate Hogwarts. Within those late 50s concrete walls I learned enough to be rewarded with mediocre exam results whilst having the time of my life. I wouldn't have swapped any of it for academic brilliance as being posh would have got me beaten up, and I didn't want to be beaten up thank you.

It was during my time there that I discovered I could make people laugh. This put me in good stead with the bullies and thugs as whilst they were being dragged off to the headmaster for vandalism and various levels of bodily harm, I was always in there for 'being disruptive' and 'mucking about in class'. It was definitely honour amongst thieves. In fact I don't ever recall being got at by any of the rougher types at all. I watched untouched from the sidelines as the weaker pupils were given the standard treatment by boys (and girls) who asserted their physical superiority over their own mental stupidity. I'm not proud of leaving them to it, but it was an approach which would become a standard situational handling mode for me in later years.

Ridgewaye was a pretty run-of-the-mill school with an array of teachers of rather Alan Bennettesque properties. There were the ones we liked, the ones we hated and the ones who came and went after giving up. We loved our Art, History, Music, French and English teachers; and hated our Maths, Religious Instruction and Sport masters. Being the seventies some subjects were split amongst the sexes – after all, girls couldn't possibly scrape bits of metal with rasps, operate welding equipment and shave wood. Equally it was unthinkable for a boy to sew or make a cake.

It was quite obvious where my leanings were pointing – I loathed metalwork and woodwork as I couldn't bear the noises and smells. The metalwork shop reminded me of Mordor, and I had no intention of ever becoming an Orc, thank you very much. The woodwork shop was run with strict discipline by a thin, sharp-faced and terminally bored-looking man called Jack Cordes. He wasn't much taller than us, which gave him a distinct disadvantage once the boys breached puberty and their hormones shot them to over 9 feet in height with fists like smoked hams. To make up for this he used sarcasm to great effect. I guess I should have liked him for that? As an adult I probably would have got on well with him, but I felt the best approach at age eleven was one of bored disinterest. Luckily I didn't have the distraction in there of my posse of girl friends who would undoubtedly have encouraged aforementioned 'mucking about'; probably not wise with so many instruments of torture freely available at every turn.

I ditched those ghastly subjects just as soon as ever I could, although not before announcing to him (and the world) in my very final woodwork lesson that I was going to make a coffee table. He did look thrilled. I managed one leg before discarding it in a bush behind the bike sheds on the way out. I would much rather have been mixing cakes and murdering pizza recipes with the girls. The sewing and needlework didn't interest me however. I had no aspirations to become a seamstress and as a gay man one never repairs anything; one chucks it away and buys new on whatever credit card hasn't yet been maxed out, thank you. Anyway it was bad enough being forced to wear knitted balaclavas without having to learn how to make the bloody things.

I struggled terribly with Maths in particular. This wasn't because I was incapable of understanding, but because we had no context applied to any of it. What the fuck is a Logarithm anyway? Why would I ever need to work out vulgar fractions? Arithmetic was obvious and I was OK with all that, but all the rest of it seemed designed only to confuse, irritate and enrage me. When forced onto us as homework this one subject became an instrument of utter torture. My parents didn't understand it either so they were no use to me. Even pleading letters from my mother to the woman who imposed all this on us fell on deaf ears. 'Gary doesn't understand what this is for, can you pleased explain it to him so he can complete his homework?', she frequently wrote (also as a thinly veiled parental plea to have it explained to her because she hadn't got a clue either). The only response she ever got from the mathematical obergrupenfuhrer was that I'd had it explained in class along with everyone else and that I should 'listen more'. Ooh she was vile that teacher. Few of my compatriots understood what she was on about either. The stupid woman could have enthused and explained and encouraged us to enjoy maths, whereas she achieved the exact opposite. I have hated working with numbers ever since. I can't be doing with them.

Those who have stuck with me so far (well done by the way) will have noticed that I didn't mention the science subjects in that scholastic love and hate list. We had two science teachers; a tall man whose name escapes me took us for Physics, whilst a small bespectacled and deeply religious elderly woman took us for biology. She disliked me as much as I disliked her. Even then my atheism was clear to all. She played the piano in our school assemblies and used to fire daggers at me and my posse of rebels for purposely and very loudly singing a semitone flat through every hymn. At one point we even started applauding each time one finished, an act which saw me back in the headmaster's office once more along with boys who had been mashing limbs in the playground.

The thought of that woman even attempting to explain procreation to our lot makes me laugh even to this day. Most of the girls I knocked around with could have given Anais Nin a run for her money, and as the boys were busy finding out what their dangly bits were for too it rather left her explanations of the marital behaviour of frogs somewhat redundant. Her religious proclivities were obviously out of sync with the sciences anyway. It baffled me how this woman could stand there professing about the wonders of the Solar System whilst proclaiming it as God's work and therefore proof of an almighty. Happily for those who endured this nonsense the vast majority of us had long ago figured out that religion, all of it, was unintelligent rubbish and we duly filed it as such.

Our RI teacher was a frightening woman who looked like a barrage balloon in a frock. Miss Collin struck fear and terror in almost all of us, sourced no doubt from her comforting faith in the Christian death cult. Whilst she yelled supernatural nonsense at us for a couple of hours a week we formulated distraction plans as a coping mechanism. My favourite involved one of my besties, Sally. The concept was to somehow drape a long piece of cotton, wool or other string-like substance over a fellow pupil's head without their knowledge and without Miss Collin noticing. If done well a visitor to the class would have seen about fifteen kids with what looked like spaghetti on their heads. The whole montage was both surreal and for me utterly hilarious. 'What's the matter with you?', she'd bark at anyone unwise enough to remonstrate with Sally if she was discovered mid-draping. Cue further sending offs for me and visits to the Head's office.

As time went on we actually became curiously fond of Miss Collin. It might have been because we felt sorry for her shoes? She was so fat and they were so tiny. I recall Jackie and Kristine elaborating theories as to how she managed to get in and out of them without the aid of industrial heavy lifting and extraction equipment. By the time we reached our fifth year all but a small number of repressed creeps had given up on the subject, but we did take part in one final hurrah. She had offered up the chance of a coach trip to an all-night religious happening in Rochester Cathedral. Well of course this was more like it; an opportunity to stay out all night was not to be sniffed at. I duly gathered the whole of my clan – Carol, Kim, Jackie, Kristine, Sally, Andrew and a few more and for the paltry fee of 50p we gathered our packed lunches and boarded the fun bus.

The event was full of weirdos busy discovering themselves to the sound of amplified rock/folk music played by bearded herberts in corduroy trousers. At one point I recall an 'exercise in trust'. Everyone was encouraged to take off their shoes and sandals (sic) and 'feel the stone beneath their feet'. Whilst they were all doing that with their heads raised piously upwards and their eyes tight shut, my gang crawled around covertly on the floor silently mixing up everyone's footwear, redistributing it as widely as possible. When they'd all found whatever it was they were looking for and came back to Earth there was absolute chaos as they tried to find their correct shoes. We were in tears of hysterical laughter at the pandemonium. Some of the beardies got quite irate with each other. We were praying for a fight to break out but as that wasn't really in the spirit of the Lord it sadly never reached that conclusion. It took the rest of the night before we saw people wearing their own shoes again. A result all round we thought. We duly finished off our corned beef and pickle sandwiches and bottles of Corona Cream Soda before heading back to reality and no further RI lessons thank you very much. I thought it was all very funny and half a quid well spent.

Our sports master was another deeply unpleasant character whose only achievement with me (and many others) was to have instilled a lifetime of hatred for the subject. His main teaching technique was psychological and physical torture, a methodology which persisted even when it resulted in broken bones and dislocations. He was a short (what is it about short teachers being sadists?), rather stocky Scottish man with a penchant for shouting at people smaller than him. Nothing was ever pleasant or enjoyable with him in charge. Sport, and in particular team events, was something to be endured. The dreaded medicine ball (a huge brown leather-coated lump filled with what felt like concrete and horsehair) was renamed by him the 'suicide ball' and it featured in most gym activities as a weapon to be hurled about until injuries forced play to cease.

At the end of each term we would be forced to play something called 'Pirates', where every piece of gym equipment from ropes to trampolines would be brought out and some poor little sod dubbed 'it'. The idea was to keep off the parquet floor at all costs, whether this be up a rope, bars, vaulting horse, floor mat (my object of choice for obvious reasons) or jumping between trampolines. Even the thought of this incredibly dangerous pursuit fills me with astonishment to this day. It was an accurate measure of the sadistic pleasure this odious man appeared to get from watching terrified kids hurl themselves around a gymnasium to the point where an ambulance would have to be called to take away the maimed and injured. He wouldn't even let us get in and out of the school swimming pool (yes we actually had one – outside and unheated) by the ladders fitted to it. We had to line up by the fence, run at it and hurl ourselves over the side into the freezing cold water. Some of the children undoubtedly thought this was great fun, whilst the plumper or less agile ones were left trembling in fear of impending doom on the slippery stone tiles which were specifically installed to make it all that much more lethal. It was a miracle that so few weren't sent home with limbs in plaster, let alone the psychological damage it inflicted.

As you might have suspected by now I ended up having a run-in with this appalling man, the result of which was somewhat unexpected. He was a die-hard proponent of rugby. At every opportunity we would be frogmarched out to the school fields and forced to endure the horrors of the scrum and the embarrassment of being dragged down into the mud by a tackle, an endeavour hugely enjoyed by the school bullies and rough types. It didn't strike me that very much skill or intelligence was involved in any of that stuff and that was enough for me to despise it regardless of it having been taught by a Glaswegian sadist.

One cold winter's day with temperatures plummeting below zero and a blizzard howling, our delightful sports master decided this was the perfect day for another rugby match. Obviously in such appalling weather it is vital to maintain body heat in order to stay alive, so he prepared himself for the important task of standing on the sidelines yelling at boys by covering his entire body with about fifteen layers of thermal coatage and a huge golfing umbrella to prevent the howling snowstorm from ruining his hair. Meanwhile we were ordered out in nothing but skimpy shorts and a rugby top. Within minutes I began to lose all feeling in my extremities and decided that I'd had enough. 'Right! That's it, I've had enough!' I bravely exclaimed to my compatriots, most of whom were now resembling snowmen at a Lapland convention. With a flick of my wrist I marched grandly off the field back towards the warmth of the cold showers in the changing rooms. A gradual trail of my cohorts followed me, obviously feeling that they'd had enough as well and even more obviously that it would be me that copped it when the shit hit the fan. Jock Petty (for that was his name) went ballistic. 'Get back to this rugby right now!' he screamed from underneath his brolly as his entire class disappeared, making him look curiously like a complaining jumble sale. When he realised he was the only one left he screeched up behind us and frogmarched me to the headmaster's office (again).

I was made to wait. It is the way of things.

And wait.

And wait.

Eventually I was called into the headmaster's office. He clasped his hands and rested his chin on his hands then after a minute or so said, 'Have you any idea how much trouble you cause me?' At which point, channelling the voice and mannerisms of Frankie Howerd, I pointed out of the window at what now looked like Antarctica and said, 'Well look at it out there. Would you? In this? Wearing these?'

There was a long silent pause.

'Oh go back to your lessons...'

Which I duly did, and not without a sense of justice having been truly done and delivered that day. The consequence of all this was that from that day onwards I had no further trouble from Jock Petty. In fact he tried to be pally with me (a most disturbing thing). I can only assume that in leading the great walk off from the field he had finally been called out. There was nothing more to be said between us. I didn't even get pressured to go down Muddy Rise, a quagmire of wet mud and puddles which featured heavily on our cross-country run route (which incidentally crossed the main London to Hastings railway line twice at track level). Petty is no longer with us, so I feel I can name him with confidence. Thanks to his teachings I have had a lifelong hatred of almost all sport; quite an achievement for a teacher don't you think?

The girls weren't immune from the terrors of the sports field either, although my impression is that they were a much tougher bunch than the boys. It would have been a brave teacher indeed to have taken on the girls from my year at that school. They made St. Trinian's look like a nursery school.

Besties Kristine and Jackie regaled me an amusing story of trial and retribution at the hands of their sports mistress Miss Markham. Apparently at one of their earliest hockey lessons the hapless mistress had yelled at Kristine to 'Kick In' (whatever that means). At which point Kristine ran up to the small white ball and kicked it with her foot sending it flying over the hedge and into the school car park.

'What did you do that for?' yelled Miss Markham, her face purple with rage.

'You said "Kick it", so I did!' screamed Kristine back at her, to the amusement of the rest of the bored group.

This very much set the relationship between the girls and their sports teacher. After getting into trouble for that episode Jackie and Kristine decided to get their own back on her by stealing her training shoes and stuffing them down the toilet pan in their changing rooms, flushing it repeatedly until the cubicle flooded. Needless to say I was enormously impressed by this. They were so much braver than I ever was. The boys were all so unutterably terrified of Jock Petty that we never got retribution for any of his cruelty, perhaps with the sole exception of that snow-induced walk-off. The girls also had get-out-of-jail cards to play that we never had; namely women's things. Jackie once told me that if she didn't fancy doing sport she just told the teacher she was 'on' and she would be let off it without any fuss. I was so jealous of this. How come the boys didn't have such a pubescent get-out like that? Wasn't your balls dropping and a voice that modulated between a squeak and a bellow trauma enough to get you off an hour of being murdered in mud? Mind you, if I'd thought I could have got away with telling Jock Petty I was 'on' I would have.

It's obvious that the drive for all pervading health and safety had barely even cranked its engine back then. I like to think of it as character building. Just like the wonderful enthusiasm of my English teacher Noddie Knight. This wonderful man enthused and encouraged his subject matter and is largely responsible for my eventual passion for theatre and writing.

Noddie was an enthusiastic Marxist and I still have the original copy of *The Little Red Book* which he gave me back in 1970. That amazing book is still as relevant today as it was all those years ago. Of course at the time it was treated as blasphemous and heretical. Odd to think that in the same era that brought Love Thy Neighbour, On The Buses and Alf Garnett to popular culture, something which actually talked sensibly about human relationships, sexuality, drugs, politics, education and how to get the best out of life from an early age should be vilified as a bad influence. Under Noddie's influence and with his enthusiastic encouragement I began writing poems, sketches and long essays of rambling imagination. I formed a school acting group and put on plays in the main hall consisting of wacky sketches, songs and flights of fancy. I was heavily influenced by my favourite comic actors and TV and radio programmes of the day; most notably Spike Milligan, Monty Python, Frankie Howerd (whom I adored), Rowan & Martin's Laugh In, Kenny Everett, Jack Jackson, Benny Hill, Marty Feldman, Do Not Adjust Your Set, Round The Horne and so many more.

When our school put on a production of *Oliver* I was given the part of Fagin. Playing an elderly Jewish London criminal type probably because I had extremely long hair (I can't think of any other obvious reason). My cohorts were all given bit parts too which gave us the opportunity to mess about and create havoc whenever we could. I'd been given a toasting fork to wave about in the 'Reviewing The Situation' number. Unfortunately it had been made by one of the boys in a metalwork class. He'd made it so that when a small clip was released at the top of the handle it dropped down and extended to twice its original length. This had great comedic potential to me, especially when walking behind players in the back row as it could be used to lift skirts and prod bottoms. It will surely have been one of the few productions of this grand musical opus to have a chorus line screaming 'Get Off!' and 'Shut Up!' every time Fagin walked behind someone. Yes of course it's childish and probably not funny either (even though we all thought it was hysterical), but I was merely celebrating being thirteen in a time when that was allowed. Anyway, I blame Jackie and Kristine; it was their fault.

All of this occurred at the time of a great musical awakening at quite probably one of the greatest decades of pop music ever. Actually the first two single records I ever bought were 'Sugar Sugar' by The Archies and 'Yester-me, Yester-you, Yesterday' by Stevie Wonder. I've still got them. There they are there, look...

points at said two singles

At this point it's worth mentioning the smells of the seventies, because it had them you know. Oh yes. The evocative aromas that instantly transport me back are newly varnished school parquet floors, chimney and bonfire smoke, whatever the explosive stuff in fireworks was, Christmas baking, tangerines and cigar smoke, fish and chips, the newness smell of a record album, the warm valvey smell of electrical equipment, my mother's perming fluid and 'Elnett' hairspray, coke in the shed coal hole (that's the stuff you burn, not the stuff you shove up your nose) and the weird fatty aroma of the milkman's invoice notebook. But more than anything was an aroma more powerful than anything else that's ever been sniffed – Brut Eau De Toilet (the extra 'te' I left off the end on purpose). It was sold in small green bottles in a hard clear plastic case for the princely sum of 50p. This prized scent was coveted by every boy and girl at our school. If we could have bathed in it we would have. Turning up at parties drenched in this stuff was expected if you were to be in with any chance of a snog. It was, from memory, completely unisex too. We all wore it until the brand's kudos was totally and utterly smashed to pieces when Henry Cooper started telling gawping viewers to 'Splash it all over'. After that we moved on to other exotic smells like Tabac and Denim, but never Hai Karate, which we all considered to be an inferior Brut copy.

The early seventies were marred with frequent industrial action in the midst of a politically unstable world, racked with oil crises, the troubles in Northern Ireland, a three day working week and the Vietnam war. At home we were being hit by power cuts which only became an issue for me in the new year of 1972. I had a dentist appointment on the 21st January 1972 in the midst of the latest round of power outages due to strikes when the miners walked out in their first industrial action since the General Strike of the 1920s. Power cut timetables were published in the papers so that people could attempt to work and live around them.

Mum had taken me up to the National Health dentist just off Mount

Ephraim in the town centre for an appointment at 9am. Unfortunately for me a power cut had been scheduled for that same time. She arrived with me respectfully early and I was dragged into the torture chamber quickly and injected with anaesthetic in a rush to beat the impending switch off. The dentist, Dr Crippen or Frankenstein, I can't recall which one of the two it was, couldn't be arseholed to wait for it to take effect so he started a scraping and a drilling and a probing whilst I was still able to feel every prick and prod. I was in agony. Fuck being brave, I screamed the place down just in time for him to finish as the lights and everything else flickered off. 'There, that didn't hurt a bit did it?' he lied. Fighting back the tears of pain I was hustled out into the freezing cold bright sunlight of the Royal Borough, with mum lying also that I had 'been very brave'.

How can you be so certain that it was this day I hear you asking yourselves? Well, actually I can't, but I'm going to tell you anyway. I am about as certain of this date as it's possible to be because it was the day that T.Rex released the first single on their own record EMI distributed label, the great No.1 smash 'Telegram Sam'. As recompense for my non-existent bravery, Mum bought me the single at the first-floor record bar in Boots. Every time I hear it now it reminds me of that fateful dentist trip. But the joy of owning that disc on its day of release by far overwhelmed the terrifying ordeal forced upon me by striking miners. In fairness to them I doubt it was anything personal.

I need to step back a bit to speak about my musical awakening. The 1970s was a truly astonishing decade for pop music. I'm no academic on this and many have written far more eloquently about the artistic side of all that. I just want to focus upon what it felt like for us as young people becoming aware of fashion, music and art as the decade commenced; think of it as a sort of front line view. The love-soaked hippy days of the sixties were alien territory to our school intake, most of whom were to hit teenage years during 1971.

Although January 1970 had launched with Rolf Harris droning on about two little boys (and the least said about that the better), it was superseded by The Marmalade, Edison Lighthouse and then at the end of February the first of the great schoolgirl crush bands, the Jackson 5 with 'I Want You Back'. The pop charts then were a wonderful eclectic mix of MOR, Rock, Pop, Reggae, Soul and the occasional novelty hit. My personal awakening happened shortly after my birthday in June 1970. Mungo Jerry had been at No. 1 for what seemed like an eternity (but was actually 4 weeks) when my cobwebs were blown away by a record that caused me to go out and purchase my first ever pop music paper –

Melody Maker. That record was Free's classic 'All Right Now' which hit No. 1 in the UK in the second week of July 1970.

I devoured every page of that paper from the screaming headlines 'Free Fever!' to the back pages filled with small ads for jeans patches, loon pants and posters of scantily clad girls (which didn't interest me at all). From that point onwards the music just kept getting better and better. We had Smokey Robinson's 'Tears of a Clown' and Freda Payne's 'Band of Gold' up in the mainstream charts, with unadvertised black reggae music from Jamaica being the most sought after discs amongst my classmates. In September we lost Jimi Hendrix and then the month after Janis Joplin, both to drugs. Drug culture which featured heavily in popular culture throughout my entire developing life was rarely an issue for me or any of my classmates for that matter. We knew it went on and that the place to pick up hash was The Sussex Arms pub near to the Pantiles in the town, but the closest we ever got to it was putting an aspirin in a bottle of cider (which was rumoured to get you drunk faster), or joss sticks. We would buy cheap joss sticks from somewhere or other and walk around with them in our mouths like ultra thin stick-like cigarettes. Of course they stank and quite apart from the possibility of ingesting microbes from them having been 'hand rolled in India' we also ended up smelling like walking bonfires. The teachers hated them and as soon as a whiff of one was caught by a Master's nose at a school disco we were told to go outside and extinguish them in the nearest fire bucket immediately!

'They're not drugs sir, they're just joss sticks,' we would pointlessly plead.

'I don't care, they're stinking the place out and a fire risk!' we'd be helpfully informed before being grasped by the collar and dragged out to the car park.

One day in assembly Dick C proudly announced to all of us that he had 'turned Hippy'. After much sniggering at how uncool this was we decided to string him along. We decided that as a Hippy he needed to be sold some drugs. A group of us boys had managed to persuade him that a roll-up fag we had lovingly fashioned was actually a joint and we sold it to him for 50p. As he snuck off to smoke it we revelled in the fact that he was actually going to get 'high' on the contents of a tea bag Andy Coleman had brought from his mum's kitchen. I'm not sure he ever really recovered from that indignity, but I still laugh at his apparent 'tripping' even now.

At the beginning of October 1970 my life was changed forever when Marc Bolan's newly abbreviated group T.Rex released 'Ride A White Swan'. I became transfixed, obsessed and enthralled with not just the music but everything about this amazing man. I had swapped my Winnie The Pooh soundtrack LP for the Rex single with a girl who lived nearby. I'm not sure how I managed to persuade her to part with it on such rubbish terms but I'm bloody glad I did. The three tracks on that record were played and played until my mother begged me to emigrate. My obsession would only ever get more intense. Despite all the other great music we grooved to back then, every time Marc Bolan released another single or album I was only further intoxicated. I worshipped him, though oddly perhaps I never actually fancied him. My bestie Sally Barrett did though. We used to compete to see who could collect the most pictures of him, covertly holding them up to each other in classrooms when teacher wasn't looking, until one day Sally forgot where she was and loudly exclaimed in the middle of an English lesson, 'I've got it!'

Just for the record our sects were divided along the following lines:

Bolan and T.Rex super fans: Me, Sally & Elaine
Bowie super fans: Jackie and David
Rod Stewart & Faces fans: Ben and my cousin Mandy
Reggae and soul super fans: Carol, Kim, Kristine and Neil
Slade fans: more or less all of us on and off depending on whether they were stopping one of our primary choices from getting to No.1
Who, Hawkwind, Hendrix and heavy rock super fan: Andy

These were my hard-core friends most of whom have stayed with me all these years. We are all, to the best of my knowledge, at the time of writing still alive and for the most part still in touch. I love them all dearly and just want to make that clear right now should they ever read this and decide to sue.

More of Marc Bolan and Glam years shortly. For now I have to go back to someone I mentioned above with whom I had fallen helplessly in love. I had no problems coming to terms with my sexuality at all. I knew who I was and what I was and was quite happy with it all. I never doubted myself even when there were no terms or pejoratives to apply. It's important to me for this to be said because there are probably many people who would still claim that a child's sexuality is fluid and that old cliché 'everyone goes through a phase'. Do they? Well I didn't, and what's more the vast majority of my close friends and acquaintances didn't either. The straight ones were busy earning their stripes at the same time as I was – in fact for most of them there was very little Miss Geering could have taught them about human biology that they weren't already aware of from late night sessions in the Calverley Grounds after the Court School of Dancing dance nights had chucked out in the town. The girls used to have me in stitches telling me everything they got up to and with whom in great graphic detail and with no holds barred. How thrilling it was that I was the only boy in the entire year who knew what was going on and all from the perspective of the girls.

Just a few years ago my dearest friend Andy and me were talking about this during a visit to the beautiful farm in Northern France where he now lives with his delightful soulmate Michelle. He was totally unaware that I had been party to all the boys' school time relationship comings and goings (mainly comings by all accounts). I was unaware that the straight boys didn't talk about any of this. Sure, they bragged to each other about conquests and who was knobbing who, but it was in no way as graphic in detail as what the girls were telling me. He was gobsmacked to hear that their every physical attribute was quite openly discussed and his flabber utterly ghasted when he found out what sort of detail it all involved. I was curious to know what they had all thought of me, because I was clearly in with so many of the girls that they couldn't get close to. He told me that they were all very jealous of my female relationships, and how they marvelled at the apparent ease I had in getting so close to them. Of course they didn't know I was gay and it wasn't something I would have shared with them anyway. I kept myself very much to myself and my own teenage loves and crushes were known only to me. I didn't even share then with my closest girlfriends. It was a sort of written agreement I made with myself. So private was this that I'm not even going there now in this story (sorry to disappoint). Unfortunately, I don't believe that times have changed enough for me to talk about this even now for the effect it might have on those whom I knew then and have since lost touch with. They may rest easy for I will not break any confidences or cause them any embarrassment now.

So how then do I tell of my first great love? Easy, I will tell what happened but not with whom. Twos and twos may be put together by those that know me well, and if they come up with any fours so be it, but I shall refer to him not as his real name but as Ben.

Even though I was totally besotted I doubt that any of my friends then (or now) will have realised. He lived a fair distance away from where I did, a trip which required a long bus ride. This obviously restricted the amount of time I could spend with him. Ben's parents didn't like me very much and it was rare for them to ever speak to me if I called. In truth I think they were mortified that their son hadn't passed his eleven-plus and gone to a better school. Instead he was lumped in with a load of council house trash like us. We spent as much time as we could together, even taking the night train to Paris together when we were a bit older for a trip that has been burned on my memory ever since. I am still deeply upset that the two photographs I had of Ben from that trip have gone missing and that as a result I now have no pictures of him at all. Quite how either of us ever managed to afford that time away I still can't recall, but it must have been after we left secondary school and perhaps when I was at college or even in my first employ up in London. In any case I adored him. As most first loves do we drifted apart with time. I was always far more up front and sure of myself than he was. Our final ever meeting ended up with us making passionate love in a wood near to where he lived (at his instigation I might add), after which I never saw him again. I do know where he is now and that Ben's 'circumstances' are radically different from the life I would have assumed he'd have had. Perhaps though I shouldn't be surprised at how things turned out for him. His family background was far more pressing than mine ever was. All my family ever wanted for any of us was that we were happy and safe, regardless of what form that took. Ben's parents seemed to put a lot of pressure on both him and his brothers to become something in the business world. Quite what his mother must have thought when he brought home the Barry White album I bought him during one particular love-crazed moment I can only imagine.

I write only of Ben in this sense and nobody else because when I think back on those days it's clear to me that my experiences were so much more guarded, more out of necessity than anything else. I learned to grow up a lot faster than any of my straight friends did. I had to in order simply to survive – especially when I eventually moved to London in 1975.

But now a step back to '71 and the glitter and glam. My obsession with Marc Bolan grew stronger and stronger. Our music teacher at school had a crush on him and to her credit decided that T.Rex's smash hit single 'Hot Love' deserved to be included in the music curriculum along with Mozart, ear-mangling recorder lessons and equally excruciating singing-in-the-round exercises. By the time 'Get It On' was released in July of 1971 it was clear at least to me that Bolan was musically on a different plane to his rivals. Sally, Elaine, Andy, David, Heather and me congealed together by the swings up at the playing fields adjacent to our school in Southborough with a small red hard plastic transistor radio every evening we could. Radio Luxembourg was our station of choice with its DJs Tony Prince, Paul Burnett, Dave Christian, Stuart Henry, Mark Wesley, Bob Stewart and if the signal held out long enough David 'Kid' Jensen. The trouble with this AM station was that Luxembourg's signal was apparently transmitted by a 9v battery. As the evening wore on the signal got worse and worse. By the time Kid Jensen came on, our chart favourites were drifting in and out in a fuzzy haze of muddled foreign voices and the weird pulsating station ident of something which sounded like 'Forza Italia' (I never found out what this was, but I'm sure we weren't alone wondering what this odd airborne intruder was).

I had grown my hair long in order make myself distinct from adult enemies. I secretly wanted groovy hair like David had. He got his 'feathered' at a unisex stylist in Tonbridge, just behind the station. Eager to get mine looking just as cool I went there too when nobody was looking, hungrily pointing at the photo on the wall of a bloke with a perfectly feathered bonce. Sadly I came out with an abomination on top of my head that made me look like a failed Apache. Damn you tall, blond, handsome, feathered David.

My flowing locks had though earned me the reward of having to pick up litter from the approach road to the school after hours, as I'd refused point blank to get it cut. Even when the deputy head offered me 50p to go and get my head butchered at a local barber's shop I declined his kind offer. The barber in question only knew one style: short, back and sides. Every client drifted out looking like they'd just been released from Wormwood Scrubs. My parents were not amused at my rubbish clearing detention duties, but credit to them they allowed me the freedom to dress how I wanted. Now I think back on it, they were terrific and fought my corner more than I realised at the time. My stepfather did have to drive me to school after lunch (as in the early days I went home to eat) when I got myself into a tizzy about a looming games lesson that afternoon. I knew we were going to be forced into doing a dreaded cross-country run and like every decent, respectable young gay man I did not like the idea of getting muddy. 'I hate you!', I screamed, blaming him in my head for everything from school-based trauma, the power cuts and T.Rex's 'Jeepster' failing to get to Number 1. I'm not sure that even he realises that the strength of response I learned from him was to stand me in great stead for the sociological battles I would face as a gay man in a society that still held us criminals just for being who we were. He will never read this, but just for the record, thanks Dad, you were a star.

Thinking of 'Jeepster' reminds me that the first time I heard it was on Fab 208 Radio Luxembourg one evening in late October 1971 before the signal left this planet for the outer solar system. I had recorded it on a small reel-to-reel tape recorder I had bought at a second-hand shop in the town. Slade had been at No. 1 for ages with 'Coz I Love You' and Bolan leapt up the chart to No. 2 all ready to clinch the coveted top position from them. But it was not to be. To my horror comic legend Benny Hill overtook and raced to the top where he sat right through the Christmas period with his 'Ernie' novelty release. Boley hung in there right up to early January 1972, but was overtaken by the fucking New Seekers who warbled their way to glory with their Coca Cola advert single 'I'd Like To Teach The World To Sing', forcing 'Jeepster' back to No. 3 and then slowly out of the chart.

Don't panic readers. I promise I won't turn this into a dreary thesis on the UK charts. I only mention all of this because many these days will not get just how much the record charts meant to us back then. One's loyalty to an artist was so all-pervading that a single failing to get to No. 1 was tantamount to contracting a deadly disease and withering away. The taunting you'd get in the playground from rivals of your idol being Top 30 trounced was a humiliation like no other. These days you only have to sell a few hundred downloads and No. 1 is yours for the taking. Hell, even I could probably get there if I put my mind to it. But records sold in their millions back then. Even now I still get a thrill from the very feel, smell and sound of a vinyl record.

It was about this time that I started carting around my most prized albums and singles to school in a blue flexible plastic briefcase affair that my stepfather had given me from British Telecom where he worked as a telephone line repair man. Although it didn't exactly leave my records in the most pristine of conditions it did mean that I had them on hand to be played whenever we could get our hands on a school gramophone. My copy of Bolan's classic LP 'Electric Warrior' still bears the scars of all that portability. Yet I still have it in my collection now and its probably my most prized LP.

Royal Tunbridge Wells was (and still is) an odd town. Its stagnant Tory politics have held it in a sort of political and social limbo for as long as I can recall. The very idea of a pop band being allowed to come and play there seemed anathema; yet play there they did at the Assembly Hall theatre, which has about as much psychedelic atmosphere and cool as a driving test centre waiting room. Its austere, interior grey walls perfectly complementing the stark, blandly functional civic building it is part of.

Along with my gang of spotty adolescent friends we thrilled to bands like Hawkwind, Status Quo, The Groundhogs and even the Electric Light Orchestra, from whom joint frontman Roy Wood had just split, putting their appearance in my home town in jeopardy. But play they did, and bloody good they were too. Frontman musical genius Jeff Lynne led the band through a set of shimmering brilliance from their recent smash hit '10538 Overture' to their idiosyncratic version of 'Roll Over Beethoven'. At one point quietly spoken Lynne came on wearing a hat with a propeller on it. 'That's a very silly hat,' shouted a head in the audience; 'Shut up or I'll make you wear it,' witticised The Lynne.

Where ELO exuded the wild musical brilliance of an unusually stringy orchestral nature, Status Quo's thrashing 1972 Piledriver tour was not only thrashing but deafening. In fact my ears are still ringing from it 45 years later. I think for sheer exuberant rock and roll excitement, that Quo gig outshone them all. They were also faithful to their recorded sound much as Lynne's ELO were too, where many bands of the time went off on musicals flights of fancy that would stretch a 3 minute hot single into half-hour marathons. The Groundhogs were good at this, although long solo breaks were not my length of joss stick.

We saw Hawkwind a number of times, usually accompanied by a rather odd hippy act called Magic Michael. Whilst waiting for the Space Ritual to start I recall hearing the glorious music of German band Can played loud over the main stage speaker system. Meanwhile as the hall tried to figure out what planet Magic Michael had wandered in from, the oil wheel and strobe light show with smoke machine cranked into life as our space heroes came on stage. The band were well known at this time for having a dancer called Stacia who'd wander on halfway through topless. Stacia had enormous titties and although this was of absolutely no interest to me whatsoever it did add a sort of frisson to the show as well as to the audience, half of whom were so stoned that they had already left our solar system about an hour before Hawkwind came on. I had gone there with my bestie Andy.

Fortunately for him he was extremely interested in Stacia's titties.

Unfortunately for him he was only about 5ft 6inches tall.

When she appeared on stage jiggling about wildly to 'Master Of the Universe', the strobe lights making her breasticles look like a David Bailey fashion shoot, everybody suddenly stood up. As the floor in this wretched hall had no rake, poor Andy couldn't see anything on stage at all let alone Stacia's titties. 'I can't see anything!!!', he cried, as the rest of us whooped and cheered. 'What's she doing, can you see them?' I could (not that I wanted to) but by the time poor pubescent Andy finally managed to part the sea of drug-crazed freaks in front of him to get a good look she had buggered off.

'Fuck it!' he shouted in my earhole, thus contributing to the 24hrs of deafness we took home with us.

Mind you, for all that he missed mammary wise he did have something that none of the rest of us did: a satin jacket. I would have killed for such a garment. It was something I'd always wanted and could never afford. My parents bought all my clothes at that time and the concept of me ever having enough money to purchase an item of unparalleled glamtasticity such as that was merely a pipe dream. My paper round only paid 50p and my pocket money was only 25p. I realised that the Ford Mustang would have to be put on hold. Sadly for poor Andy not only did he not get to see live breasts but whilst squatting on the floor he'd managed to get chewing gum all over the back flap of his purple satin jacket. Try as he could the sticky Wrigley blotch was never eradicated. It was a tragedy we all felt deeply as we lived through the period vicariously through Andy's jacket.

Sadly I never got to see my hero Marc Bolan play live. On October 27th 1971 the band played the Dome in Brighton. Our troupe were hell-bent on going as the tickets were only 50p and I could afford that! Just one big problem; how the hell was I to get back from Brighton to Tunbridge Wells after the gig? We mused over the swings on a bottle of cider with an aspirin in it. This enabled Andy to come up with a brilliant plan – we would sleep under the pier!

'Mum, me, Andy, Sally, David and Elaine want to go to the T.Rex concert, is that OK?'

'Where is it and how much?'

'Oh it's only 50p don't worry. I can pay for that from my paper round money and still have enough for the train fare'

'Where is it?'

'Err, not that far.'

'How far is not that far?'

'Brighton sort of far.'

'Oh yes, and how exactly do you propose to get back from there then?'

'Oh don't worry about that, we'll stay there and come back the next morning.'

'Stay where?'

'Andy's got somewhere.'

'Where?'

Thinks: Curse this woman! Will she never give in?

'It's very close to the venue so we won't have far to go afterwards.'

'Where?'

Pause…

'Under the pier.'

'YOU ARE NOT SLEEPING UNDER A PIER, AND I DON'T CARE IF MARC BOLAN HIMSELF IS STANDING GUARD OVER YOU WHILST YOU KIP DOWN MY WORD IS FINAL!'

Henceforthwith I never got to see my hero play live. How unreasonable can you get? What responsible parent wouldn't allow their 13-year-old child sleep rough under a seaside pier? I hate parents. Selfish sods.

Apart from school discos, which were held during summer months whenever we were able to persuade the teaching staff that it wouldn't result in a mass brawl under a cloud of joss stick smoke, there were various other avenues of teenage club life in the area. Most of these seemed to revolve round Churches in some way, shape or form. The Christian Death Cult (as I personally think of it) had three main branches into local youth – the Protestant Church of England fiddled with the minds of children (apart from other parts) by infusing itself with the Scouting movement. Its pseudo-military structure fitting well with Baden-Powell's bizarre outward-bound, jingoistic attempts at recreating a benign version of the Hitler Youth. Throwing beanbags to each other in order to win a crappy badge didn't appeal to my pubescent leanings in the slightest.

The Methodists seemed to have youth clubs everywhere. In odd little chapels built in the late Victorian era they lured their spotty boy prey in with a promise of table tennis and even snooker. The only pay-off was that you had to sit through a religious lecture at the end. Fat chance of getting any of our lot to sit through that, however much we enjoyed the ping-pong. The Pastor who led the High Brooms club where we went was a sharp-faced, intense-looking man of the 5 feet 6 inches variety. What is it with short men and sport? He used to slick his dark brown hair down with so much oil that the playing area would end up like a skating rink. Music was forbidden in this club; couldn't have the devil's tunes fiddling with God's work could he? As 9pm approached we'd go through the weekly lecture, usually punctuated with awkward questions from the floor like 'How could Mary have a baby if she was a virgin?', 'Do you believe in ghosts and if so why are they always so miserable?', and if we were really antsy 'How did man develop from Adam and Eve if they gave birth to two sons?' (That was always my favourite one).

The final club on our social event roster was the Catholic one, St Dunstan's in Southborough. This one allowed music, didn't have any religious twaddle and was THE dance club to go to in our area. It usually ended up with someone being discreetly informed during the course of the evening that one of the rough lads was 'going to get you' after chuck out. This didn't remotely bother me as I knew that my gang would not only look after me but see off the attackers on my behalf too. I was a lucky lad. Indeed so confident was I that I'd have no trouble with this that I frequently taunted the yobs with rather silly jibes. One of them once called me a poof. That's not very nice is it? My team instantly leapt to my defence and when the inevitable chase sequence started I laughed and shouted back at my would-be assassins as we fled up the London Road. I don't ever recall being beaten up during my whole school life, although thinking back I did push my luck on more than one occasion. In a strange way it was that odd mutual respect between the bullies and me I spoke of earlier. I made people laugh; they battered the meek in training for GBH in later life. Whatever else I was I certainly wasn't 'meek'. I think 'insufferable' probably best described me through most of my early life.

My best friends outside of school were Mark B, Mark C and Gary J, all of whom were very straight and a million miles away from the group of people I would eventually get in with when my sexuality became apparent.

I can't remember how I met Mark B, although I suspect he may have been a year younger than me and that it was probably through school. He lived in a huge house in a very swish part of Tunbridge Wells. He and his older sister Jane had the entire ground floor to themselves with French windows leading out onto the garden. We had wonderful parties there, played music, loafed around, smoked, drank and munched goodies when we could afford or purloin them. They had a great stereo system and it was there that I learned to love the music of Steely Dan and German avant-garde electronica pioneers Can. Jane had had a fling with one of the band and spent some time getting stoned with them in a cave somewhere recording bat sounds for the title track on their Future Days album. If you listen to the intro you can hear those very sounds backing the swirling, menacing synthesised composition. My favourite album of theirs was Ege Bamyasi. Apart from my beloved Marc Bolan's work, nothing takes me back to those halcyon days quite like that album. It is at this time that my life started to split almost into two distinct paths; the first with Mark B and Jane's bohemian friends and wild parties, and the other with my dearest and more conventional friends Mark C and Gary J. I shall return to them shortly, but it was during the course of the St. James's Road parties that I was to meet my first out gay man. Obtaining alcohol was dependent upon us obtaining money (oddly enough). This wasn't easy, but we managed. Christmas could be lucrative with myself, Jackie, Kristine and Carol terrorising the neighbourhood with carol singing. We would stroll up the driveways of better off houses, murder 'Good King Wenceslas' and if they didn't come to the door with a suitable offering Kristine would open the letter box to shout 'And a bloody Happy Christmas to you too!' It was appalling and not something I am proud of at all, but we laughed and laughed through it all and it usually ended up with enough money to buy some cider and ten Sovereign ciggies from the Bottle & Jug at the Cross Keys pub on the main road.

Mark and Jane's parties were altogether more sophisticated. Their kitchen was huge; full of pale painted bespoke cabinets and a big wooden table with real chairs. Our kitchen had a melamine coated table as a centrepiece surrounded by functional furniture. Like everything in Mark & Jane's house the kitchen was a wonder to behold for a council house boy like me.

All drink brought in to a soirée, whether alcoholic or not, was poured into a huge tureen on the giant kitchen table. We would then connect multiple paper straws together so that they reached into the vat of noxious liquid right down to under the table where we would sit and drink through multiple mini pipelines. The mixture was known as 'Filth' – which was extraordinarily accurate as a description. All the lights would go off, music turned up, incense swirling in the air and everyone under the table sucking away at whatever it was above. We got appallingly rat-arsed at these do's but they were wonderful. If we so desired we would dress up too. As Jane was at St Martin's Art College in London she seemed to be able to source all sorts of costumes and coverings. I have a wonderful photograph of her and me in the back garden of their house – she as Alice and me as a bishop. It seemed somehow to fit the house and occasion nicely. The sounds of Bill Withers' 'Who Is He And What Is He To You?' from the album 'Still Bill', Neil Young's 'Old Man' and of course multiple tracks of our beloved Can wafting through the windows into the warm evening light before festivities kicked off.

Jane's rather camp gay friend Alan used to attend these parties. He and his older boyfriend ran a sort of a junk shop in Camden Road. I never quite got the hang of how the pair of them made money. It was full to bursting with all sorts of rather grimy stuff, presumably obtained from house sales? Who can say? I never saw a single customer in the shop in all the times I visited. I had a terrible crush on Alan. He was so good-looking, so forward and so unlike anyone else I had ever met. One night after a classic Filth party we left together for a secret assignation in the grounds of St Luke's church down the road. I thought this rather appropriate given the shit I'd taken as a result of finding the vicar's clothing funny whilst at my primary school. Let's just say I got my own back on his hallowed turf. Alan was so late in getting back that his boyfriend John had been calling Jane to ask where he was. I suspect that she had an inkling, because she didn't breathe a word.

Despite having Alan yearnings it never actually went anywhere. John clearly fancied me and always seemed to be in the bath whenever I went round there. I wasn't daft though, I knew what was what and I didn't fancy him in the slightest. Even in my teens I was tough enough to put up the barriers if I needed to. This tactic stood me in very good stead when I eventually moved up to London. But for now I was still at home and stuck in Tunbridge Wells. One day whilst at the junk shop I happened to comment that I liked the old Fry's chocolate machine on the wall on the other side of the road. I arrived next day to find it sitting in the shop waiting for me. 'It's yours,' said John, 'You said you liked it and I want you to have it.' 'It's beautiful John, but what did you do that for? I can't take that home with me! Put it back. I want to see it just where it was when I come back next time. Please.' I was really angry with him and I needed to show it. I don't think either he or Alan had removed it. I suspected it had been prised off by a rather roguish man they knew who Alan had told me was a burglar. I didn't think burglars either should or could be good-looking (which he was). He wore very tight pale Brutus jeans, tight white cap-sleeve T-shirts and had long curly blond hair like a pop star; you know, fucking gorgeous.

The chocolate machine didn't get put back. I suspect they sold it or moved it on. Either way I was just glad I didn't get lumbered with it. Whatever else illegal I was or was developing into it wasn't thieving. In retrospect I now realise that this whole episode was a first example of my apparent capacity to meet extraordinary people and soak up their auras like a movie camera. It was almost as if my earlier childhood feelings of floating around the ether were made real. That's exactly what I did. It was like I was there invisible and untouchable and observing everything whilst contributing nothing.

I was now coming to the end of my secondary school life. This charmed, magical period would end all too soon. I somehow managed to scrape through my CSE exams, excelling only in English, History, Music and (surprisingly) Maths. That I managed to obtain any educational qualification in Maths is astonishing not just because I loathed the teachers I'd had and manifestly failed to grasp any context from any of it apart from arithmetic, but also because in the latter years my gang had made life hell for a temporary teacher who'd been drafted in during our fourth year. She was from New Zealand, dressed in frumpy all-beige clothing and had an accent that you could cut cheese with. Kristine and Jackie started calling her 'Man At C&A', which to this day strikes me as one of their more bizarre flights of nomenclature fancy. Despite being (too) easily distracted by my gang members I actually liked Man At C&A and she helped me finally unravel some of what had been previously unfathomable. She will never know this of course. Isn't that sad?

I decided to do my fifth year studies and O level exams at West Kent College in Tonbridge rather than stay at Ridgewaye and the distractions it offered. Our last day at school was heartbreaking. Most were glad to escape, but our group were so close that the July 1974 break-up was profound. Sally in particular seemed to realise this was truly the end of an era. She burst into floods of tears as we left the school gates for the last time. She could never have known that despite the ravages of time and experience we would still be close friends for over 40 years. She went on to marry a stunning, handsome local guy called John to whom she is still very happily with, have three beautiful boys, become a proud granny and remain one of my dearest lifetime friends. Yet when I look at her I still see that perma-happy blonde girl triumphantly waving pictures of Marc Bolan in *Jackie* magazine across classrooms, having hysterics whenever Judge Dread's 'Big Six' was played and made me laugh so much by draping bits of cotton over people's heads. Bless your heart Sal' – love you!

The summer of 1974 is something of a blank to me. I had earned some money fruit-picking in the small Kentish village of Brenchley. A lorry would turn up in Silverdale Road and fill with old ladies and the boys from my little clique (including my beloved Ben) eager to earn enough money to buy records, fags and cider. And money was there to be earned too. The most lucrative fruit was raspberry, which were easy to pick, filled the trays in no time and an easy day's wage. 'How much are you going to pick today?', I used to ask old Mrs. Cheesman, who was at least 100 years old and bedecked in black from head to foot. 'An 'undred pound,' she'd say. And she said this every day regardless of how much she'd picked or what the weather was doing (this mattered as most of the fruit was only fit for jam if it was wet).

The nightmare crop was blackcurrants; fucking things, I hated them. You could pick for hours and barely fill a tray. You were paid by weight and with each fruit a different rate per pound. That's why raspberries were so good – easy to pick an 'undred pound and at a high rate. But those effing blackcurrants took forever mainly because the berries seemed to hide under leaves in ones and twos rather than in convenient bunches and even when you'd found some they were bloody awkward to pick. Bastard supervisors would come round to inspect the bushes to make sure pickers weren't just taking the ones on top and leaving the others. After a hard day's work sometimes you were lucky to reach 40 or 50lbs, and at a low per pound rate this would barely fund the purchase of a single record let alone fags and booze. It was a hot summer though and made better by my being able to spend time with Ben with the sounds of the Hues Corporation's 'Rock The Boat' and George McCray's 'Rock Your Baby' as the year's memorable number one hits.

I wasn't looking forward to college. Ben had decided to stay at Ridgewaye to do his 6th year exams and the rest of my gang had mostly decided to leave and start working. It was handy having Kristine, Jackie and Carol working in Woolworths, especially if they were in the tobacco booth near the entrance for reasons I think it's prudent not to go into. September of that year marked a change in my close-knit group of chums. I'd lost daily exposure to my old gang, although we did still socialise. I continued to spend more time with Mark C and Gary, but drifted slowly away from Mark B and Jane. Like you do.

It seemed logical to me to pick GCSE 'O' level exam subjects in which I thought I would do reasonably well. I couldn't wait to ditch the maths and science subjects that I'd suffered for so long and now loathed. Anything sporting could fuck off too. That left me with pithy subjects like English, Music, Art, Drama, French and the like. Piece of piss I thought. Unfortunately for me it was during that year I discovered that however hard I tried I simply couldn't paint, draw or sculpt anything that didn't end up looking like a road accident. My musical proclivities were curtailed early when the rather anal music tutor discovered that I was attempting to play recorders left-handed by twisting the bottom of the instrument round to suit my fingering technique. 'You'll get penalised for that,' he instructed me with rather too much glee.

English literature was taught by a fierce lesbian woman who hated the very air that surrounded me for some reason. I struggled terribly to cope with picking the dreary set books to pieces to analyse what the writers had been thinking when they wrote them. I wasn't interested in all that rubbish. I just wanted to let my imagination roam from chapter to chapter without making hard work out of it. *Far From The Madding Crowd* was hard work enough as it was without being expected to write essays about Hardy's motives. I thought it might all become a bit easier to manage when I discovered that John Schlesinger's 1967 film version was being shown on the telly one weekend. I watched and hated the book even more. Incredibly my loathing of it resulted in huge arguments with my tetchy tutor. 'I couldn't care less what YOU think of the plot devices, and neither will the examiners who will simply fail you for not bothering to answer the question!', she helpfully explained in a voice so loud that it parted my hair.

French at least was taught by somebody nice. An extremely camp man who in the middle of a lesson would suddenly flit over to the window, hurl himself up onto the ledge and exclaim in a beautifully effeminate French accent, 'Oh, look at diss little birdies in diss tree, so sweeeeeeeeeeeet!' Despite having at least some synergy with his mindset if not his manner, I only achieved a mediocre pass in French too, grammar being my eternal downfall.

The brightest part of the year was drama. Despite being rather strict and remote our music tutor put together a couple of shows during my year there, both of which enabled me to show off my thespian bent to great effect. We performed the (then) unfashionable classic musical *Salad Days*, which is always good for a laugh, and then followed it up with a revue at the end of the academic year. I have only vague memories of both of these shows, perhaps because the guy chosen to lead in *Salad Days* was taller than me and better-looking.

I was also a member of one of the local amateur theatre groups doing shows like *The Pyjama Game* and *South Pacific*. There were very few young males in this company, so the chorus of 'There ain't nothing like a dame' must have looked very bizarre with the line-up consisting of retired policemen and building society managers in their late 60s, a couple of bearded beefy blokes who were in it mainly to score with as many female dancers as they could cop off with, and me, an overconfident teenager in tight jeans. I decided to make myself look older by parting my long hair down the middle and wearing a roll neck top. This failed to make me look as distinguished as I'd hoped and instead made me look like I was trying to impersonate Des O'Connor. The line-up was further confused by the vast variance in bodily heights. Whilst we strode downstage trying to look all butch and Navy-like, the line looked like a badly arranged identity parade. It was impossible for anyone to look anyone else in the eye without either looking upwards or staring down towards the floor. Thank Christ we didn't have to do kicks like the Tiller Girls or we'd have been utterly fucked.

The direction of these hackneyed shows was also hardly of West End quality. Most of the big musical productions follow a fairly standardised presentational format: big opening number with full chorus and lots of pizazz followed by a bit of exposition business between the leads up front, then another song, then a slightly bigger chorus number, then back to a bit of two-handed up front whilst the scenery is changed... And so it goes on; the structure allowing for maximum flexibility of staging.

None of that seems to be taken on board by amateur directors though, who get into terrible trouble by having to somehow get a large a number of chorus people off the stage through very small exits at the side and at the rear. Some smaller locations may even only have one exit at the back of the stage, which up to 20 elderly and confused chorus players have to use to get off. This is made worse if what follows the big number is a bit of tender billing and cooing up front between the lady and her beau. It's hard to maintain an ambiance of burgeoning love when all the audience can see is two up front and a large number of haphazardly and massively frocked people jostling and queuing through a small hole behind them. As the love song is also likely to be quiet the effect isn't helped by the racket of shuffling feet to the rear and the curious way that the male lead has to behave in order to convey that there's nobody else there whilst he plights his troth. Needless to say all this was highly amusing to me and I found keeping a straight face very hard. I always look out for this basic staging error when going to see the largest possible amateur production in the smallest possible venue. *Oklahoma* is especially good for a laugh as the curtain goes up after overture as the opening scene has herself on stage churning butter whilst matey wanders on murdering 'Oh What A Beautiful Morning' and pretending there's nobody else there; hard to carry off effectively if the stage has roughly the same floor area as someone's living room.

I was once in a truly bizarre show called 'Midnight Cabaret with Cyril Fletcher' at the Assembly Hall theatre in Tunbridge Wells. It was a fundraising charity event attended by the Mayor, his wife and dignitaries, starring comic variety artist Cyril Fletcher (he of the BBC's *That's Life* TV fame) and local music and singing act Mark Adam, who also happened to be my music tutor at West Kent College. As usual I was in the chorus line. We had the advantage of a much bigger stage for this show and therefore the sets were similarly more impressive if a little on the hazardous side. The Sammy Khan Medley routine utilised a huge sweeping staircase built by men who obviously had no concept of the varying physical capabilities and costume requirements of the cast that would have to use it. As we burst forth with 'Three Coins In A

Fountain' and 'The Tender Trap' we were all directed to slowly descend this stairway from heaven arm in arm, lady to gentleman in the traditional fashion. Unfortunately each step was about 18 inches deep. The women were all wearing huge frocks and high heels, with the men done up in tight-trousered dress suits and top hats. As we clomped down the stairs it not only sounded like we were all wearing hobnailed boots, but there was a real risk of a total body count collapse. None of the women could actually see the stair edges because their frocks blocked the view. Therefore they were holding onto us for dear life and then pushing their frocks in the middle section to attempt to see where they were treading. It must have looked like the disorderly evacuation of first-class diners on the Titanic.

In addition a rumour had been sweeping the dressing rooms that the janitor there was a dirty old man and that he'd been seen peering through a small knothole in the stage floor to look up women's skirts as they passed over. The director kept asking why the women were all swishing their frocks to one side when they reached centre stage? He hadn't told them to do it, so why were they? 'There's a dirty old man trying to see my knickers,' explained my partner Dot. 'This might be a charity show, but that doesn't mean he's getting a freebie out of it too!'

Whilst Mark Adam was very professional and formal when singing his lovely songs (whatever they were), Cyril Fletcher was kind, friendly and chatty. We talked about poetry (one of his specialities) and comic writing and he was full of enthusiasm and encouragement with myself and the few other younger members in the show. It's unusual for a major star to spend so much time with the rest of the cast but it was appreciated. A genuinely nice man.

The show dragged on later and later, well past midnight and heading North towards 1am o'clock hours. Many of the more elderly in the chorus were yawning and struggling to stay awake. Even through the lights we could see that half the audience had nodded off and there were complaints by the ladies in the cast distracted by snoring noises coming from the stalls.

I don't know why we overran so much that night, but I do recall the director moaning at the orchestra conductor for dragging out the musical numbers. Most unfair. Never upset the band, that's a cardinal sin in a musical show!

That Christmas my stepfather managed to get me a temporary job working in the Tunbridge Wells postal sorting office. There were records to be bought and I needed the money so I accepted. Because my uncle was a postman there I was given a cushy job based in the sorting office itself and taking out special deliveries in the town centre only. It was a cold and snowy winter that year so being mainly in the warm and only venturing out a few times a day seemed ideal to me as opposed to traipsing around for miles in the snow with a two-ton bag of mail.

I set up stall around a huge table onto which thousands of cards and letters were poured for sorting into the relevant slots underneath. Most of the workers doing this were old ladies, with whom I had a great affinity. They had a marvellous sense of humour which came in handy when it was announced that our local Tory MP Patrick Mayhew was to pay a visit with his wife and delightful children. We were all accordingly told to behave ourselves and speak only if spoken to. This didn't go down too well with either me or the rest of the sorting ladies, most of whom looked like Les Dawson and Roy Barraclough's famous TV characters Cissy and Ada. As Mayhew was fawned over by the management his vile kids ran amok in the office, taking already-sorted mail out of the slots and throwing them back on the table. This infuriated the old girl sat next to me who suddenly grabbed the arm of one his boys as he'd attempted to pilfer her hole, gave him a sharp slap on the head and told him to piss off. The sound of the slap and the ensuing cry made all the officials suddenly look round. Cue sixteen stony faces round their table and one cowering boy. Well done her. No nonsense from the Tory boy that day!

After a while I began to realise that I'd drawn the short straw with this cushy job. All my compatriots were coming back from their rounds laden with Christmas tips, whilst I was getting bugger all. The snow fell deeper and the cold dug in as we approached Christmas Eve and the last shift clocked off. As I prepared to leave I noticed a parcel on the table outstanding for delivery and addressed to someone in Royal Chase, a posh area of the town on my way home. 'I'll take that if you like and deliver it on my walk home,' I said to the office manager, thinking that I would surely get a tip if I laid it on thick. 'Nah, fuck 'em, leave it there,' he helpfully exclaimed. 'They can have it after Christmas now, you get yourself home.' 'I don't mind, I haven't had a single tip all week, I'm bound to get something for this one!' 'Go on then, up to you,' he said, and I duly took the package and toddled off as he locked up and switched off all the lights. I trudged up the steep hill from the sorting office and eventually arrived at the huge gated house in Royal Chase. I pulled the doorbell cord and eventually a rather elderly lady came to the door. 'There you are, Madam,' I said with a great flourish as I handed over the package. 'This is the last parcel to leave Tunbridge Wells sorting office this Christmas!' 'Oh, do let me give you a little something for that,' she said in rather withering upper-class tones. 'That's quite alright Madam,' I said, with a sweep of my hand to express my modesty. 'Merry Christmas then,' she said and slammed the door in my face! Cow. 'Let that be a lesson to you,' said my mother when I got back home and told her. 'If someone offers you something, you take it.' She was quite right of course. Yet that was a lesson I don't think I ever really took to heart. To simply take without questioning goes against every brain cell of my psyche. I'm just too nice you see?

Probably.

My exam results came through in the summer of 1975 and were predictably mediocre. I passed six GCSE 'O' levels to add to my six equally mediocre CSE passes. I had always wanted to go to Drama School to fulfil my lifetime ambition of becoming an actor, but without a 100% grant or a scholarship there was no way I could have afforded to do that. The theatre was overwhelmingly elitist back then (and some may say it still is) and gaining Equity Union membership, which was mandatory, seemed an almost impossible dream.

I was getting pressure from home to apply for a job locally. My parents had no idea how much I wanted to escape from my home town and get up to London. I duly applied for two jobs, one as a warehouse assistant with international logistics company Transfesa in Paddock Wood near Tonbridge, and the other as a mail room boy with Pye Records in London. My stepfather drove me to the warehouse for an interview. I hated it. The smell, the environment, the language, the dirt and its very reason for even existing. Of course they offered me the job. Desperate not to be forced into it I went up to London and had the interview at Pye. Frankly I was so desperate to work for a record company that I would have paid them. But they insisted I lived too far away and when I heard they'd turned me down I was devastated. In a fit of pique I applied for a post with a classical music publishing company in Wardour St in Soho and to my delight I got the job.

And so began my first full-time job and my love affair with London.

3

Young Hearts Run Free & I Feel Love

1975 to 1980

The Managing Director of my first full-time employer, Peters Edition Ltd, looked like the tall man from the horror film *Phantasm*. His name was Jonson Dyer. He was at least 9 feet tall, had enormous hands and a cultured, silky upper-class accent. Why on earth he picked me I have no idea – I was just a gobshite from the sticks, albeit with a bit of boyish charm? Perhaps? The showroom was staffed by just four people. Myself and my manager Graham, and in the copyright office next door a very pretty little Jewish lady called Sandra and her assistant Ian (who would later write the original music for a show I was to appear in at the Royal Court Theatre in Sloane Square).

Graham was a very cultured, tall, thin-framed and extremely effete gay man whose closest friend Donald used to come into the showroom, hurl himself on top of the filing cabinets, flamboyantly cross his legs and make lewd comments about how gorgeous he thought I was. Even more outrageous was a man called Michael who worked at the head office in Baches Street in the city. If I answered the phone to him he'd say, 'Yesssss pleasssssse!' in a very salacious way. I never met him. He remains to this day just a disjointed voice that stuck in my mind. I'm aware that it sounds as though the company was crawling with perverts. Actually it wasn't, but that didn't stop us from having a great deal of fun. I adored Graham and he was very kind to me, as was Sandra.

Peters Edition is a world-famous music score publisher and as a result we frequently entertained well-known celebrities in the field of classical music. I say 'well known', at least to everyone else but me. One day we received a call from the PA to the great opera singer Elizabeth Schwarzkopf. Graham went into paroxysms of delight when he realised she'd be coming in. 'You are not to serve or even speak to her,' he ordered me. 'When she comes in you come and find me and then disappear until she's gone!'

Later that morning the showroom door opened and in swept La Schwarzkopf (not that I recognised her). I looked into the adjacent office and Graham was nowhere to be seen. Realising I couldn't just abandon her I politely started to serve her with some Schubert Lieder and other twiddly stuff. At which point his Lordship reappears from the loos out the back and sees that the great woman is being attended to in the showroom by a gobby little Kentish shitehawk (me). Aghast, he rushed in and practically kicked me out of the way. I slunk round the back to the post room and listened to him crawling obsequiously. After showering her with compliments so sweet she must have put on at least a stone in weight from it he reached his flattery crescendo.

'You know you really are my most favourite singer,' he oozed. Her reactions suggested she was told this by every person she'd ever met and she swept out laden with scores and the till was bursting with the cheque she wrote.

'Creep,' I said, having enjoyed the spectacle he'd made of himself.

He was a lovely man though. I wonder what happened to him? If anyone knows would you pop me a note through? Thanks.

The Peters Edition showroom was next door to the offices of Associated Television – ATV – and therefore the business base of the famous Grade brothers. Sir Lew Grade used to park his Rolls-Royce right outside our showroom door. At this time the IRA were busy planting bombs and blowing things up for freedom all over the place. London was on high alert. We were like coiled springs, ready for action should a package suddenly be spotted. One day I saw just such a contraption wedged under the rear wheel arch of his nibs' Roller. In a panic Graham and I called the Police who dropped everything and raced to the scene an hour later. During which time we had made complete prunes of ourselves out in the street trying to stop people from walking past what we thought was a bomb. In true British style nobody took any notice of us whatsoever. Despite the fact that there had been high profile emergencies and deaths all over the place as a result of this terrorism, Londoners were seemingly oblivious to it all. And they certainly weren't going to be deterred from going on their way by two queens running around waving their arms like demented cheerleaders. It turned out to be hoax, but only after the bomb disposal unit turned up to prod and poke it. These days I don't bother. I've lived long enough really, but back then I really cared.

One day I was in the showroom when another very prim and proper lady came in for some Chopin. I turned on my naive charm and happened to mention that I came from Tunbridge Wells. 'Oh, how posh!', she said with no obvious hint of sarcasm. I was thrilled and when she'd gone I marched into the copyright office where Sandra was sitting going over some legal papers. 'I've just been talking to a lady in the showroom and happened to mention I came from Tunbridge Wells and she said it was posh!', I enthusiastically reported. 'Yes, I always thought that,' said Sandra slowly and without even looking up from her papers, '… until I met you.'

I worked there for just over a year and had a wonderful time. I adored Soho, with its tramps, buskers, exotic foods, hints of danger and vibrant culture. Even the prostitutes who called out to you from seedy flats above the street were all part of this extraordinary place's allure. It's almost all gone now; sanitised and cleansed and made corporate and family friendly. It's lost its heart and soul; such a shame.

During my time there I met one of my first boyfriends proper. A really beautiful guy called Keith, with whom I fell madly in love. He lived way out in Elm Park in Essex where he rented a room in a house owned by a kindly lady who understood the 'complications' her gay tenant had in finding somewhere to live. Keith came from the West Midlands and all was fine until he lost his dad very suddenly. Things were never the same after that and he split from me, torn between staying in London and going home to be with his mum in the Black Country. Of course suffering from a broken heart was hard to bear. Who hasn't been through all of that and felt like ending it all dramatically from a bridge somewhere, with music underscored by John Williams? Happily for me I didn't and within a short time I'd moved on to Tom, who this time had fallen madly in love with me rather than vice versa.

He was a flautist with Goldsmith's College Orchestra. I was only then really coming to terms with gay politics. This wasn't as easy as people now might imagine. Homosexuality was of course illegal under the age of 21 and there was I just 17 and quite sure that the establishment was in no way going to tell me what to do. Rather than being scared of this, through the bohemian facilities that this great city afforded I could grow and flourish and throw the trammels of oppression off. I really didn't care. I knew who and what I was and if anyone else didn't like it then that was their problem.

Tom was a gentle and kindly man a few years older than me. At that time I was still living at home in Tunbridge Wells and commuting every day; up on the 0723 train, back home on the 1720 – wash, change and then run back down to the station to get the next train back to London and then home again on the last train at 2345. I did this frantic travelling every weekday for almost 18 months until it became impossible even for me to keep up.

When Tom became too clingy and started playing Diana Ross's 'Theme from Mahogany' to me all the time in an attempt to make me 'know where I was going to' I realised it was time to move on. I ended our relationship after about 6 months doing to him what had been done to me previously.

You'll either be relieved (or disappointed, what do I know?) to hear that I have no intention of going through an entire list of dreary detail about every lover or relationship I ever had. Who wants to read that? Not. Me. I'm just sticking to the main players and to people who were around me during so many fascinating and exciting times; in other words the ones I would want to read about if I was reading your story.

Sometime in the late summer of 1975 I had plucked up enough courage to purchase a copy of *Gay News* from a magazine stall at the entrance to Charing Cross station. Convinced I would either be instantly arrested or beaten up I stuffed it under my armpit and hurried to the very end of Platform 6 as far away from all civilisation as it was possible to get in central London. As my long, thin-bodied 12-car Hastings diesel train thundered in I made my way to the single seat located at the end of the carriage and from where I could secrete the offending paper inside the socially acceptable *Evening News* – except that this didn't work! For reasons best known to soon-to-be-criminal Denis Lemon, editor of 'You Know What News' it was about an inch bigger all round than the London evening papers. I tried hiding it but whichever way I manoeuvred it the word 'GAY' was still visible from the front. This made it look like I was reading the *Gay London Evening News*. Hardly the sort of thing the bowler hat brigade who commuted on my train to and from Royal Tunbridge Wells was used to seeing. Fart, bum and knickers, I thought. I would have to wait until I got home where I'd be able to read it in the safety of my bedroom with a stout bolt drawn on the door.

I didn't just read the paper, I devoured it. Every last page, column, photograph and word. I read, reread and re-reread until I could have staged a production of it. As a paper written by and for gay people it was fantastically eclectic for its time. Aside from news stories that would strike fear and astonishment into the hearts of today's supposedly enlightened society, within its pages were adverts for art studios, professionally installed security systems, exotic holiday hotels in Key West, book, record, theatre and film reviews, and an extensive pink page section of pub, club and social group listings. I know this all sounds a bit obvious, but knowing this was aimed at such a specific audience, and one that was effectively alienated from almost every other medium of the day, was fantastically comforting. Even more so when I found a small classified advert for the newly formed 'London Gay Teenage Group'. With the sounds of Van McCoy's 'Hustle' driving me on I plucked up courage and called the meeting's organiser to find out when and where the meeting was. It had to be done in total secrecy and with military precision. I felt like Jane Bond.

The group was founded by a guy who was to have a profound effect on my whole life. Philip Cox lived with his flatmate Paul in a council flat at Old Street in the City of London. The shabby-faced block was a two-minute walk from the tube there. Its delightful stainless-steel lifts stank of stale pee and frequently broke down. I was given the address and told that the next meeting was to have a guest speaker on the subject of 'Rubber'. I was baffled as to what this had to do with being a young gay teenager, but what the hell? I assumed it was perhaps an effective cover mechanism in case we were raided by the Police; 'Nothing to see here officer, just a group of young men discussing the economic development of Malaysian rubber plantations.' Well, you tell me? What on earth else was there to discuss about rubber? Tyres? Surely not rubber rain macs? Such waterproofed garments were for dirty old men and flashers, we were young and fresh and wore tight denim and cap-sleeved T-shirts.

The fetish elements of rubber were lost on me. I didn't have a clue. I arrived and was given a warm welcome by Phil (and totally ignored by his rather strange flatmate Paul, who appeared to be jealous of everyone and everything). There were about twelve young guys present, all nervously checking each other out and marvelling at what for most of us was the first time we'd been amongst our own kind in a safe environment. It's impossible for me to convey just how much this meant to us. It wasn't just a social gathering – it was a revelation.

Phil had cooked a vegetarian stew which was duly served to us all along with a hunk of bread. I picked at the stew wondering what the large white lumps it was full of actually were? I nudged the arm of a quietly spoken, curly blond haired Irish guy I was sat next to and asked him if he knew what they were?

'God, I think they're whole cloves of garlic! He must have put about ten whole bulbs of it in there. I won't be able to speak to anyone for about a week!'

Garlic was a foreign flavouring of fear as far as I was concerned. I had smelt the effect it had on breath and there was no way I was going to let that interfere with the aroma of Tabac aftershave I was liberally drenched in. Together we picked out the deathly lumps and hid them in uneaten bread chunks to save offence. Phil may have been a pioneer of gay liberation, but he sure as hell wasn't a cook. At the end of the evening I discovered that Phil and I shared the same sense of humour and we made plans to meet up again in town.

Meanwhile I had to somehow get back to Charing Cross to get my last train home at 2345 o'clock hours. With nearby Old Street tube station being on the City Branch of the Northern Line it may as well have been on Mars and I began to fear I'd miss my train. The kindly Irish guy with whom I'd been hiding the garlic earlier on (not a euphemism) said he had come on his motorbike and that he had a spare helmet. He would give me a lift back to Charing Cross 'no problem'. We said our goodbyes and agreed to leave in pairs for safety reasons. I behelmeted myself and clambered on board my new friend's huge black bike. I held onto him for dear life as he hurtled through the deserted streets of the City towards St. Paul's, Fleet Street and eventually the Strand. With minutes to spare I dehelmeted myself, thanked him profusely and ran to Platform 5 for my train home. Alas that was the last I ever saw of him. He didn't come to any more meetings. I wondered if it was because I'd left scorch marks on the back of his leather jacket from all that garlic? Maybe I had held on just a bit too tight? For all that I have never forgotten him. I wonder if he will ever read this and remember that same event? If it's you reading this, then thank you again. You may never have realised how much that lift meant to me.

Phil and I became the closest of friends meantime, despite the aggressive unfriendliness meted out towards me from flatmate Paul. Both of them worked for the Greater London Council on the South Bank. I would sometimes pop down there to see them in their subsidised canteen at lunchtime, during which time Paul's clothing I had noticed was getting more and more outrageous. I was strictly a high-waisted flared trousers and tight shirt kinda guy, but Paul and his friends I noticed were starting to wear incredibly tight PVC drainpipe trousers in fluorescent colours that could stop traffic. The catalyst for this fashion change appeared to come from a friend of theirs called Steve. Steve was sharing a flat in a rather seedy house in nearby Lower Marsh Market. The girls who plied their trade from the other rented rooms in the house were really very sweet.

Steve, Paul and their friends were the original punk fashionistas. It was they who started the style revolution way before it hit the mainstream. Most of their outfits came from from Vivienne Westwood and Malcolm McLaren's shop 'SEX' in the King's Road, although much of it was also home-made by Steve, who was also an accomplished stylist in his own right. Although the GLC was a Labour-dominated seat of local government and not known for its conservative habits, I am not sure they were over-enamoured of Paul turning up with ripped T-shirts sprayed with the words 'FUCK' and 'GAY' all over them.

Steve was fabulously good-looking and very, very scary. His wide staring eyes had an emotional and artistic anger which I had never come across before. It was both terrifying in its intensity and thrilling at the same time. I loved going to their parties, even though they could be violent drink-and drug-fuelled affairs. The music was good anyway. At one I went to with them in a suburban semi-detached house up in Wembley I recall Steve punching his fist through some glass door panels. There was blood and spilled drink everywhere. Yet every time he came up to speak to me he seemed perfectly calm and lucid. Many years later I came across Steve again when he was running his own shop selling imported luxury Middle Eastern carpets, rugs and bags in Seven Dials, Covent Garden. During the course of our conversation and remembrances I recalled those manic punk days from years before and how baffled I was that it would all be kicking off one minute and then down to earth with me seconds later. 'That's easy to explain,' Steve told me 'You were totally unshockable. Nothing we did or said seemed to have any effect on you at all, so we never aimed any of it at you.' This seemed strangely comforting to me. I just soaked up all that was going on around me, the more outrageous the more I loved it. And yet for all that I remained strangely conventional in my psyche. This would stay with me throughout my life, with the same attitude carrying me through my theatre career and eventually doing live television.

In typical Gemini style I was leading a double existence in London. With Phil and the teenage group on one side I was also frequenting the cafe bar of the Institute of Contemporary Arts (the ICA) in The Mall, just down the road from Buckingham Palace. There I meet and became fixated upon a handsome, dark-haired brown-eyed man called Gerald Chapman. Gerald was an up-and-coming theatre director who had just started working at the Royal Court theatre in Sloane Square. I had been desperately trying to get into drama school to train as an actor, but although I'd been accepted at both Central and Mountview drama schools I could not get a grant to enable me to study. Kent County Council wouldn't give me one as I'd left home in Tunbridge Wells and the London educational authority wouldn't either as I hadn't been living in London long enough to qualify. I was especially pissed off because I had somehow managed to learn a great tract of Shakespearean monologue for audition purposes. I hated Shakespeare as I didn't understand any of it, but it had to be done and was a requirement of practically every audition back then. At the Mountview audition I had stood awkwardly in front of the panel, with the Principal, Peter Coxhead, sat in the middle peering at me. I spluttered out the lines that had caused me so much pain learning…

'Now I am alone. O, what a rogue and peasant slave am I!
Is it not monstrous that this player here,
But in a fiction, in a dream of passion,
Could force his soul so to his own conceit
That from her working all his visage wann'd.'

At which point I could see Mr Coxhead staring at my crotch. Valiantly I carried on trying to avoid his gaze.

'Tears in his eyes, distraction in's aspect.
A broken voice, and his whole function suiting
With forms to his conceit? And all for nothing!'

I hadn't got a clue what any of this stuff meant, yet as I was saying the words they seemed somehow to end up more as a comment on the way that I was being rather lasciviously ogled. I felt pretty sure that the Bard hadn't had that in mind when he wrote it. I rambled on awkwardly until I came upon my final speech line:

'… Swounds, I should take it: for it cannot be.'

With a flourish of the Coxhead's hand I was asked to come back later for the verdict. Incredibly I was accepted, although that last Shakespearean line proved to be oddly prophetic as I couldn't take it and it wasn't to be. I just couldn't get a grant and without the money from a rich mummy and daddy it was beginning to look as though my stage career was disappearing Hamlet style. Amusingly I even wrote to my home MP, a certain Patrick Mayhew, to try and get the funding decision reversed somehow. I assume he was unaware that I had been sat at the sorting office table when one of his vile kids was clouted for misbehaving, though I managed to convince myself that he'd had MI5 on to me and had been waiting for an opportunity to accordingly slap me down. He wrote to me claiming to be 'extremely sorry', although I failed to detect any tear stains on his parliamentary notepaper.

Even and despite all that, I was lucky. If I had attended a drama school I would undoubtedly have been skilled not only with stage crafts, but the discipline that is so important and which I lacked in abundance. I would also have been subjected to dance classes and general show business capabilities that didn't interest me. Although I was a reasonable (untrained) singer my ongoing experiences in chorus lines had taught me I was certainly not a dancer and with every production I was involved with I was convinced I resembled Norman Wisdom in ballet shoes.

Gerald Chapman came to my rescue. The ICA cafe was impossibly hip and literally crawling with literary geniuses. In the latter months of 1975 as Rod Stewart 'Sailed' and David Essex 'Hold Me Close' in the main pop charts, I had discovered Disco in the shady upper floors of London's gay pubs, there being no large clubs at that time. Silver Convention sang 'Fly Robin Fly' and our very own Donna Summer crooned and groaned 'Love To Love You Baby' all over the place as our 'community' (such as it was) musically split once and for all from the mainstream to find a dance, fashion and music subculture all of its own.

Gerald lived in a basement flat in Warwick Avenue in North West London with a gentle and kindly stage designer called Barry Parr and a couple of rather lovely butch lesbians whose names escape me now. Through them I got introduced to London's mainstream subversive theatre and arts culture.

When I wasn't slumming it round at Phil Cox's tower block flat I was loving it at the ICA and at the parties that Gerald took me to. He seemed to know everyone there was to know even though I'd never heard of them. Who was David Hockney anyway? Eh? I liked his glasses and very blond hair but withdrew somewhat in conversation as I lacked any artistic gravitas. Still, I was a bit on the rough side even though I was something of a pretty boy. I recall sitting through a showing of Hockney's 'A Bigger Splash' at the ICA cinema and thinking just how distant it all was from the front line gay politic I was experiencing through association with Phil Cox. I don't recall the two 'sides' ever meeting, although it is perfectly possible that Phil came to see the first production I was in at the Royal Court and which dealt with the lives and experiences of gay teenagers.

Gerald had been taken on by the Royal Court to form a new theatre workshop company called the Young People's Theatre Scheme. He'd been given an office round the back of the theatre just off Sloane Square, and next to an old garage which had been disused for years and which belonged to the theatre.

Gerald's office was something of a safe space for us and it was lovely to have somewhere we could simply be ourselves without fear of harassment.

The moniker 'YPTS' just didn't fill anyone with enthusiasm though, as it rolled off the tongue like a brick. 'We need to find another name for it. Let's hold a competition and see what turns up.' And so we did. The winning entry gave us the name 'The Activists'. Its logo being a capital letter 'A' made up of pins. I was enthralled to be enrolled as member number 2, with Gerald himself at number 1 on the roll call. The newly formed company was split into two at a very early date as Gerald decided to focus his attention on a workshopped play devised by and for young gay men and women. The other 'straight' company worked with writer Edward Bond and directors Max Stafford-Clark and John Schlesinger. Edward Bond always seemed so serious and the play he wrote for The Activists was a real no fun zone as far as I was concerned. John Schlesinger though seemed both passionate and genuinely interested in our development as actors. He gave us boundless enthusiasm and encouragement, together with that discipline we lacked and so desperately needed.

Gerald meanwhile had gone off on a holiday to Greece and whilst there had sent a postcard of a small classical statuette with an enormous willy to my home address at Tunbridge Wells. His handwritten message said how much he was missing me and ended with 'Love Gerald' and a swathe of kisses. At first my parents ignored it, but eventually my mother came to me and asked me if she minded her asking me 'a question'. Not so much 'a question' as 'the question' really. I was relieved to confirm her suspicions and she assured me that both she and my stepfather still loved me just the same and that all they ever wanted was for me to be happy. Wasn't that sweet? Mind you, I could have killed Gerald for provoking it all – most probably quite deliberately.

Considering the times, I really did get off with family politics as easily as that. It simply wasn't an issue for me and I certainly didn't have any of the hysterical dramas that so many of my friends went through. Doesn't make for much of a story really does it? One erotic postcard with a willy on it and a heart to heart with mother and that was it. However it did convince me that I had to move out once and for all. I couldn't keep up the commuting as it was cramping my style. My torrid affair with Gerald didn't really last that long for reasons that whilst burned as they are on my mind I don't think you'd care to have burned into yours. We did however remain close friends. I shall return back to the Royal Court shortly, but before that I need to get back on the tube to Old Street.

Through Phil I met Iain, the guy I would leave Tom for in that long hot summer of 1976. Whilst Wings were riding high with 'Silly Love Songs' and Melba Moore's 'This Is It' was ringing in our ears at the gay disco above the Green Man pub at Great Portland Street, Iain and I were struggling to spend time together as both of us were living at home; me in the Wells and he in Ealing, West London. At least he had a car though. He also had a friend called David who was conveniently studying at Kingston University and living in their halls of residence on Kingston Hill. One day during the summer break Iain and I concocted an elaborate plan to spend the night together in David's room there whilst he was going home for the weekend. We had planned to go to a new disco just off of Oxford Street and then drive back to Kingston afterwards for a night of passion in David's room.

There was however one flaw in this grand plan: the halls of residence were guarded by an fierce old dragon who kept an eagle eye on every coming and going. David had given Iain a key to get in so all we had to do was drive up, park and let ourselves in the back door, creep up the stairs and bob's your uncle, a night of passion at last!

We had a great time bopping around at the Hanover Grand in the West End and clambered into Iain's Austin 1100 for the 45-minute drive back to Kingston Hill. As the car scrunched up the gravel driveway with the silence of adjacent Richmond Park amplifying every engine throb and tyre squelch we winced at the racket we were trying so hard not to make. We parked and crept up to the door in the almost total darkness. After fumbling with the bloody keys for a painful eternity we finally gained entrance. The dragon's lair was an office to the left of the door we had just creaked open. Hardly daring to breathe we picked our way across the parquet floor tiles and got about halfway up the staircase in front of us when suddenly from behind us came a booming voice that could have woken my family in Australia.

'WHO ARE YOU?!' boomed our nemesis from behind us. I froze in abject terror, when to my astonishment Iain, who was actually not the most demonstrative person I'd ever met, wheeled round and threw the compliment straight back at her.

'Why? Who are YOU?'

'I am the bursar here and responsible for the security of the residence. Now who are you and what are you doing here?'

I was still frozen in terror.

'We have come to see David,' lied Iain.

'At a quarter to one in the morning?' burst forth she.

'Why not? You live your life your way and we live ours in ours. David gave us a key so we wouldn't disturb anyone. What's so strange about that?' said Iain with an air of confidence that belied our situation.

'Well, then let's see if David is in shall we? And whilst we are at it I will have that key back,' she said, grabbing the dangling metal from Iain's hand and frogmarching us up to David's empty room.

She hammered on the door waking up the rest of the residence and the inhabitants of several nearby graveyards.

'DAVIIIIIIIIIID!!'

Silence.

'DAVVVVIIIIIIIIIIIIIIIIIIIIIIIIIIIIIIIIID!!'

Painful silence.

At which point I suddenly regained my voice and some backbone.

'Oh no! Don't tell me we've driven all the way from central London and he's gone out? Typical! Oh well, when you see him will you tell him to call us to let us know he's OK?' I said with an actor's conviction as we hurried back down the stairs and out of the back door to Iain's still warm 1100, leaving Miss Trunchbull glowering in the doorway.

We clambered in and drove off not knowing what to do or where to go. We couldn't go to either of our homes and it seemed there was no option other than to find somewhere to park the car and sleep in it until morning. Iain found a quiet lane and duly parked. He slept in the front and I scrunched up in the back seat. At least it wasn't cold.

As dawn broke and the sun crept into the car we stirred on hearing odd noises all around us. Wiping the condensation squeakily from the windows we were horrified to discover that he'd actually parked the car in the middle of a riding stables. All around us were stable hands and horses peering into the car which looked like it had been deposited there by an alien spaceship.

The living situation couldn't carry on this way. And so I consulted the classifieds in *Time Out* magazine and found myself a room in a house in New Barnet on the topmost end of the Northern Line. Keith drove down to Tunbridge Wells with me to collect my things as I moved out of the family home for the first and final time. My mother was terribly distressed and assured me that I would certainly be back before very long. Of course, I never did. It was as final as a closing curtain with no encore. At last I had broken free of Tunbridge Wells for the excitement and wonder of living in the capital city I simply couldn't get enough of.

Hey, at this point how about a bit of supernatural stuff? Just to perk things up a wee bit? Yes? Alright then, here we go. I should perhaps point out that I am not only an atheist but also a complete non-believer in the occult and the supernatural. I do however love the gothicness and drama of it all, henceforth the stories I shall now relate. I have no idea what caused the events I shall tell of, and I offer no solutions. They are as much of a mystery to me now as they were when they occurred. In all these years I still have no explanation for any of it. And yet I can assure you that everything I relate is exactly as it happened.

The house I moved to was at 10 Shaftesbury Avenue, New Barnet. A largish semi-detached Victorian house owned by a short bespectacled gay guy in his late thirties. He lived there alone and rented out his spare rooms to young gay guys for six months at a time. I had the biggest of the rooms and a very sweet young blond Scottish guy called David had the room next to mine. I think the landlord was involved with the local council in some capacity but I can't recall exactly what. He frequently worked overnight and often spent time away from the house at his mother's nearby. This left David and I totally alone in the house.

One night, with the landlord away and the house locked up, David and I had said our goodnights after bathroom duties had been taken care of and repaired to our respective rooms when a strange noise on the upper landing stopped me in my tracks. It sounded like glass marbles being rolled around on a tin tray and it appeared to be coming from the upper landing and staircase. I tapped on the adjoining wall between mine and David's room and called to him. 'David, is that you?' 'I'm in here, is it you making that noise?' he whispered through the plaster. 'Of course it's not me!' I cried. 'I'm not going out there, I'm too scared,' said David. 'Me neither,' said I, and with that we both hurried to our beds and pulled the covers over our heads. The noise rattled on for a while and then stopped as suddenly as it had started.

In the morning after a sleepless night for us both we met on the landing and made a thorough inspection. We found nothing. The house was locked up and just as we had left it when we had retired just a few hours earlier.

Neither of us had any idea what had just happened and we never did find out. The house was desperately creepy though and we were both glad to move on, I to a new flat share in The Barbican in the City of London and David back to his native Scotland. I have tried to locate him after all these years and through the wonders of the internet found him through LinkedIn at an educational establishment in Scotland. I wrote to him hoping to talk through old times but sadly at the time of writing this he hasn't responded. Told you I was a handful didn't I? I wonder if he thinks it was me playing a trick on him? It really wasn't you know.

My next experience was far more terrifying than that though. Ready? Here we go then. Don't say you're not getting your money's worth.

Through Phil Cox I had been introduced to a guy called John with whom I had had a dalliance, although we became friends more than lovers. John worked at the BBC at Television Centre and knew lots of media types. After leaving the New Barnet House of Horror I needed somewhere to live, preferably close to my then job as an international telephonist at the old Faraday telephone exchange in Queen Victoria St. near to St. Paul's Cathedral. It was John who introduced me to a BBC TV director called Peter Butler. He had a fabulous flat in the Barbican; 268 Ben Jonson House to be precise. This was one of the long concrete blocks on the ultra-modern estate and accessed from an above street walkway known as The Podium. Peter's split-level flat was on the bottom corner of the building, opposite Shakespeare Tower and the ancient Whitbread Brewery, with Whitecross St. market adjacent at street level. The whole thing was a vision of 1970s futurism; stark and brutal in architectural design. Its other great advantage was that it was a mere five-minute walk from where my dear friend Phil Cox lived at Old St. Result!

Both bedrooms in the flat were located on the upper floor and either side of the front door, which was at the very end of a long corridor seemingly stretching for miles. It was like a carpeted luxury prison. In all the time I lived there I never saw a neighbour or had any idea who they were. My bedroom had one entire wall of glass, split into two as huge sliding doors leading out onto a balcony which went right round the end of the building. From the very day I moved in I was convinced that I could hear whispering outside my room coming from the balcony area outside. John was convinced I was just hearing the wind, which used to whistle around the estate like a parochial Mistral. However what I could hear was not the breeze, it was definitely hushed speech of some sort.

Peter was frequently abroad, mostly back in Australia where he hailed from, and as a consequence I was often in the flat on my own for weeks at a time. I grew to hate the telephonist job that I'd taken to earn myself money whilst trying to figure out how to progress my acting career. During one of Peter's trips away I fell ill with tonsillitis. Feeling exceptionally shitty and it not being helped by having to talk all day in the switch room it developed into an acute infection and then into an abscess in my throat. This required me to go to my doctor every day so he could check I was able to drink water (and thereby evade a hospital event). I glugged gallons of penicillin during this time and was genuinely a very poorly soldier.

Right, that's the scene set – now onto the scary bit you've all been waiting for. One morning I was due to walk round the Podium level to my doctor's surgery and have him check I was still alive. As I prepared to leave the flat for some strange reason I felt compelled to check that all the glass doors were closed and secure on the upper level. I checked my bedroom and all was good, walked round to Peter's bedroom at the front of the building and all seemed fine there too. As he mainly directed classical music productions he had an upright piano in his room with a reading light on top just above its sheet music holder. It wasn't in my nature to venture anywhere near Peter's room as I totally respected his privacy, but on this occasion I had somehow felt compelled to check all was OK before leaving the flat.

I duly shut the door and got into the lift to go down to the Podium level and walk round to the surgery. For some odd reason though I pressed the wrong button and instead went right down to street level. I have no idea why. When I exited the lift I crossed the road and considered trying to get to my destination from there instead of schlepping back up to the Podium. All of a sudden I was overcome with what can only be described as absolute dread. I turned back and looked up at the flat and into the windows of Peter's bedroom. I saw nothing but had an indescribable urge to go back up to the flat. To this day I have no idea why, I just knew that I had to go back. I crossed the road and caught the lift back up to my floor. With absolute terror gripping my head and heart I opened the front door to the empty flat. All was quiet and yet I was more frightened than I had ever been in my entire life. I noticed that Peter's bedroom door was ajar and this was not how I had left it only minutes before. I slowly walked across the landing and pushed the door open. To my horror the reading light which I had seen just a short time ago on top of the piano was now laying about ten feet away on Peter's bed with the flex and plug trailing on the floor; an impossibility that to this day I cannot rationally explain. Gripped by utter terror I fled the flat, slamming the door behind me and rushing down to the nearest phone box to call my friends Clive and Mike over in Victoria. In a state of complete panic I gabbled some old nonsense and asked if I could go over and stay the night with them as I didn't want to be in the flat on my own.

When I reached them I was in a terrible state. Feeling ill from the terrible sore throat I had and still confused and frightened by what I had seen and felt back at Ben Jonson House, my friends managed to calm me down over a nice meal and with the assurance of a safe place to stay the night. I struggled to find the right words to explain just how terrified I had been and what the fear I had experienced was caused by. The lamp incident seemed almost secondary to the feeling of dread I had experienced. The following day dawned bright and cold. After the boys made me breakfast they managed to persuade me that I couldn't stay away and that I needed to go back if only to put my own mind at rest. I caught the Circle Line all the way round from Victoria to Moorgate and strolled back in the winter sunshine to Ben Jonson House, approaching it from the same location I had looked back up from only the day before. This time though I felt no dread and no fear. It was as if nothing had happened at all.

I ascended in the lift and let myself back in. Once again, no feeling of foreboding or anxiety. I walked round to Peter's bedroom and there was the lamp still laying on his bed with the wire draped curiously down the side of the bed with its plug on the floor. I picked it up and put it back where it belonged, went down the open staircase to the kitchen and made myself a coffee. As I was sitting contemplating what had happened and wondering how I could have been so rattled I heard a knock on the front door. This was unusual as entry for visitors was by the intercom from the Podium level entrance. Whoever was knocking was obviously already inside the building. I opened the front door to find two men who introduced themselves as representatives from the Police by flashing their credentials. They asked if they could talk to me and if I had been in the flat the previous evening and if I'd heard or seen anything unusual? I told them I had only just returned after visiting friends the previous evening, where I had stayed the night. Curious as to what this was all in aid of I asked them what was going on and why they were inside the building? 'I'm sorry to have to tell you that a backpacker was murdered last night on the podium level underneath the room at the rear of your flat,' explained Detective Inspector whatever his name was. This was immediately underneath my bedroom window and balcony. They duly left when my movements were corroborated and they realised I could not help them in their enquiries. I can report that from that day onwards I heard no more whispering and there were no repeats of anything untoward in the flat. Make of it what you will. It's as much of a mystery to me. There's no logical or practical explanation for any of it, yet it happened exactly as I have described here.

My final weird experience happened about two years after this in Muswell Hill, North London. I was staying with my then boyfriend Paul and his flatmate

Chris at their rooms on the ground floor of a huge semi-detached Victorian house in Cranley Gardens (oddly enough in the same street that years later serial killer Dennis Nilson would butcher his poor victims). We had retired to bed after an evening of fun and games when we heard odd sounds coming from the hallway. All was deathly quiet in the house as we were the only inhabitants there at the time. We could clearly hear hard and defined footsteps walking around on the polished tiles in the hall immediately outside the room we were in. 'There's somebody out there!' whispered Chris in a no-shit-Sherlock moment. 'It must be burglars because there's nobody else in the house,' mouthed a terrified Chris as we agreed we would find something large and heavy to cosh an intruder with after rushing them in a surprise attack! Failing to find a handy cosh of any sort Paul grabbed the first thing he could lay his hands on, which happened to be a small and utterly lethal milk saucepan. We prepared for an assault as the footsteps grew ever louder and appeared to be right outside our room door. With a sudden burst of energy we hurled ourselves out of the room and into the hallway, assault kitchenware aloft.

It was completely empty. Nobody there. Front door locked as it had been earlier and no sign of any life anywhere in the rest of the building. All three of us were totally stunned. It didn't make any sense. We had heard someone walking with hard-heeled shoes right outside the door – for certain. Yet it was dark, empty and full of nothingness.

And that dear reader concludes the supernatural stories. Nothing has happened to me of any note in that vein ever since. I can offer no explanations or theories; make of it what you will. As I said earlier, I'm a total non-believer in the occult and have always treated the supernatural as entertainment rather than anything from the great behind. The latter incident is noteworthy however as there were three people who all experienced the same thing. Otherwise I'd openly suggest that perhaps I am just bonkers?

For the moment I need to return to my dear friend Phil Cox. Writing all this has made me realise just how much he meant to me and how much I miss him. I'm afraid the postscript on Phil isn't a very happy one, so for now I need to stay with happier times. Our friendship developed alongside our shared sense of humour and love of music, gadgets and politics. With regards to the latter it could be a scary thing to be out with Phil. He was highly... err... demonstrative and would think nothing of suddenly grabbing hold of you for a big overt, flamboyant kiss out on the street if he spied Police watching. Whilst this amused me it has to be borne in mind that as gay people we were still social pariahs even in the supposedly enlightened late 70s. Our pubs and clubs were regularly raided by the authorities on the flimsiest of pretences; agent-provocateur tactics, although illegal, were employed to lure gay men into traps and subsequent arrest. The Police would think nothing of exposing gay people to humiliation and outing in front of their friends, family and employers, such tactics frequently resulting in heartbreak, job losses and even suicide in some cases. It was against this backdrop that our political stance was formed. As out gay teenagers we were acutely aware that we had no legal status and were subject to arrest and blackmail by the status quo, and yet for all that our group of friends grew stronger and more active in our desire for change.

Phil was one of the kindest and most genuine people I ever met. He would provide a place to stay for people who had been thrown out of their homes and would lend money to those who needed it in an emergency. The tower block he lived in was tough. Phil was frequently abused, beaten up and had all sorts of objects pushed through his letterbox (the details of which I won't go into here). He even suffered a few attempted arson attacks, which were foiled owing to his prescience in placing a secure box on the inside of the door. Despite this he would help elderly neighbours and those with small children if the lifts were out of order (which they frequently were). With three flights of stairs between each floor it was no mean feat getting in and out when the urine soaked lifts were out of order.

As time went by we came up with the idea of the first radio programme made and presented by and for gay men. This would eventually become 'Gaywaves', the first such radio programme anywhere in the world. Of course we realised that the established media wouldn't touch such a thing with a 20-foot broom handle, so we decided to go it alone and do it for ourselves. The first programme would not be broadcast until May 1982, but the conception and development commenced a long time before that. I would write and record sketches, make jingles, and we'd play our favourite music to make taped mock-up programmes over four years before we actually found a way of broadcasting them. I spent most evenings with Phil and he became one of my most trusted friends, although he was not always the easiest person to get along with. He had a ferocious and furious temper. It was not wise to get on the wrong side of him, although I learned quickly that his outbursts were always very temporary and that if he said sorry he really meant it. These mercurial changes of temperament were alarming for those unprepared for it, and not everyone stayed the course with him.

Although he didn't smoke, he had a particular fondness for home-baked hash brownies, which he made tray loads of and shared with anyone daft enough to tuck in. As I mentioned earlier, Phil's cooking was more 'cordoned off' than 'cordon bleu', so I generally avoided it, quite apart from the fact that drugs scared me and I had no intention of partaking; I wanted to stay aware of what was going on around me.

One night Phil's baking almost cost him his life. The dope he'd got hold of for the tray bake that night must have been bad as after eating it he became increasingly disturbed, tripping with nightmare visions of the building being on fire (which of course it wasn't). It is just as well that I was there with him as the drug-induced paranoia grew so bad that he tried to climb onto the flat balcony handrail and jump off. From that height he would have been killed had he succeeded. I managed to lock the balcony door and spent all night talking him down. I had no idea what I was doing, but my sixth sense told me to just keep him occupied with soft voice, mild humour and constant reassurance. I held him tight if things got really bad. Eventually after several hours I managed to rock him to sleep. I was physically and mentally exhausted and fearful of allowing myself to fall asleep in case Phil woke up in the same state. When he did finally awaken the effects had worn off completely. He had no recollection of the previous night and just how close to death he'd been. I decided not to tell him but just to make sure he knew he'd been ill and that the dope was to blame. I'm pleased to say it taught him as much of a lesson at it did me. I never took drugs again – ever. That experience would, I am certain, protect me from the effects and consequences of the excesses I would confront later.

As the long hot summer of '76 faded to the halcyon disco-fuelled new year of 1977 we danced the night away to Rose Royce's 'Car Wash', Thelma Houston's 'Don't Leave Me This Way' (incidentally one of the first newfangled 12" singles I ever bought), Cerrone's 'Love In C Minor' and El Coco's 'Let's Get It Together'. London's gay discos were almost always above pubs in rented rooms. The London scene was dominated by a guy called Tricky Dicky, who ran the majority of down-to-earth, low-end gay discos at various pub venues around the city. I was yet to experience the high-end club scene based around Bond Street's Embassy Club.

Our queen was Donna Summer. Her records ruled all without exception. The arrival of every new Giorgio Moroder-produced disc would be met with fanatical excitement. In July of 1977 I was in my favourite inner London record store browsing the latest import singles which included a new one by Donna

Summer called 'Can't We Just Sit Down And Talk It Over'. 'You won't think much of that,' said the guy behind the counter, who knew that I was seeking fast dance music with plenty of high hat and bass riffs. 'But the other side is sensational, give it a listen,' he said handing me a set of headphones. The B side of the single was a track called 'I Feel Love'. The sweeping, swirling, surging, throbbing electronic sound was a revelation. I had never heard anything like it before. I played it twice in the store as I couldn't wait any longer to get it to the decks at the Sols Arms disco next to the Euston Tower at Warren Street that evening. That record remains in my opinion one of the most groundbreaking pop records ever released. It changed everything; overnight the gay disco dance scene transformed into a whirling frenzy of electronic sound, with Moroder at the forefront. Although there had been previous electronic sounds from the likes of Can, Kraftwerk, Faust, Eno and Roxy Music – they were all fairly rock based and rarely troubled the dancefloors. I still have that same vinyl single now and play it whenever my mood needs a boost. I'm instantly transported back to those wonderful days when it was all new. The gay discos had a very different feel to straight clubs – the fashions and dancing all totally different. They were places of sheer joy, fabulously free and never with any violence or trouble. Even when we were raided by the Police the 'community' generally stayed calm and just put up with it. This would eventually change following harassment on a grand scale by the Police outside London's Coleherne bar in Earl's Court. Phil called me to say that there was trouble brewing there and that we should all go and demonstrate to show we wouldn't be pushed around. The Coleherne was a famous leather bar, which wasn't my scene at all. I don't recall why I didn't go there, but it certainly wasn't for fear of arrest or violence – like all of our clan we were up for whatever was needed. However for some reason I stayed away. It's possible that I was in rehearsals at the time? Who can say?

Meanwhile at the Royal Court, Gerald and the Activists theatre group was developing nicely albeit split into two groups: the gay group and the, well, I suppose the straight group? In the early days we had stayed fairly close and I was very friendly with a sweet, incredibly good-looking blond-haired guy called Maxwell Caulfield. Max had been dancing at the Raymond Revue Bar and the Windmill and struggling to be taken seriously there. He was incredibly strong-willed and focused upon making it in the business, and I admired him hugely for this. Max was also one of the very few actors who 'crossed over' and socialised with those of us in the 'other' group. I don't recall anyone else doing that. He would often come out with us to bars and parties and had a wry, and rather raw take on things which went down well with our crowd. I got the sense that some in the other group were a bit intimidated by him; he wasn't someone to be messed about with for sure. However I always found him to be genuine, good fun to be with and kind hearted in a masculine straight sort of a way. Even when he told us of the time that he had stormed out of one of the shows he was doing because one of the other male dancers had groped him inappropriately on stage, it all seemed perfectly reasonable to me. Despite the other dancer concerned knowing Max was straight he had continually fumbled with him in the groinage area. Fed up with this Max told us he'd 'sloshed him' after deciding enough was enough, walking out of the production. There was nothing homophobic about it, it was a matter of professional pride; they were there to do a job and not be interfered with whilst doing it, especially in light of recent revelations regarding the behaviour of some men in our industry. These were the days when gaining the required Equity union membership was really tough. You had to have one to be able to work professionally and yet it was almost impossible to get qualifying work if you didn't have membership. It was a terribly unfair system which forced many of us towards qualifying contract jobs that otherwise we would not have touched with the proverbial bargepole. Incredibly, working in the 'adult entertainment' sector was a source of much prized qualifying contracts. If you were young and good-looking it was relatively easy to get one of these jobs and to put it towards the requisite number of continuous weeks professional work that Equity needed for a union card. The whole pukka entertainment industry was a closed shop at that time too; you want the work then you have to be in the union. I was to come a cropper with this later on whilst working on TV at Tyne Tees, but more of that later.

The last time I saw Max he had decided that the system here in the UK was too restrictive, stuffy and old fashioned. He was young, fabulous looking and dynamic. As we sat in a bar just off Dean Street in Soho he enthralled me when he said 'I can't do this here, I can't breathe in this environment. I'm off to the States and won't come back until I've made it.'

All credit to our Max, he did indeed go to the US, met and married Juliet Mills and later landed parts in the film *Grease 2* and Aaron Spelling's lavish internationally camp TV series *The Colbys*. Good on you, Max. Though I doubt he'd ever remember me and I never saw him again after he left I will always remember him as one of the nice guys.

When it comes to being groped and interfered with in general I only ever had one negative experience and that was when I went to see a potential room in a house at Putney Bridge in West London. I turned up to find it was in a house owned by an actor who I recognised as a bit part player in several *Carry On* films. I was offered a seat in a rather high-backed chair and then interviewed mainly by the actor's boyfriend, a much younger model and far better looking. As you'll have gathered by now, I am not the sort of person to be messed about with and when they started making comments about the contents of my trousers and then getting 'feely-touchy' with my frontispiece I told them I wasn't interested and made a hasty exit. They seemed to find this highly amusing. I didn't. I could name names, but I won't. I don't have a grudge and I'm happy with the way I handled it. Mind you, I still can't look at this actor in those films without recalling what happened.

Though I hate to disappoint anyone who's got this far hanging off the possibility of lurid sex stories I'm afraid that nobody else ever tried anything on in my entire career. I guess I should be happy with that, although I have no idea why when I heard so much stuff going on from my friends and colleagues. I was twinky and quite pretty back then, though at the time you don't recognise that do you? Sort of. I suppose. So much for sex, drugs and rock and roll. I lived my life on the periphery of it all. If I was a superhero I would be called 'PeripheryMan', always there on the sideline of a major incident being vigorously left alone. Don't be under any misconceptions though, I got invited to all sorts of spectacular parties at houses where the pop stars now sport wigs and false teeth rather than spandex and eyeliner.

My love life meanwhile was as all over the place as you'd expect from a new boy about town. In the summer of '77 I had fallen deeply in love with an actor called Tim Wales. For me this was one of those awful obsessional affairs that only ever seem to end up in heartbreak. I utterly adored him and even though I knew he was living with somebody else (a common theme in relationships on our side of the social paddock) I had hopes he would be my one true love for all time. He'd sent me a card and a photo which I still have to this very day for goodness sake! How could it not have been true love? After it all became a bit random as far as meeting up was concerned he'd agreed to meet me at Moorgate Station one evening and we would go out together somewhere from there. I arrived half an hour before our scheduled 7 o'clock rendezvous time. At 7 there was no sign of him. I waited and waited. As 8 o'clock approached I managed to convince myself that it was me that had got the time wrong and that all would be good when the clock struck twenty hundred hours. As the time approached 9pm there was still no sign of him. Of course he never arrived. I was utterly heartbroken. As an adult I guess we would summarise such disappointments as part of growing up. But do you know, even after forty years have passed I still wonder what happened to him. I have tried searching the internet to find him but to no avail. Even though I know what productions he had been a part of I can still find no trace of him at all. It's almost like he never existed. Except he did, and I have the photo and card to prove it.

Are you crying your eyes out yet? Good. Well don't use up all your tears just yet, there are more heart wrangling episodes to come.

At the Royal Court we had started devising the play that would put the theatre on the front pages of the national press in a scandal that would rock the western world. Well, that's how it seemed. It was pretty controversial in London's Western Boroughs anyway.

Gerald Chapman had hired Royal Court writer in residence David Lan to help construct a play about the experiences of young gay men and women, the script being compiled directly from the life stories of the ten actors in my group. In addition to the drama, the play also had a superb original music score written by composer Ian Stewart, with whom I had worked during my first job at Peters Edition. I sang the main song, which told of teenager Lionel's extraordinary experiences of having been a young hustler on the Piccadilly 'meat rack', a notorious pick up location for male prostitutes.

Over forty years later the play's powerful monologues are still extremely moving. One scene contains a piece where a seventeen-year-old gay lad is goaded into electric shock therapy by his outraged parents. They rant and rave at him blaming the 'perversion' on him being in London, a place where 'all these sorts of things go on...' When he explains it 'actually happens everywhere', they respond with 'Not in Norwich!' And that is how the play got its title.

Although we played ourselves in the production the stories we enacted were not always wholly our own. It was just as well my folks didn't see the play because they had been nothing but positive and incredibly supportive. Yet there was me up there seemingly being berated and harangued by ignorant parents suggesting I was in need of treatment usually meted out on death row.

Just before the show was launched the *London Evening Standard* newspaper somehow got tipped off and decided there was a story in it which didn't quite fit what we'd intended. They ran a hysterical, screaming front page headline 'LONDON CHILDREN IN SEX PLAY'. In time-honoured British media style the article was completely twisted and factually incorrect; most of the cast were not from London, we were certainly not 'children' and there was no sex in the play at all. Although the senior management of the theatre went into meltdown to their credit they stuck to their guns and the play went ahead unhindered, eventually transferring from the adjacent theatre space at the Court in the aptly named 'Garage' (for that's what it had once been) to a tour of schools and fringe theatres.

Far from being scared out of wanting to perform the play, the furore was treated with laughter and derision by everyone in the cast, driving us on with even stronger resolve to tell our story with an even louder and prouder voice. Each performance was followed by an open discussion between audience and cast, with consequential highly emotive responses from both sides.

I still have what must surely be one of the only surviving original scripts and music scores for the production. David Lan appears to have disowned it for some reason as it never gets mentioned in any résumé of his subsequent successful career at places like the Young Vic. I remained in touch with Lionel, Ian and Mark, but what became of Paul, Catherine, Lynn, Robert, Hayden and Geraldine I don't know. How I would love to see them again and to reminisce over a huge magnum of champagne. Lionel and I were keen in 2017 to restage the play with a new cast for its 40th anniversary, perhaps with us appearing out of the mist at the very end as potentially the only survivors of the original cast and whose stories still resonate even today.

Gerald Chapman sadly passed away in New York in 1987. Just one of so many talented people who lost their lives to HIV/AIDS. The final words in the play were spoken by Mark. They serve as a moving tribute to Gerald and to all of us who have fought ignorance and bigotry over the years:

'We don't want you to do anything. Some of us want to change the world. Some of us don't. We work. We think. We talk. We listen. We play. But nobody knows we're here. We're not asking you to do anything special. We just want you to know. We don't want to be covered up people. We just wanted to tell you: We're here.'

Gay politics has changed so much over the years. Yet that paragraph sums up so much for me. It isn't all about screaming at people. I have never subscribed to the 'Deal with it' slogan we see so much these days on T-shirts, posters and even the sides of buses. I find that unnecessarily aggressive and somewhat unintelligent. The crux of what we did back then was actually to celebrate difference and diversity for what it was. These days there's an uncomfortable drift towards the politics of 'same'. That's not what we fought for. We weren't about being accepted by a hostile society on its terms. We didn't want the crux of our societal acceptance to be judged on whether our relationships were as durable as straight ones; to be married with kids and to be acceptable to established religions. Fuck that. We knew who we were and all we ever wanted was to be equal in rights and to do what we wanted to with freedom.

The 'We're here' statement is incredibly important as it provides the lifeline of hope for those people who know they are different from the overwhelming norms presented to them. Although things have undoubtedly moved on greatly since the seventies I think we kid ourselves that we have achieved social equality. As I write these words the political right appears to be resurgent, Trump is still president in the US (incredibly) and we continue to see huge injustice and persecution of gay people all over the world. I reread the play script before writing this and it seemed as relevant today as it was over forty years ago. That's quite sad in a way I think.

Thank you.

music swells

As 1978 flowered into another classic seventies year Phil and I continued building on our ideas for what would eventually become the Gaywaves radio show, and in between my acting at the Court I was working to earn money selling advertising space. How I ever got into this I will never know. I am the world's worst liar and let's be honest if you're trying to sell advertising you need a lot of conviction (honest or otherwise) and even more chutzpah. I had neither. My first exposure to all this nonsense was for a green grocery trade magazine called *The Fruit Trades Journal*. It will come as little surprise to anyone that I had no interest in fruit and vegetables beyond what got plonked down in front of me to eat. The greengrocers I had to canvass were almost always hulking great male specimens who could lift sacks of potatoes with one finger and whose knuckles trailed across the floor on the return journey. I hated it. Although the people I worked with were very sweet I realised I had to go before they got rid of me. So instead I went to work for a new magazine called *Homes & Jobs*. Wasn't that imaginative? Its content was even more thrilling – it was full of classified adverts for… err… well, homes and jobs. About thirty of us sat in a cramped, stuffy office in Regent Street swilling copious amounts of coffee, chain-smoking whilst dissecting all the classified adverts from the day's newspapers – national and local. We would divvy up pages of each paper to each other and then call every single one of them to try and persuade them to place the same ad in our magazine. It was utterly soul destroying. Beside me sat a fiery woman called Jackie. She had an extraordinary ability to sell anything to anyone. Hell, I swear she even managed to sell advert space to us sat next to her. She was loud too. It used to baffle me how she did it. She wouldn't just ask the advertiser to place their ad with us, she would actually tell them that's what she was going to do and then bill them for it. A typical call would go as follows:

'Put me through to the person who deals with your advertising would you love? Thanks.'
(Short pause for connection and two long draws on a B&H King Size.)
'Hi my name is Jackie and I'm calling from *Homes and Jobs* magazine. Who am I speaking to?'
(Susan from the admin office unwisely provides her name.)
'I notice you have a classified ad for a Telex operator in Hammersmith? Well that would fit very nicely into our magazine and it would work well for you. The rate for an eighth of a page ad will be two hundred pounds. I'll go ahead and place that for you then shall I and we'll invoice you on publication. Thank you dear.'
(Puts phone down and books another two hundred quid.)

This went on all day. She would rack up thousands in sales. Meanwhile I rarely ever got beyond the woman that answered the phone on reception. If I ever did actually reach the person responsible for advertising I would balls it up within seconds as I had no conviction whatsoever. I knew that they didn't need our magazine and my dialogue clearly gave the game away every time. As time went by I was so embarrassed at how bad I was that I stopped using my real name and gave out purely made up ones. I became Chris Garland (Judy's long-lost son?) on one call and then Martin Flowers on the next. As I grew more desperate the names I chose got more and more silly. One minute I was Harry Crabs and the next I was Duncan Horseradish. I finally realised that the game was up for me when after almost three days of selling nine and five eighths of fuck all I told someone on the end of the line that my name was Fred Minge. It was the final realisation that I simply couldn't go on trying to sell fridges to Eskimos. I left and wandered down the road to Reed Employment and signed on as a temping Telex operator (which I was rather good at). This had the advantage of being non-permanent, giving me time to earn the money I needed to live and as much as I could afford in acting and rehearsal time.

One day it was Friday April 28th 1978 and 'Night Fever' by the Bee Gees was at Number 1 in the charts. I was still in touch with Carol from school, so whilst sitting at my desk drumming fingers I called her and said in a silly Monty Python type voice 'Christ I'm bored!' 'Yeah, so am I,' she said. 'Let's go to Paris tonight for the weekend,' I said, 'I will call Chris and Paul and see if they want to come too.' And so, whilst Paul didn't want to go, Carol, Chris and I met on Victoria station for the night train to Paris and off we jolly well went. Just like that. We didn't care did we? None of us had any money to speak of. In those days you couldn't take out any more than twenty-eight pounds in foreign currency anyway. How did people ever manage to travel? It didn't bother us though. We took sandwiches and bought bottles of wine to oil the rigours of the 12 hours it was going to take to get there. We took the train from London Victoria to Dover Marine, then cross-channel ferry to Calais and then the long and slow train from Calais to Paris arriving around rush hour the next day. None of your door-to-door, two-hour trips on the Eurostar in those days my dears, this was a full-scale expedition.

Phil had persuaded me that it might be fun to record the whole trip on a portable cassette recorder. For some odd reason we decided to make audio reports as though we were in an episode of *Star Trek*. I became Captain Kirk, Carol was Uhura and Chris just a crew member (bless him). We didn't know who we were talking to or even why, but we were so shitfaced by the time we reached Calais that it hardly seemed to matter. Listening back to it all these years later it is a very curious and rather embarrassing taped travelogue. So strange to hear us laughing at appalling jokes, insulting each other and getting drunk to a background of ambient Parisian street sounds.

Carol always made me laugh and this helped when I was recovering from my having been violently sick on the first night after a dodgy cheap repas Chinoise for a paltry 12 francs. It didn't help that we'd been steadily quaffing bottles of even cheaper duty free wine almost non-stop for the previous 24 hours. I was so ill afterwards that I was vomiting blood, turning the grimy Hotel Moderne bathroom into a scene from a budget slasher movie. It taught me a lesson though. I was never a big drinker, and I rarely ever drank to that extent ever again. The following morning I felt bizarrely bright and breezy considering I had thrown up most of my insides. To celebrate this we hiked up to Montmartre for a mince round La Basilique du Sacré Coeur. We decided to split up with me and Chris walking round one way and Carol the other making a taped report of each trip for posterity. As we passed a statue of Mary I said, 'Ooh look, it's God with a garden of roses up his cassock.' When we played back what Carol had recorded on her way round she had said exactly the same thing on passing the same statue. Isn't that fascinating? We spent a hilarious time visiting the sights and whilst standing next to them asking locals if they knew where we could find it? For some odd reason we found asking where the Arc De Triomphe was when we were standing underneath it hysterically funny. Whilst experiencing the gothic majesty of Notre Dame Cathedral I said to Carol, 'Something comes over you in here dunnit?' 'Yeah, pigeon shit,' she said. How we roared.

On our last day we ran out of money and the three of us had to survive the journey home on one large baguette and a bit of *fromage du jour*. We would follow up this winning formula by recording two further trips that year – one to Hastings on the East Sussex Riviera and the other a trip home to Tunbridge Wells on Christmas Day. Earlier I mentioned how much Jackie's joke telling made me laugh. 'Tell us a joke, Jack,' I said as we swilled beer up The Kelsey Arms that Christmas Day in 1978. 'Bloke working on a building site had his ear chopped off,' she said with glee. 'The foreman picked it up and said to the bloke, "Is this your ear?" and the bloke said, "No, mine had a pencil behind it."' That simple little (old) gag was delivered with utter perfection and reduced me to hysterics; incredibly. Those tapes remain much-treasured records of halcyon seventies days and of absolutely no interest whatsoever to anyone else. I don't even know why I wrote about it here. Forgive me. I will get back to London and more interesting things almost immediately.

(Note to editor, you might want to cut out all of that last bit. I'd had a gin before I wrote it.)

When *Not In Norwich* finished its run I was approached to join the Gay Sweatshop theatre company who were planning a new play called *Who Knows?* written by long-term LG activists Sarah Hardy, Bruce Bayley and Philip Timmins. I was to play a nasty piece of work called Colin, a sixteen-year-old schoolboy and trainee thug. This was a much grittier play than *Not In Norwich* and it contained real menace and threat of violence. The company was to tour with it to fringe theatres and schools all over the country, including one gig in Coleraine in Northern Ireland.

The eight cast members and the director, Philip Timmins, gathered for the first read-through and rehearsals at the Oval House in south London. Most of the actors were around twenty years old, apart from two women who appeared to me to be in their late twenties. It all started reasonably well, although I was never a great fan of the long, drawn-out warm-up sessions that this company seemed to want to start every rehearsal with. We hadn't done any of that at the Royal Court and quite frankly I couldn't be doing with it loosening up my arms and mouth. My gob was a quite wide enough and ready for action thank you. Despite this every day commenced with one of these ghastly, drawn-out mind and body workouts. One day one of the older women came in with a pained look and told the group that as she was having a particularly bad period our warm-up session was to reflect the pain that women have to go through every month. The younger cast members, male and female, glanced at each other in slight bafflement at this, but played along as we went through a dreary, wail fest. At the end of that I wasn't so much warmed up as withered down. One of us, and I can't remember who, then ventured to suggest that our group shouldn't have to go through something like that again. This was met with the angry response that as far as she was concerned 'All men are potential rapists'. This came as something of a shock to the four young gay guys in the room, none of whom had any experience with the opposite sex at all and all of whom had no interest whatsoever in associating willies with front bottoms.

As you can imagine the atmosphere by now in the room was not overly positive. Sadly the negativity festered throughout the whole time we were together. Rehearsals were fraught and touchy. One word out of place would set off arguments and personal attacks. It was without doubt one of the most difficult productions I have ever worked on. I was able to draw on a whole host of boys that I had encountered from my schooldays in finding Colin's rough edge and menace. The dialogue was well written and the situations generally believable. I employed a particular sort of blunt tonality that I knew to be typical of bullies and rough types. It didn't help that the most radical lesbian feminist in the group was playing my character's girlfriend. Consequently I had a lot of dialogue with her. She helped me to develop my role by telling me that I was 'monotone and couldn't act'. Wasn't that thoughtful of her? I wasn't put off by that and as I had no intention of BBCifying my delivery I carried on exactly as directed and ignored her negativity. The only aspect of this play which didn't ring true to us were the scenes set in a gay disco where the gay guys and gals freely mixed. Even though I hadn't been on the scene that long I knew this wasn't what actually happened outside in the real world. Bars, clubs and discos were heavily split between male and female and it was rare to find a venue where gay men and women mixed freely. In perhaps the biggest irony of all, the only places I ever saw this happen regularly were the big drag show pubs like the Black Cap in Camden Town, which had a very mixed clientele. It seems a bit strange thinking back that the only entertainment which would regularly draw in both sexes was one where one sex was dressing up as the other.

The other thing we disliked in this play was the choice of music, every one of which I hated. Although most of it was from either 1978 or 1979 they were all tracks that had been hits about six months previously, and six months in music terms back then seemed like a lifetime. Anita Ward's 'Ring My Bell' always put my teeth on edge as she sings so much of it out of tune. Don't believe me? Then just listen to it again and get ready to stick your fingers in your ears when she warbles that ghastly chorus. Then we had Michael Jackson's 'Don't Stop Till You Get Enough', another song I loathed and which you'd rarely ever hear played in a top rate gay clubs or discos of the day. The final track in the play was Tom Robinson's 'Glad To Be Gay'. This was one of dear Phil Cox's favourite records, but again it was one I hated. I think however that my view may have been coloured by having been told by an older gay friend of mine who had been to school with him that back then he'd been an 'absolute tosser' and that the song was probably 'just one big gimmick'. Of course I had no proof of either gossip element, but as I didn't like his music anyway it just became a convenient excuse to wince every time it came on. And that was the other thing, we heard these same tracks over and over and over again in relentless rehearsal and then performance. That killed three of the other bits of music in it that I had always liked up to that point: Sister Sledge's 'We Are Family', Edwin Starr's 'H.A.P.P.Y. Radio' and Elton John's 'Your Song'. Even after all these years I can't bear any of these tracks, great songs though they undoubtedly are.

I had moved in to share a flat in King's Cross, next door to the play's author and director Philip Timmins. In what was probably the most unstable time of my entire life as far as living quarters was concerned, I felt deeply unsettled and this didn't help my peace of mind, especially when we left to go on tour around the country all crammed together with a ton of scenery in a tatty hired Ford Transit van. When the company arrived in Liverpool we stayed over at a flat on the Dingle council estate lived in by some gay friends of Philip's. Sweet, lovely people but I had no idea what they were saying as their accent was so heavy. I'm such a southerner. After the show we were driving back past Lime Street railway station just as the pubs were chucking out. With perfect timing our van broke down. We were stuck in the middle of the main thoroughfare, a van load of pooves and lesbos and hundreds of drunken straights milling around us, waving beer bottles and cheering at our predicament. I was absolutely terrified, and convinced that we were about to be beaten up and murdered to death. But something amazing happened. Instead of getting duffed up by the boozy hordes they all came over and offered to help us. We were astonished. They helped us push the van over towards the nearby slopes from where we were able to get the van moving and the engine started again. I've adored Liverpool ever since. Really.

Gay Sweatshop was partly funded by a modest Arts Council grant. Margaret Thatcher's Conservative government had been elected on May 3rd 1979 and already her vile and divisive policies were beginning to take effect. Though her attacks on the very working class voters she lured with promises of curbing union power and flogging council houses were yet to reach their zenith, other swingeing cuts were already hitting hard. Predictably the arts suffered the razored handbag pretty quickly. We returned from the show in Liverpool back to some bookings at Action Space just off of Tottenham Court Road to discover that our grant had been cancelled. The rest of the tour over to Ulster after the final London dates would not be able to go ahead and we were effectively out of a job. The thought of having nowhere permanent to live on top of having to sign on the dole again didn't appeal. Signing on was bad enough for anyone, but for actors we always got a lot of extra hassle as nobody in civil service quarters considered our work as valid employment to start with. That stigma hangs heavy over all of us who work in arts and entertainment. It's an industry that is so often taken for granted. People will think nothing of switching on their TV sets, radios, cinema and theatre without giving a second thought to the huge numbers of people who both deliver and enable it all to take place. And whatever else you might think it is, it is certainly work. Bloody hard work too. Rewarding when it all goes well, but brutal in its execution when it doesn't.

I had fallen out with the guy I was sharing with who had become threatening and unreasonable, so I went to Phil Cox and opened my heart to my predicament. 'Don't worry, you can stay here or I'll lend you some money for a deposit if you find somewhere else to live,' he said casually. Bless his heart. I hated the very idea of asking anyone to lend me money, and actually this was to be the one and only time I ever did it. I found a flat share up in Willesden Green in North London with a nice big room and all gay men in residence. Perfect.

Although *Who Knows?* still had a few more dates to run I could stand the bad atmosphere in the cast no longer. Knowing that the company's finances were about to hit the skids I decided to throw in the towel and leave. I was gutted to leave behind my close friends in the cast Geraldine and Kenny, whom I adored. I don't manage stress very well and had been a grouch during those last tour dates. As we gathered for the evening's performance for the first and only time in my entire career I simply could not go on. I so loathed the two women who had made my time on the production such a miserable experience that I had to get away. As the threat of violence back at the flat had grown it had all simply become too much for me. I'd already gathered my things and decamped it all to Phil's flat temporarily before the move up to Willesden Green. This just left me to face the rest of the company. When I got to the theatre I received the usual offhand welcome from the Sisters Grimm. I confided what I was going to do with Kenny and Geraldine as I suspected it wasn't going to be pretty when the rest of the group found out. I knew that our director Philip Timmins knew my part and that he would be able to cover for me for those last few performances. And so with a quiet exit I left the building and left them to it. Although I am not proud of having done that it was a measure of my extremely disturbed state of mind that for the only time ever I simply had to escape.

Although I stayed in touch with Geraldine and Kenny for a brief time afterwards I eventually lost touch with them. This saddened me terribly and I have always wondered how they got on and how they are now. I didn't hear from Philip Timmins again for many years until a short while before I started writing this. I am pleased to say that we are now back in touch and our friendship is rekindled.

I needed money. Badly. The following day I went back to the Reed Employment agency and restarted my temping work so I could avoid having to sign on, afford the rent on the new flat and also pay back Phil in instalments. However I knew I couldn't bash T15 Telex keyboards for the rest of my life and so whilst riding on the Metropolitan Line between Baker Street and Finchley Road I suddenly realised that I needed a job with shift work that I could do to earn money and leave me with the option of continuing to work in the theatre. So I applied for the job of a Guard with London Transport on the Underground. I had always loved trains and railways and was somewhat obsessive about them. I would have loved to have become a train driver. How unutterably butch and fabulous would that be? The romance of hurtling through tunnels at a hundred miles an hour and swooping through the leafy suburbs of the great Metrollops was just what I needed to restore my creaking equilibrium.

Ed: What on earth does that mean?

Me: No idea, but run with it as it was getting boring. They'll never notice.

I could be on my own in the luxury of the driver's cab and manage my drifting mind streams whilst earning a decent wage for the first time in my life. I filled out all the forms and was overjoyed when in December 1979 I was accepted for training at the White City Railway Training Centre in West London, almost opposite the iconic BBC TV Centre.

My mother was horrified when I told her what I'd done. Sensing that the railways would be full of rough, uncouth, homophobic yob types she said, 'Darling do you really think this is wise?' I reassured her that it was something I really wanted to do and that I was more than capable of handling any negativity. Phil was supportive too and I began to feel that at last my life was about to change for the better. I don't intend to write very much about my railway career in this account, so don't panic about being bored to death by train stories. However there are a few key moments that I will have to touch on or I won't be being true to myself.

The day I joined I arrived at White City with about twenty other newly recruited herberts and was surprised to find that actually there were very few yobs and criminals after all. One of the women, a delightfully alternative woman called Audrey, had been a roadie for Siouxsie & the Banshees on their first couple of tours. We had a lot in common and it was nice to have someone I could relate to during the somewhat unexpected militaristic treatment we got as new trainees. On the first day we were all herded onto an old red London Transport double decker bus and driven to a huge reception facility at Acton to collect our uniforms. It was just like some bloody awful army conscription. We were frogmarched into a building with a huge long wooden counter. Starting at one end they would pile up your uniform jackets, coats, shorts, trousers, ties and boots until we resembled a jumble sale on legs. We changed into one of the outfits and carried the rest of it away in huge white plastic bags. Back at White City we congealed into a large training room and told that we would be 'welcomed' into London Transport by the current Operations Director, a severe-looking man who went by the name of Charlie Cope.

The room went quiet as this important dignitary strolled to the front for his royal address. Sensing that this would be profound and life-affirming stuff we all sat to attention ready to receive wise words of wisdom.

'Right!' he yelled, 'Anyone in 'ere who don't like bad language can FUCK OFF out that door NOW!'.

Audrey and I looked at each other in absolute horror. What on earth had we done? I should seriously have listened to Mother. I immediately began to plan my will whilst yearning for the theatre life I had just walked out of.

Cope gave a bizarre speech littered with profanities to the point where I actually started to find it amusing. That helped a great deal. Together with the ludicrous ill-fitting uniform they'd given me which made me look like a cross between Worzel Gummidge and a charity shop clothing bin, it all began to take on a surreal air. When I got back to the flat and told my housemates what had gone on I found myself describing it all in a way which made them laugh. I quickly realised that I was able to divorce myself from the daft, pseudo-naval militaristic atmosphere which pervaded the Underground way of things from my personal life and my other interests. This was a revelation to me and would actually serve me well for almost my entire working life. I regaled Phil Cox with all sorts of hilarious stories from my new endeavour, which proved to be a rich source of creative energy. I was also earning more money than I ever had in my entire life. At last!

I shall tell just more three railway tales in this book and then I'll shut the fuck up about it I promise. There'll be two funny and one tragic tale. Here's the first funny.

After I had finished my training I became a guard on the Metropolitan line way up in the frozen north at a place called Rickmansworth. It was certainly a lot more upmarket there than where I was living then in Neasden. The train crew mess room (for that's what they called it – somewhat appropriately as it was indeed a mess in there), was located at one end of the northbound platform. There was a sort of greasy spoon cafe adjacent to the southbound platform from where we obtained suitably butch snacks like bacon and sausage sandwiches, fried egg rolls and the like. Well, you need that type of foodage when you're doing a fabulously manly job on the railway. The only drawback to this was the schlep from the messroom through the subway to get to the other side. If you weren't speedy and sharpish your fried delight would be stone cold by the time you'd got back. The official railway workers' term for anything resembling food is the delightful term 'grub', as in 'Where are you having your grub?' and 'I'm fucking starving, what time's grub?'

In addition to my own nutritional requirements, and because I was but a mere guard, I was expected to go and fetch my driver's grub (sic) too in a sort of working class fagging type arrangement. My driver was a nice, fairly jolly man whose entire family had been on the railway since prehistoric times. I had been duly fetching his breakfast grub every day for a while and was starting to get fed up with it all being cold by the time I got back. And all this because the woman on the ticket barrier buttonholed every member of staff that passed her and would not stop talking. I don't wish to be unkind but she really was one of the ugliest women I've ever seen. She looked like Ernest Borgnine in drag. And boy could this woman talk! Yabber, yabber, yabber and all the while my bacon was solidifying. It was impossible to get away from her and it was driving me nuts. Now I was always friendly and would accommodate the nattering as much as I could without appearing rude but enough was enough and after a few weeks of this I could stand it no more. Carrying yet another bag of cold breakfast fare I stormed back into the room where several members of train crew were gathered. 'Jesus fucking Christ!' I yelled, slamming the sandwich bags down on the blue melamine-topped trestle table, 'Who is that ugly old bag on the ticket barriers? She's driving me bloody crazy. Every fucking morning my bloody breakfast gets back here stone cold because all she wants to do is talk! I don't give a shiny shite about her bloody kids or her bloody husband! I just want to get back in here with a hot snack and not a cold lump of congealed lard!'

I stopped.

Absolute silence.

One of the other guards beckoned me over with a wiggle of his finger. Their heads all turned slowly to follow me as I walked over.

'That "old bag" on the barrier? It's your driver's wife.'

Oh. My. God.

I wanted the earth to open up and swallow me. Then, quite unexpectedly, I detected a ripple of laughter. I turned to find my driver in hysterics. When he started so did everyone else. I guess I had dug a hole so big that there was no escape. He forgave me my outburst, even telling me that she drove him up the wall too. He'd just never heard it from anyone else quite that bluntly. If that wasn't embarrassing enough I had an equally appalling experience not that long afterwards when I progressed to driver training. I was paired with a dear old queen called Terry, who been driving trains since he was demobbed from the war. A large, quietly spoken avuncular man, Terry was an utter joy to work with and I adored him. We all did. Many of the old boys working there were cantankerous old bastards and it could be an unpleasant experience to be paired off for a week of duties with one of them, especially for delicate flowers like me. Terry however was kindly and helpful and he taught me how to drive the old Met line trains with all the knowledge he'd amassed over the years. One morning rush hour I was driving the train and approaching one of the dead end platforms at Baker Street. My train was jam packed with commuters on their way to London from the suburbs. The signals on the approach were speed controlled to make sure that the train was not at risk of entering the platform too fast. I passed the first one on the tunnel wall and it cleared from red to green just as it was supposed to given my slow speed. The next one was only about a few metres ahead and Terry assured me that it would clear to green just as I reached it. Only this time, for whatever reason it didn't. I slammed on the brakes to stop the train as quickly as I could. As the train jolted to a halt the red signal just passed the cab window on the side by a few inches and out of my line of sight. As this happened I let out a long, loud and rather camp screech, which beautifully accompanied the jolting stop.

'You should be OK,' said Terry with a smile on his face as I sat there trembling with fear and he apparently not even remotely bothered. 'But there's only one way you're going to find out if that signal has now gone to green. You'll have to open the cab door on the inside of the carriage where the passengers are and check it from the passenger window.'

My skin crawled with embarrassment as I opened the cab door to see all the passengers who had heard me screaming like a schoolgirl seconds before staring straight at me. A man sat on the seat nearest the window then said, 'It's OK mate, the signal's green now.' As I thanked him and apologised for the rather rough stop, a small ripple of applause went round. I slunk back to the safety of my cab and to record that as one of the most embarrassing experiences of my life. Terry meanwhile will figure once more in this history, although I am afraid as a consequence of something tragic rather than amusing. Bless him.

The gay scene in London changed rapidly and profoundly in the late seventies and into the early eighties. When the first really big club opened up the smaller 'community' based pub discos started to dwindle in number and quality. The first one I recall opening up was BANG at the Astoria in Charing Cross Road, near to Tottenham Court Road tube station. This was a cavernous space compared to the rented function rooms above bars we had been used to. Tricky Dicky Discos suddenly looked and sounded very old hat. Where previously the atmosphere and ambiance was more party-like, at BANG guys just gathered in the darkness and cruised 'a la Americain'. It seemed to me that people just stopped talking. In any case it was so loud that you had to practically scream simply to get a drink at the bar. The light shows there made the pub disco effects look like traffic lights. Worse was that you could spend all night either cruising or being cruised and come out either alone or having not spoken to a soul all night except the queen serving drinks behind the bar. It dehumanised and flattened what had up to then been a highly interactive way for gay people to meet and entertain.

The pub scene carried on for a few more years but gradually the disco nights petered out. Gay pubs carried on with their main entertainment offering of drag acts which, with the exception of comic geniuses Regina Fong and Lily Savage, I had always found a bit intimidating, threatening and weird. There was an aggression to drag acts I found deeply uncomfortable, and to this day it isn't an entertainment I find easy to experience. I mention Reg and Lily in particular, but I should also mention David Dale, who along with them made up the legendary 'Disappointer Sisters'. This threesome were the only ones who ever made me laugh and all of whom were able to elicit genuine affection from their adoring audiences. Most of the pub drag circuit players mimed to rather hackneyed prerecorded soundtracks consisting of Garland, Streisand, Bassey and the like. The few who could actually sing did so usually with repertoire from the same genre as the mimes only with voices that could blow the froth off a Guinness from 20 feet away. Reg, Lily and David had a unique talent that, in my opinion, far outstripped any of the others. They were genuinely funny in their own right, Reg with his stunning visage depicting 'her Imperial Highness the Grand Duchess and last of the Romanovs' persona which would eventually make him famous as a solo act, Lily the brash Liverpudlian tart with not much of a heart, and David with his extraordinary rubber face seemingly able to pull his top and bottom lips in different directions which had the crowds cheering and laughing. Whilst I would get to meet both Reg and David out of drag I never met Lily. I think I would probably have been too scared of Lily (the alter-ego of the British now mega-TV star Paul O'Grady). David was going out with a guy who I had worked with on the Underground and for a short time I used to run into them quite a bit outside of both trains and drag shows. Reg I only ever knew through talking to him at the venues he played. I recall going with him to a place the other side of Heathrow Airport one night, a location well away from his usual stamping ground and adoring fans known as the 'Fongettes' (of which I was proud to have been one of the originals). He was terribly nervous about this gig as his act depended a great deal on audience participation, and this was a new venue at the arsehole end of nowhere. The core Fongette group travelled there especially to support him and hopefully to whip up this foreign location into the same frenzy we experienced every Tuesday night at the Black Cap in Camden Town. Sadly the club was sparsely attended and despite our best efforts we were onto a hiding for nothing. Reg gave it his all, but our fevered whooping and hollering just made the cavernous space seem even more desperate. We finished off with Regina's signature grand finale dance to Helen Shapiro's 'Tell Me What He Said' and then repaired to his 'dressing room' (a storage space with a sink in it next to the toilets). We sat there smoking and drinking while Reg (over) analysed every painful moment epitomising what every performer in almost any branch of entertainment will go through at some point. The scooping lows that occur as if to punish the elation brought by incredible highs. It is a profession alike no other in that regard. And the lows force self-examination which can eat away and haunt the player for always. It never goes away. In one regard Reg was lucky, he had an incredibly loyal and adoring fan base who genuinely loved him. His bizarre humour and seemingly unfathomable stage act gave him a cult following for whom he could do no wrong. Experiencing Reg's act from the 'other side' eventually helped me manage some of my toe-curling moments on live TV too. A couple of years later I would spend an afternoon with Eartha Kitt up at Tyne Tees TV in Newcastle and Reg came to mind frequently during that unforgettable encounter. More of that later though...

Around the same time that BANG opened, the huge club called Global Village which was under the arches of Charing Cross station started a roller disco night. I absolutely loved it there and despite being the world's crappiest skater I would swirl around the floor like a tart on wheels to the sounds of Sylvester, Rose Royce and El Coco. I got to know the DJ there, a wonderfully flamboyant guy whose performing name was Talulah. He was rapidly gaining in reputation as a major club DJ, but at the time was augmenting this by working as a restaurant manager at a swanky eaterie in Old Brompton Road. I absolutely adored him. He was funny, kind and generous and one of the few really camp guys that I became close to (most of my close friends were either geeks, nerds or punks). I was devastated when Global Village was closed to make way for a new gay super club called Heaven. How dare they take away my roller dance nights! Even though I could hear my battered ankles breathing a sigh of relief, it was still a bitter blow. Talulah carried on DJing there but as a club it was not really my scene. I wasn't interested in the twinks they employed to mince around the club in tight gold lycra shorts, and couldn't be arsed with the sex and drugs freely available in the toilets. Excuse me? I can't be doing with that! I am from Tunbridge Wells after all.

I found the transition between the glorious seventies and the dour eighties a real jolt. Everything changed. The seventies had been a decade of luscious colour, future promise and beautiful rebellion. It had started with a bohemian explosion of glam and glitter. It lurched from a soul and reggae explosion to dance and disco magic, with rock music screaming out of prog rock excess to punk rock outrage. Each with its own distinct fashions, culture and passions. Every shift in music and fashion, like the two decades that preceded it, was original and innovative. The eighties by contrast seemed stark, fluorescent, cold and retrospective. It was by comparison a cruel decade. It seemed as though everything positive the seventies had promised had been pushed towards a cliff edge.

Sure, we'd have fun, but at a price.

Strange little boy 1962

First birthday June 1959,
Father & Mother on right, Grandparents on left, Uncle holding me

Me with a haunted look at a family wedding in 1968 next to Dad 2 with my mum and sister Karen, who looks as enthralled as I was.

Photo booth mugshot 1975

A 'filth party' as a bishop with Jane 1974

Royal Court Theatre Sloane Sq.
London 1976

Pissed with Carol in Paris – the night of the great throwing up!

With Iain & gang Kingston Summer 1976

With Phil Cox at Waterloo 1975

Beautiful pic of Gerald Chapman circa 1976
(Photo courtesy of Stuart Round)

With my school besties (L to R) Carol, Kristine, Jackie,
getting hammered up the Kelsey Arms on Christmas Day 1978

Singing 'The Meat Rack' in the Royal Court Activists'
production of *Not in Norwich* 1979

Hastings with Carol and Phil 1978

Playing Colin in *Who Knows?* 1979

Recording 'Gaywaves' in Phil's flat 1980

In the film: *Watch Out There's a Queer About* 1980

Michael & record plugger Ian G messing about in my grotty
Queen's Park council flat 1984

On the beach with one of Phil's Gay Switchboard messages
chalked on the sea wall – 1984

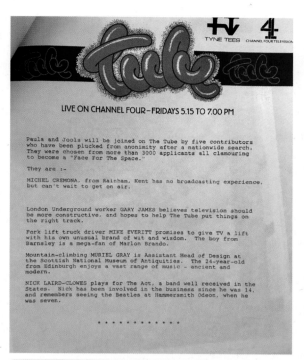

LIVE ON CHANNEL FOUR – FRIDAYS 5.15 TO 7.00 PM

Paula and Jools will be joined on The Tube by five contributors who have been plucked from anonimity after a nationwide search. They were chosen from more than 3000 applicants all clamouring to become a "Face For The Space."

They are :-

MICHEL CREMONA, from Rainham, Kent has no broadcasting experience, but can't wait to get on air.

London Underground worker GARY JAMES believes television should be more constructive, and hopes to help The Tube put things on the right track.

Fork lift truck driver MIKE EVERITT promises to give TV a lift with his own unusual brand of wit and wisdom. The boy from Barnsley is a mega-fan of Marlon Brando.

Mountain-climbing MURIEL GRAY is Assistant Head of Design at the Scottish National Museum of Antiquities. The 24-year-old from Edinburgh enjoys a vast range of music - ancient and modern.

NICK LAIRD-CLOWES plays for The Act, a band well received in the States. Nick has been involved in the business since he was 14, and remembers seeing the Beatles at Hammersmith Odeon, when he was seven.

* * * * * * * * * * * *

THE TUBE RUNNING ORDER   TT.84.06.1.   TX 10.2.84

DIR: GAVIN TAYLOR   PA: ELIZABETH MARY BAGE

I/TIME   17.31.00   C/B's   1 x 2.10 (before 18.00)
R/TIME   78.10   2 x 2.40
O/AIR   18.56.30

----

1. VTR A " OPENING TITLES" R/TIME   1.04

· JC
2. FRENCH & SAUNDERS/RECEPTION
    Vox Pop or FRENCH & SAUNDERS
    Piece 1 + ASTON
    CAMS 6 & 7   1.00

CC
3. JOOLS/GREEN ROOM/Intro to
    Programme * ASTON CAM 5   0.30

LO
4. VTR B"THOMPSON TWINS + SIOUXSIE
    & THE BANSHEES" + ASTON

SL
5. MURIEL & LARGE SIOUXSIE PAINTING
    RECEPTION- Intro to Painting +
    ARTIST ALAN DICK
    CAMS 6 & 7   0.30

SL
6. VTR A"ALAN DICKS PAINTING &
    MUSIC"

SL
7. MURIEL/ALAN DICK/CAROL KENYON
    RECEPTION - Chat + ¼"Warriors"
    CAMS 6 & 7   3.00

    (Cam 6 to studio)
    (Cam 7 to Green Room)

✳ 8. GARY JAMES/GREEN ROOM
       Intro to Top Five
       CAM 5   0.45

KS
✳ 9. VTR B "GARY'S NUMBERS 10 - 5"   2'·06"
       + ASTON

KS
✳ 10. GARY JAMES/GREEN ROOM
       link - CAM 5   ~~1.00~~ 30'

KS
✳ 11. VTR A " GARY'S 5 - 1"   1'56"
       + ASTON

The Tube 1982 -1984
Note me and Muriel in the infamous 'morning after' photo, both utterly blitzed after getting plastered the night before.
(Photo ©ITV/REX/Shutterstock)

The Tube 1982 -1984
Series one presenters Muriel Gray, Michelle Cremona, Nick Laird-Clowes
& yours truly
(Photo ©Mirrorpix)

Michael, Phil and me in Phil's Old Street council flat – 1984

With school friends Carol and Sally 2008

Driving on the other tube 1984 and Gay Pride March London 1981

Gary James – First independent publicity shoot photo 1985

4

Smalltown Boy – 1980 to 1982

Two days ago I received an email completely out of the blue from Philip Timmins, the co-writer and director of the Gay Sweatshop production *Who Knows?* The email header read 'How about this blast from the past – we're both in it… remember?' There was no message text, just a web link to a page on the London Community Video Archive website and a short eight-minute film called 'Watch Out – There's a Queer About'. I had never heard of or seen this film and therefore assumed that Phil was referring to him and his partner Sean in reference to the 'we're in it' of his message header. I watched the film with great interest and then stood up in utter astonishment whilst pointing at the screen when I saw that not only was Philip in it, but both me, my mate bus driver Lawrence and his partner Jimi Somerville! Admittedly mine was a very short part; apart from some excruciatingly embarrassing period dancing I only had one line. In fact not even a line really; I just said 'Nineteen' as a response to a policeman asking me how old I was. Actually in 1980 at the time this film was apparently made (it is dated January 1st 1980, but one assumes that it was actually filmed in the latter months of 1979) I would have been 21 and therefore 'legal' for the purposes of the film's subject matter. The LCVA website gives the following synopsis:

> *'Police Cadet Training Film No. 69… Male Homosexuals and the criminal law. In wonderful spoof style the tape uses actors to reconstruct scenes of police investigation and harassment of gay men… from the point of view of the police. Despite the humour, the message is a serious one, giving information*

on the law and acts of parliament affecting gay men. The tape is not about excesses and abuses of power nor about prejudiced police officers, but rather about the routine everyday enforcement of contradictory, sometimes absurd, but nonetheless consistently oppressive legal machine, the implications of which affect many people beyond the gay community. All is not quite lost however – in true epilogue style our friendly Dixon (of Dock Green fame) gives advice on what to do if you are arrested.'

I was utterly dumbfounded to see this. I had no memory of seeing it let alone making it. I immediately wrote back to Philip to ask him if he could throw any light on how I came to be in this film? He told me that his friend Andy Lipman had developed the project through Oval House (where we had suffered those ghastly rehearsals I spoke of earlier) and which had a broader arts portfolio called 'Oval Video'. I didn't recall ever meeting Andy but the LCVA website gives an interesting biog of him:

'Andy Lipman the television producer and writer was born on 27 January 1952. Originally trained as a lawyer, he left the legal world behind to work in video television. He made Watch Out – There's a Queer About *with Oval Video, and then, with Philip Timmins, was a* project coordinator *of the low-budget video* Framed Youth. *The video won the Grierson Award for best documentary in 1984. Lipman submitted the proposal that became* The Media Show *on Channel 4 and became its producer. From 1990– 1992 Lipman edited and produced four series of the Channel 4 programme* For Love or Money *on the art and antiques' market. He also produced* World in Action *in 1993. He died on 3 March 1997.'*

I must have been cast in this at the time of *Who Knows*, but it's truly bizarre to me that I have no memory of it whatsoever. It was a very strange experience to watch this for the first time 38 years later, to see oneself in a situation at odds with one's own memories. Although the film location is listed as 'unknown', I am almost certain that the club scene in it was filmed at the Carved Red Lion, a pub in Islington in North London which was a favourite dance club for those of us seeking an alternative to the growth of the London mega clubs like Heaven and Bang. The location seems familiar as the ceiling in there was so low that anyone over 6ft tall was in danger of knocking themselves out if they dared even attempt to Pogo. For now I am still buzzing from having discovered after all these years that I have actually been in a film, the one medium I had always wished I'd had some involvement in but was convinced I hadn't. How on earth could I have forgotten this? Perhaps I'm going senile after all?

I won't dwell too much on the content on the film or you'll accuse me of going all political and serious, which would be tedious and cause furrowed brows all round (the precursor to crows' feet – and we wouldn't want that, would we?). I can't let it go completely though as the film's scenario is one that would surely surprise a lot of people these days. We were used back then to our pubs and clubs (and even homes) being invaded by the Police on the ludicrous premise of 'outraging public morals' and 'indecency'. The straight world back then had terribly high standards which were under threat from political agitators, social pariahs and perverts like us. Residents of Jerry and Margot's BBC Surbiton private roads and avenues had their respectable lifestyles at risk not only from Tom and Barbara's *Good Life* self-sufficiency, but from the seething working class minorities who would insist upon having a valid lifestyle of their own. How very dare they! Films like *Watch Out There's a Queer About!* should be shown again to remind us all of just how far we have come and how much we had to fight for what we have now.

With the HIV/AIDS crisis about to hit our community so hard these were not easy times. Social history isn't exactly a ratings winner on TV or in cinemas nowadays, where in the 60s and 70s it had been a prominent part of the arts scene and been instrumental in changing the attitudes of a staid post-war majority still hung up on Victorian family values and a rotten class system. Although the US didn't have 'class', it was fighting the rise of religious fundamentalism from vile death cult evangelists like Billy Graham and fellow charlatans who discovered that God could be big business, especially if the masses could be whipped up into an emotional frenzy by the very mention of fags and commies. The work of pioneering film-makers and dramatists such as Ken Loach, John Schlesinger, Joe Orton, Otto Preminger, Mike Leigh and so many others gave powerful testimony to much needed social change. We seem to have lost this at the time I am writing this. Here in 2018 we have a moron in the White House, a UK government apparently attempting economic suicide and the threat of social breakdown still ever present. Who is making stuff like this nowadays? Where is the social commentary? Am I ever going to belt up about all this and get back to the story and something more interesting? Eh? Oh, alright then...

Back in the mundane world I was travelling more and more with my new found wealth from the day job on the trains, perhaps to escape the rather depressing place I was living in at the time. I had somehow managed to get myself a council flat on the notorious Stonebridge Park council estate, not far from Wembley in North West London. This was handy for my railway work over at Neasden and provided me with an escape from private landlords and rented rooms. I was sharing this ghastly flat with another gay guy I worked with. We had no money for carpets, beds or furniture so we made do with a second-hand sofa and mattresses on the floor. As with Phil's flats the lifts in our block were frequently out of order and reeked of the joints which everyone on the estate seemed to be smoking.

One night in April 1981, just after the anti-Thatcher Brixton riots which had so rocked London, my flatmate and I had decided to go for a night out in Notting Hill. On our way home we were forced to walk back from the bus stop in Harlesden High St towards the estate as there had been some sort of incident in the road involving a car and some bystanders, which had stopped any traffic from getting past. We walked past the pulsing blue lights, police and ambulances with that rather resigned air that all big city residents seem to have to such things. As we neared the major road junction on the outskirts of the estate we heard someone shout something at us from across the road. Ignoring it at first we then became aware of a large if somewhat splintered crowd of guys moving towards us from the other side of the road. One of them was calling, 'What have you done then?' at us. It didn't make any sense and we ignored it and carried on walking. Then, with a sudden rush of shouting and screaming a large mob of about sixty to seventy young men streamed across the road directly towards us dodging the traffic as it roared past seemingly oblivious to what was happening. Neither Peter nor I had anywhere to run. There was fast-moving traffic to our left and a tatty hedgerow in front of houses to our right. When it became obvious we were about to be attacked I yelled at Peter to run. As I did so I felt a crack to my forehead as I was coshed with what (coincidentally) looked like a strap hanger off of a tube train whilst the guy yelled that same phrase 'What have you done?' angrily at me. Fearing for my life I ran and ran until I could barely breathe.

To this day I have no idea how I managed to escape the raging crowd baying for our blood. I'd tried to reason and recall crying that we were on their side. Such was the hatred of what Thatcher's divisive government was doing to working class people and the multitude of communities that it comprised that it was hard to come to terms with. I recall feeling aggrieved that this crowd of angry black youths, with whom I had so much political and moral empathy, was attacking two guys from the gay community which was also suffering appalling discrimination and bigotry from the same source. This wasn't right. We were on the same side weren't we?

I had somehow managed to scramble myself up just as I saw a flash of something silvery and metallic swoop down and miss me by inches. Taking advantage of the confusion and mass of people I broke through the crowd and made it to the other side of the junction and into the darkness of the outer edges of the estate's moribund concrete towers and shady walkways.

I got back to the flat and let myself in panting for breath but relieved to be in a safe place at last. My flatmate's boyfriend who had been working and hadn't come out with us rushed out of their room when he heard me come in. In a panicked state he asked me where his partner was. It was only then that I realised I had lost sight of him in the melee of the attack. I didn't know where he was or what had happened to him. 'I'm so sorry Shaun, I don't know where Peter is. I just told him to run. There were so many guys coming for us. There was nothing I could do,' I cried. We were both frantic with worry as we heard the wailing sounds of police sirens tearing through the constant background white noise of traffic. 'You need an ambulance, look at you,' he said as for the first time I took stock of what had happened to me. I was covered in blood from a gaping wound on my forehead. My shirt and face were soaked in blood and I had started to feel nauseous as the reality of what had just happened hit home. At first I brushed off any suggestion of going to hospital, but then when the extent of my injuries became apparent I changed my mind. About half an hour had passed when the ambulance arrived and there was still no sign of Peter. As we lurched through the streets of North London towards the hospital I overheard the driver and the paramedic talking.

'What happened to the guy they brought in earlier from Harlesden High St?'

'Oh he's dead, didn't stand a chance.'

I felt sick as I assumed this was Peter. I had left him and they'd got him. It was all my fault. If only I could have helped him. How was I going to tell Shaun?

They dressed my wounds whilst refusing to answer my questions about the person I'd heard the ambulance men talking about earlier. Eventually the police came to talk to me for a statement. They didn't know whether I was an attacker or a victim at that time, just that I had somehow been involved in the night's affray. I explained what had actually happened and enquired frantically about Peter. When it became apparent to them that I was indeed an innocent victim of the riot they opened up more. The earlier incident in Harlesden High St had been an attack on a car during which the driver had been stabbed and killed in front of his girlfriend. The same crowd had then dispersed and reformed to attack Peter and me about 20 minutes later. It was mildly encouraging to learn that the guy who so nearly stabbed me had however been apprehended and was in custody.

They drove me back to the flat and I was relieved to find that Peter had finally made his way back after having sheltered in (of all places) the Conservative Club near to the junction where it had all kicked off.

Somewhat incongruously, I had been due the following day to attend a final audition for the pop duo being put together for the 1982 Eurovision Song Contest; the group that would eventually become 'Bardot'. I was in no fit state to do this as I had a large cut on my head and was covered in bruises. Hardly appropriate for international Boom Bang A Banging. With a heavy heart I called the agency and told them I was pulling out. As luck would have it this turned out to be fortuitous as it was during my recovery from the operation I subsequently had on my forehead injuries that I saw the advert in *Melody Maker* that would change my life forever and give me the biggest break I could ever have wished for. Bardot eventually represented the UK at Eurovision with their terrific song 'One Step Further', although the song reached No. 2 in the UK charts it only managed seventh place in the competition itself as their performance was seemingly hit by technical difficulties putting their singing pitch at odds with the orchestra backing them. In an odd coincidence the male half of that duo, a guy called Stephen Fischer, would go on to work as a keyboardist with Boy George and Bob Geldof, both of whom were about to figure in my own endeavours.

Following the street attack neither Peter nor I felt safe in that area any more. I'd lived in rough places before and it wasn't so much that which bothered me, it was the thought of what had so nearly happened and having to walk past that spot every day filled me with anxiety. The event changed me forever. Whereas before I was happy-go-lucky and open armed to all the experiences of my incredible city, I now became cautious and hyper-aware of what was going on around me. This has never dissipated. I am still like it now. It fed my dreams and gave me nightmares for years afterwards. I hate what happened for doing this to me. I have always wanted my old gay abandon back, yet that glorious free spirit somehow never returned. Whilst there were plenty of people around me ready to put the blame for all this on racial conflict, at least I never let that opinion get the better of me. I knew it had nothing whatever to do with that. I could just as easily have been ambushed and beaten up by gay bashers in a predominantly white area of London. My attackers may have been a different colour to me, but I knew instinctively that I couldn't go through my life blaming that for what happened. Racism of any type had always appalled me and just going back to working on the trains with my many friends and colleagues from all backgrounds was a tonic, not a trial. To this day I still love London for its diversity and mix of cultures. It's what makes the city feel like home to me. I count myself lucky to have grown up with the Indian neighbours whom I adored in Tunbridge Wells and I'm sure that helped with having to vocally argue with a small number of people I knew who used the attack to proffer their own stupid bigoted rationales.

Peter and I put in an application to be moved from our council flat to one in another area, which was thankfully granted and shortly afterwards we moved what little we had to another shitty flat at the attractively named 'Crone Court' in Queens Park, about 4 miles south of where we'd been. I was going through another Andy Warhol worshipping period and decided to paint my bedroom walls in great blocks of bright red and blue in an attempt to make my bedroom look like The Factory in New York. Sadly it looked more like an abandoned warehouse in Queen's Park than the most creative space in the known universe.

Once again, I couldn't afford to buy a bed so I plonked my mattress on the floor and decided that it looked cool, hip and groovy. My beloved vinyl record collection was once again propped up against the wall with my turntable, tape deck, amplifier and speakers balancing on the cardboard boxes I'd carted them there in. Though this flat was equally bare with no furniture or carpets, it did at least feel like home for a short while. For some odd reason I have never really been able to fathom Peter and I rapidly drifted apart as friends after we moved to Queens Park. As a result I spent very little time in the flat, preferring instead to stay at Phil's, especially after a long night of recording sketches, jingles and interviews.

As I mentioned earlier, at the beginning of 1980 I had started going to a small club in the basement of a pub called The Carved Red Lion in Islington. The disco there was run by a couple of guys who styled themselves 'Hipper Than Shit'. It was refreshing that they played alternative music and not the dance stuff which almost all of the others did. Favourites of the time were 'Papa's Got

A Brand New Pigbag' by Pigbag, 'Fiery Jack' by The Fall, 'Lava' and 'Quiche Lorraine' by the B-52s, 'It's Obvious' by the Au Pairs, 'Death Disco' by PIL and so many more. Sprinkled liberally with plenty of Velvet Underground, Bowie, Bolan, Bauhaus, New Order and even vintage reggae, it was a joyous place to be.

Editor's note: Stop listing records – it's beginning to sound like a mix tape. Get on with it...

Gradually some of the crowd who had mainstreamed at the Blitz Club also started to come here before decamping wholesale to the Camden Palace along with Steve Strange. I remember Boy George in particular as he was so tall, especially including his head creations. The ceiling was incredibly low in there and I am not sure how he managed to manoeuvre around without becoming wedged between the floor and the roof. The DJs would be up for playing almost anything you asked them to. One night they even played the Velvet's 'Sister Ray' – all 17 minutes and 29 seconds of it. Even if a lot of what they played was impossible to dance to, somehow it all seemed perfect; the antidote to disco.

It was here that I became friends with a guy called Lawrence and his other half Jimi. Lawrence was a bus driver at Riverside garage in Hammersmith. It doesn't get much more exotic than that does it? Lawrence was beyond cool. With his sharp-as-a-razor haircut, super laid back attitude, tight black jeans and skinny, loose T-shirts I totally fell for him, even though Jimi (who had the bright ginger hair I always lusted for) and I were also good friends. Somehow it didn't seem to matter. We sang, laughed and drank together regardless. We obsessed about the B-52s' songs and had the time of our lives at the Wild Planet tour gig in Hammersmith that year. I think it's fair to say that Jimi loved the booze slightly more than most of us did. He got particularly shitfaced one night at the Carved Red Lion. Lawrence had an open topped Triumph Herald. As he drove us back down the Euston Road towards Ealing with the stereo on full blast, Jimi and I were both standing on the back seat wedged through the roof singing and waving about. For reasons best known to him he was shouting 'Oot of ma' heed' in his glorious thick Glasgow accent at passers by and then collapsing in hysterics as they looked back bemused. How we didn't get pulled over that night is beyond me.

One night we turned up for our regular weekly session in the basement to find that the entire upstairs pub was seething with rowdy, drunken, chanting football supporters. And what they were chanting was definitely not of the Buddhist variety. Now of course we could more than match the rowdy and the drunken, and possibly even the chanting, but as Hipper Than Shit cranked up the volume for our disco the noise drew the fans downstairs.

George was there that night done up if I recall a la Leigh Bowery and this didn't make for an easy interaction with the rumbustious ball kickers. Sensing that this could very quickly become a bloodbath the landlord tried desperately to steer the straights away from the 'private party' downstairs. For a while it got very scary indeed as one of them yelled 'They're all poofs!' up the stairs as laughing and jeering fans descended en masse. Somehow the pub staff (who were wonderful) managed to relocate the interlopers back to the upstairs bars. We were then told to stay where we were until the upper floors emptied at closing time. The pub was about 7-8 mins mince to Angel Tube station though and I became convinced that we would be murdered by death en route. In a rare and unusual turn up for the books the Police were called and we were given peculiar protection. Indeed some of us decided that this was too good an opportunity to miss and we started playing up to it, asking how big their truncheons were and where we could buy furry handcuffs. The incident probably doesn't sound very dramatic now, but it sticks in my mind for two reasons. Firstly because there was real fear in that room when it so nearly turned into a brawl. I have always been afraid of physical violence and although we would have fought if we'd had to it was an oddly incongruous sight seeing so many 'alternatives' mingling with our very opposites in football shirts. Secondly it's hard to convey just how weird it was that the Police who were still causing our communities so much routine hassle were actually affording our group protection.

The Thatcher years had angered us to the point where we actively sought to enrage and provoke the status quo. We supported the miners in their fight for justice (in stories already told elsewhere) and fought against the ignorance of her bigoted regime throughout the most divisive years of politics I have ever experienced. These days it is hard to convey just how much we loathed and hated her and all her vile Tory cronies. Together with Ronald Reagan raving in the States and threatening a second nuclear holocaust these were deeply troubled times. The establishment represented a past we could not accede to and a future we didn't want. Politics, fashion, art and music were all interwoven into one giant anti-establishment protest against fascists, racists and nuclear power, the miners' strike and eventually the ten-week Falklands War which would erupt in April of 1982. By that time the cumulative effects of popular protest had made the Thatcher government deeply unpopular and deeply polarised voters. We were convinced she was on a path to be routed in the polls until she engineered the ridiculous war with Argentina in the South Atlantic. With the nationalistic jingoism she encouraged, the bitch cow from hell clung on in power and was re-elected for a second term.

Although I had no choice but to put my stage career on the back burner for a wee while whilst I was busy establishing myself with a line of financial stability on the tube trains, Phil and I had been hard at work recording the sketches I had been writing and making plans for what would eventually become the world's first ever gay radio programme 'Gaywaves'.

I don't think we really had a fixed idea of what this should be, but we knew it had to serve as an effective news medium apart from anything else. With no internet, social media and a very small periodic dedicated gay press there was no easy way of sharing what was going on, even in a city as huge and frenetic as London. People outside in the other cities, towns and in rural areas were even more disadvantaged. Phil in his geekery was obsessed with pirate radio. He'd somehow managed to get in with the people that ran a station broadcasting in the London area called Thameside radio. This was predominantly a music station, but they often held parties effectively serving as outside broadcasts. Moving locations helped keep the whole thing away from the Home Office detector vans, which were always on the lookout for illegal broadcasters. If discovered they would confiscate equipment and arrest anyone found with it. Phil's flat was a great place to broadcast from as it was so high up. It was also convenient to hide the transmitter aerial around the washing line on his balcony. Thameside literally pushed the Beatles through Phil's underwear. How about that? It was easy to keep an eye on the street below from up there too and even if a van had drawn up outside, the piss-soaked lifts were usually out of order, meaning it would take the officials bloody ages to get up the stairs. By which time it would all be packed away and hidden. Part of the trade off for this was that Thameside would broadcast some of our material. I don't know how Phil wangled this but wangle he did. Our reports went out sandwiched between records along with a few of my rather incongruous jingles and sketches. It wasn't ideal, but it was a start.

Our friend BBC John then introduced Phil to some guys he'd met at a pirate outfit called 'Our Radio'. This station was radically different as it acted as an outlet for all sorts of minorities that the status quo had ignored. Through negotiation Phil and John managed to secure a weekly spot for the truly groundbreaking Gaywaves programme. On the 5th of May 1982, as the Falklands War raged away thousands of miles away, the one-hour pilot programme went out starting with one of my jingles recorded in Phil's flat some months earlier and (for security reasons) with Phil using the fictional announcer name of 'Anvil Chime':

Sound FX: *Series of pips pinched from the BBC time clock.*
Gary in BBC cod announcer type voice: 'The time in Britain is seven o'clock, in Hong Kong it's five, in San Francisco it's three fifteen, in Shanklin it's seven o'clock as well, but all over the place it's time for Gaywaves on 103.7!'
Music Cue: *Record of theme from naff old BBC radio programme 'Two Way Family Favourites' distorted by slowing down and speeding up.*
Anvil Chime: 'Hello, as our Jingle says this is Gaywaves on 103.7 VHF. We're being brought to you by courtesy of 'Our Radio', and in a minute we'll go through what we're about and why we're here… so… the two members of the Gaywaves team here today are Neil and me 'Anvil Chime', and we've got taped contributions from another member of our team Gary, who we hope is going to have you laughing at, of all things, his 'Epilogue'. When it comes to explaining why we're here… We are a small group of gay men who felt that the coverage of gay issues by the radio, TV and Fleet Street is at best poor, and at worst heavily biased against a fair say for gay people. By one of those lucky coincidences a couple of us heard that Our Radio were looking for other groups to produce their own programmes… by the people, for the people.'

Phil then went on to explain that whilst the programme was made by gay men, we would not be ignoring women's issues, but that we could not presume to present things from a woman's perspective. This all sounds a bit strange in light of current political thinking, but back then there was little real integration between gay men and women beyond sharing a common dislike of discriminatory laws and the ridiculous social pariahs we all were treated as. It was this separative factor which caused my dislike of the disco scene in the *Who Knows?* play. Men and women simply didn't mix like that in many bars and discos. It wasn't really thought of negatively then either, we just accepted that we had different needs and motives.

For the purposes of Gaywaves reporting though the news items did contain a considerable mix of Lesbian and Gay items. Listening back on them now is sobering. I'd forgotten just how bad things really were. Horrendous prejudice and discrimination in the workplace (from organisations like WH

Smith, Marks & Spencer, Barclays Bank and many others that you now see supporting and sponsoring major social events like Pride), the police regularly employing 'agent provocateur' tactics to entrap gay men, pubs and clubs regularly raided under the slimmest of pretences, and violence on an appalling scale. Gaywaves news captured it all. The vox pops that Phil conducted with his roving microphone are astonishingly moving to listen to. You can hear the disdain and tacit acceptance that this is just how things are in the voices of those whose views he captured and which now speak back more than two generations later.

I live in hope that one day somebody will broadcast these wonderful recordings once again. They are a fascinating record of a troubled time.

Oh, in case you're wondering? The 'Epilogue' Phil mentions refers to a sketch I wrote taking the piss out of the religious programme which the BBC used to show at the end of the day's TV transmissions. It was usually presented by some clapped out old cleric and consisted of rambling nonsense designed to put the viewer to sleep easily. I invented a character that Phil adored: The Reverend Q.F. Pubies. Even the mention of this name used to make him laugh. Pubies' voice was a sort of dribbling, aged old man and the text was a wandering nonsensical parody of daft bible stories. The sketches always ended with a silly moral. In fact it was largely indistinguishable from the real thing. I could have saved myself time and just repeated the TV programme text.

I am also really proud of my jingles. Phil and I recorded everything on reel to reel tape in his flat, overdubbed and then edited them by marking, splicing and then joining the tape. It's a skill that is now largely lost and took a great deal of patience and practice. But it worked for us. My favourite jingle was recorded with Mrs Mills playing 'The Lambeth Walk' (off a record, she'd never have made it up the stairs to Phil's flat) and went as follows… (You can sing along with it if you like? Go on, spoil yourself, you know you want to!)

'Listen to the wireless every day
There's now't that they put out that's really Gay
Now there's no need to despair
'Cause Gaywaves is on the air
Now Wednesday night is full of glee
We're fifty times more camp than the BBC
And *rasp* to the IBA
'Cause Gaywaves will save the day

Everything's bright and cheerful
We'll give you a bona earful
We're on 103.7 for an hour prime
Even Prince Charles listens when he's got the time*
So if you're feeling rather blue
Now you know just what to do
Don't tear out your riah**
'Cause Gaywaves is on the Air***'

*Rumours were rife back then that Prince Charles was actually a whoopsie. A ghastly thought I know, and it was with some relief to our community when he finally married Di and established himself as a confirmed breeder.

**'Riah' is gay slang for 'hair' (spelt backwards, geddit?).

***'Air' was mispronounced humorously to rhyme with 'Riah'.

Another rather delicious jingle was sung to Mrs Mills playing the 'Hokey Cokey'. It went (and you can sing along with this one too if you like, although if you do make sure you check who's listening as I use the word 'homosexual' an awful lot. It might upset your neighbours.):

'You bring your new self in and chuck your old self out
Become a homosexual and find out what fun's about
You scream around the city looking like a bunch of Glads
Oh why don't we all come out!
Oh oh the homosexuals
Oh oh the homosexuals
Thank the lord we're homosexuals
And that's what we're gonna flout
You bring your Gay News in and chuck your Express out
Become a friend of Dorothy and shake it all about
You tune your set to Gaywaves on a Wednesday night
And guess what we're all about!
(You've guessed it)
We're raving homosexuals
We're campaigning homosexuals
Thank the lord we're homosexuals
And that's what it's all about
Oh, don't stay in the closet – come out!'

Many years later when I listened to the shows for the very first time since we recorded them I discovered many more jingles and sketches I had completely forgotten about. Although I had some cassette tapes of our rehearsals and rough cuts, it was a joy to finally hear these in complete programmes.

We even included a very strange interview Phil did with me after I had arrived back from a holiday in Majorca. I'd brought back bottles of a painfully cheap Spanish brandy and we decided to do a sort of travelogue for gay tourists going to Palma. On hearing this again it was apparent that we had drunk a bit too much of this foul brew and I was ever so slightly tipsy. It had also been the first time I had ever flown and I remember being fascinated by how the plane's wings appeared to flap. I rambled on about where to find 'trade in the bushes' on the gay beach and how odd their discos were, with them all starting long after I usually went to bed, everyone filling one club for about an hour and then it emptying out as everybody moved on to the club next door... And so on. It was the clubbing equivalent of musical chairs.

We had such fun making these programmes. I am not sure we ever realised just how much of a time capsule they would become and the value and importance of what we were doing was probably lost on us. Now I think I am more proud of these broadcasts than almost anything I have ever done (perhaps with the exception of the shitfaced Palma Travel Report).

By happy coincidence just as the first of these broadcasts went out I answered an advert in either the *New Musical Express* or *Melody Maker* (I can't remember which one), which said 'Are You The Face For The Space?' Well I thought I was. I wasn't that bad looking, despite the scar on my forehead, which I'd decided in the face of Hobson's Choice adversity made me look butch. I don't recall there being a great deal of information about what the job was, but it must have mentioned TV presenting and music somewhere in it or I wouldn't have bothered. After all I was hardly likely ever to present *Blue Peter* was I?

And so began my path from one Tube to another Tube.

5

The Tubes – 1982 to 1985

I answered the advert with some old self-promoting nonsense or other and posted it off to the anonymous Post Office Box number. I didn't seriously expect to hear anything of it (not many auditions I ever got were via secret PO Boxes. Well, not the legit ones anyway). To my astonishment I arrived back a couple of weeks later at our shitty flat to find a letter from Tyne Tees TV calling me for an audition. I wasn't to know at the time but 3,000 other Herberts had also been sent the same audition call. My audition was at a place just around the corner from Marble Arch, up the Edgware Road in London and was attended by about 100 other hopefuls. The day had been marked by torrential summer downpours, much to the despair of girls who had arrived tarted up like dogs' dinners. 80s fashion was signified by big hair and this did not combine well with heavy rain. Consequently a long damp queue of semi-hysterical wannabe women (and a few queens) formed to gain access to one small lav' where they desperately tried to rescue and rebuild.

The auditioners from Tyne Tees TV were all sat behind three wooden desks just below the stage in the small church hall they had hired. It was very impersonal and incredibly open and therefore not much chance of being able to do your pitch privately. I had devised, what I thought then, was a sure-fire way of getting through the audition; I was going to rush up to the desk when I was called, bang both fists on the table and demand to know what it was all about. It makes me cringe to think about it now, but it did seem to fit with the rebellious spirit of the day, as provoked by Thatcher's Britain. These were dark days and troubled times and the Punk attitude of young people was still very powerful.

It all seemed to be about yelling. Yes, that was it for sure. In order to get myself noticed and to make my mark I deffo had to yell. I had picked a suitably yelling type of outfit consisting of faded jeans so tight you could read the label on my pants, a black T-shirt (no logos or pictures of cowboys kissing – one didn't want to scare them off before even the get go) and a short black cotton bomber jacket infested with silver zips and red piped epaulettes. I'd had my hair bleached to buggery and arranged with a sort of TinTin-esque quiff up the front. I thought I looked reasonably passable for my age.

It transpired that the TTTV bigwigs sat sitting at the desk I got sent to were newly appointed Programme Controller Andrea Wonfor and Producer Paul Corley. It was clear by now that each interview was conducted and concluded in only a couple of precious minutes, so clearly I needed to make an impression sharpish. When it came to my turn I duly rushed up to the table, but then, in a sudden fit of good taste, I decided that it would be naff to bang my fists. Instead I sat down and told them what I had planned to do and what a rubbish idea it was. This made Andrea laugh and Paul smile. At least I think that's what he did, as it was hard to see through his magnificent ZZ Top type bushy blond moustache, beard and long hair arrangement. But his piercing blue eyes sparkled so I guess I'd hit the spot. After my time was up I hung around a while and then managed to find the nearby pub that they'd all repaired to for a drink afterwards. I did a bit of mixing and mingling, like you do and spread my wit and wisdom to as many people as I could. God knows who I ended chatting up. By the time we chucked out I'd probably sold myself to other customers and the bar staff. Not that I really cared. I'd had fun and didn't seriously expect anything to come of it. Whoever heard of anyone from Tunbridge Wells making it on TV? Although I didn't know it at the time Andrea Wonfor was quite a powerful TV exec in those days, and would become even more so later on in her career. I adored her. She was a tough cookie, but absolutely fair and great, great fun to be with. Sadly Andrea is no longer with us, but I will always remember her with great affection.

I duly returned to work on the trains the next morning and went back to writing sketches and jingles for Gaywaves. A couple of weeks later I arrived back at the shitty flat from my Metropolitan Line Guard's duties to find a telegram laying on the grubby tiled floor by the front door. It asked me to telephone the producers at Tyne Tees TV in Newcastle immediately for some 'good news'. I could barely believe my eyes. To me this was simply the most exciting thing that had ever happened to me in my entire life, with the possible exception of getting off with Ben all those years previously. I ran around the empty flat shouting 'I've got it! I've fucking got it!' It was an indescribable high, and a legal one at that! I phoned the number in the telegram and then realised that this gig was not yet 'in the bag'. I was asked to go up to Newcastle for a screen test. A few days later I was sat in first class on the train eating a prepackaged cheese sandwich and loving every minute of it.

I was given the task of a prepared piece-to-camera then a live interview with someone of their choosing. My interviewee turned out to be a local radio DJ from Newcastle's Metro Radio, though I can't remember his name sadly. Mike something or other. I do recall that he did the night show, and we therefore spent the entire interview having the most bizarre conversation on how best to stay awake when you were being bombarded with calls from crazies and insomniacs. Just as in the London auditions I hoofed it and had fun. I didn't have anything prepared, so just camped about invoking the spirits of my comedy heroes Frankie Howerd and Kenny Everett topped off with as much me as I could get away with. Tyne Tees wasn't a huge regional ITV franchise and the studios were much smaller than the BBC at White City where I used to go 'exploring' with my friend John who worked there. The biggest difference though was how friendly everyone was, from the ladies in make-up to the technical crews and production staff, everyone I met was down to earth and with the glorious Newcastle accent and attitude that I grew to love.

Not long after returning back to London I was called by producer Malcolm Gerrie and told that they'd decided not to go with just one presenter to add to the already selected celebrity team of Paula Yates and Jools Holland, but to have five newbies who would share the co-presenting task on a weekly rotating basis. I was one of the five. My goodness gosh I was chuffed, although the realities and practicalities of what was about to happen to me hadn't really hit home. I had a secure if mundane day job and was earning good regular money; something I'd had little experience of whilst acting as I was still trying to accrue enough qualifying work for my Equity card. How was I going to do TV work and then come back to the trains afterwards? This was far removed from stage work and plays where I was seen only on a nightly basis by relatively few punters. Then there was Gaywaves, which was being broadcast on a pirate radio station and gaining in strength and credibility with every broadcast. This was also a project very dear to my heart and important politically. I wasn't sure how I was going to square legit TV work with transmitting my poofy stuff through the washing line aerial on Phil's balcony. What would TTTV do if they found out about that?

I figured out that at least the TV show was going to be broadcast on the soon to be launched Channel 4, a station that had been purposely set up to be the 'alternative' to everything in the world and Albert. Perhaps then if it did get out then it might enhance my street cred? On top of all that I hadn't actually 'come out' to TTTV in the process of my auditions, though in hindsight it must have been pretty clear which side of the bathroom cabinet I stored my toiletries. I duly signed my contract with them to appear 'as myself' and was to be paid £50 a day plus expenses of £35 a day (excluding hotel and travel costs) for the 105 minute live TV show. It might not sound like much now, but at the time it was a lot of money to me.

The five people Tyne Tees picked were myself, Muriel Gray, Michelle Cremona, Nick Laird-Clowes and Mike Everitt. It wasn't just me that had to decide what to do about existing jobs. Muriel had a job that she really loved at the Scottish National Museum of Antiquities, Michelle was working in accounts at a small furniture company in Kent and Mike was a forklift truck driver at a company in Barnsley. Nick was a musician with a band called The Act (post-*Tube* he went on to form the group Dream Academy, who had a massive worldwide hit with 'Life In A Northern Town'). All of us except poor Mike managed to get round the problem somehow. Mike was a really talented presenter but he was married with a family and he told me that when his company refused to let him take part (as they thought it would show them up in a poor light apparently) he was forced to make the choice of *The Tube* or his day job. There was another rumour knocking around as to why Mike couldn't do the show, but I choose the version he told me as I liked him a lot and simply will not entertain anything more salacious. See? I told you I was loyal to my friends. It's a great shame that he gave up this wonderful opportunity although if it was for the reasons he told me then they were understandable. I am convinced to this day that had he taken the chance he would have gone on to have a successful career in the media. Not only was he a talented presenter, but a really lovely guy. The producers must have thought so too, because they broadcast the only filmed interview that Mike had ever done on the show anyway. Mike – you were a diamond.

It wasn't long before the new programme's publicity machine came to life and we were all called back up to Newcastle for production meetings and to meet the team. Muriel Gray and I were bivouacked at the Station Hotel on the Tyne Tees TV expense account. We had hit it off right from the minute we met. I just adored her. We shared the same silly sense of humour, politics, fashion, music and love of the arts. My goodness how we chinwagged. We decided to celebrate all this by stuffing our faces with the most expensive items we could find on the hotel dinner menu and augmenting it by getting absolutely shit faced on champagne and fine wines. We had a great time at zero cost to us and duly repaired to our suites with our stomachs bursting and our bloodstreams having been replaced by alcohol. The following morning we both had hurricane force hangovers and had to be helped into a taxi, imploring the driver to take it easy going round corners as neither of us knew whether we'd make it there without throwing up. We both looked like we'd been dragged through an unploughed field, but poor Muriel had high spiky hair and hadn't had time or inclination to put any make-up on. To our horror the first order of the day was a photo shoot outside the studio with Jools Holland for the press pack. I stood at the side half asleep and barely able to raise a grin. Muriel secreted herself as far back as it was possible to do without disappearing from the photo altogether, peeking over Jools's shoulder and trying to make her distressed state look mysterious and alluring. Neither of us were successful. To this day that photograph makes me laugh. Needless to say neither of us ever got in that state before a studio trip again. I don't recall much more about that day except that Paula Yates wasn't there. Not sure if that was because of her pregnancy or other work commitments, but I don't recall meeting her properly for the first time until we had the show's press launch in Covent Garden some weeks later.

Meanwhile back at my day job I had somehow managed to persuade London Transport to let me change rest days and move shifts so that I could do this show called *The Tube*, but without being specific about exactly what it was. In the simpler times of the day they just assumed that it was about the tube railway in London and to my relief left me to get on with it. I am also struggling to recall what I told Phil Cox and my other close friends about all this. Somewhere in my mind I have the idea that I had kept most of them in the dark about it, as if I had come clean I am sure they'd have figured in my recollections of the time. I know I had carried on making Gaywaves with Phil right up until at least December of 1982, after I had started appearing on TV, but I may have started to withdraw from that by then. The Gaywaves show broadcast on December 15th 1982 was still packed with my jingles and sketches. By that time after just 6 short months the programme had become much more slick and professional sounding. It is fascinating to look back and wonder if the coming of Channel 4 itself didn't have an effect on media coverage of gay political issues which up until that time had been largely ignored by the establishment at the BBC?

Back at *The Tube*'s press launch at the Rock Garden cafe in London's Covent Garden (now the Apple Store) we were setting the scene for the first programme on Friday November 5th 1982. Muriel was to be the 'guest presenter' on show one with me doing the second show a week later on 12th November. I got on well with Jools Holland especially when I found out that he had also loved Marc Bolan's music with T.Rex. He was suitably blokey and very straight, but I'd learned to deal with all that back at the railway so it didn't phase me. All of the other guest presenters were there too and for the first time we met Paula. She was an extraordinary woman, one minute great fun, the next aloof and curiously cold. At the start of the show's run I got on with her well and I think she clicked with my detached campery and sense of humour.

During the course of the press launch it suddenly hit me that I had not actually considered what I was going to do on the show itself. Incredibly nobody had actually discussed this with us. Sure we knew that we would be introducing bands and interviewing people, but in all seriousness I hadn't actually thought about how I would do this. We had only ever experienced the BBC way of conducting pop music programmes, and there it was a toss up between the staged and stylised DJ delivery on *Top Of The Pops* and Radio 1 and the laconic, rather nerdy presentation style of *The Old Grey Whistle Test* on BBC2. Whilst we all knew this to be naff, what on earth was the alternative? We just knew that we didn't want to be like that. We wanted to be true to ourselves and honest in a way that we didn't think the status quo was. I could hardly scream about like I'd been doing on Gaywaves. At this point I started to worry that I had actually got myself into something I didn't really know how to deal with. It was also live TV, no scripts, no talkback and no autocue. There were no second chances. If we fluffed we did so in full view of millions and with no opportunity to go back and do it again. My only solace at the time was knowing that the new TV station Channel 4 was not yet being broadcast to the entire nation as many transmitters were not ready. Maybe I could be an embarrassing flop and nobody would see it? As ridiculous as it sounds I really did think that.

As Friday November 5th 1982 loomed I got landed with another problem. I had been sent to the Underground's training school in White City for training as a Train Driver. It couldn't have come at a worse time. I was busy in every waking moment outside of work with either Gaywaves recordings or planning for travel up to Newcastle, which in the early days involved three days per programme. After studying the technical issues to butch up to being a driver I was suddenly given my final examination the day before I was due to go up to do a programme. I was desperate to get out of it so I ballsed up almost every answer to the examiner's questions, until the examiner began to get suspicious. In the end he stopped the exam and took me to one side. 'I don't know what you're up to but I'm baffled as to why you appear to be deliberately sabotaging your own promotion', he said. 'Look, I can't explain now, but please would you just fail me and have done with it so I can get out of here,' I pleaded. My answers had been getting silly to the point where if he hadn't let me go then I might easily have lost my job as a Guard let alone any promotion. My one saving grace was that the Instructor concerned knew that I really did know my stuff (as dreary as that sounds). He obligingly failed me and sent me back to Neasden as the Guard I still was, and for which I thanked him profusely. Not often one gets to be so pleased at being a failure is it? How we laughed.

The night before the first show I had spoken to Muriel on the phone. She was in a terrible state of nerves after discovering she'd been given the job of interviewing Paul Weller, who was to play with The Jam in what was to be their final TV performance, quite an exclusive for the show. I did my best to calm her by helpfully reminding her that she was good and I was rubbish. Not a very sophisticated argument, but at least it was heartfelt and accurate. I promised to call her at home on the Saturday afterwards to get all the dirt on what happened.

I went to work as usual on Friday 5th November, Bonfire Night. Channel 4 itself had launched successfully that Tuesday the 2nd with shows like *Countdown* and the Liverpudlian soap opera *Brookside*. Funny choice of launch night I thought, but then it was to be the new alternative and launching on a Tuesday night seemed pretty radical to me.

In the early days of *The Tube* we would arrive up at Tyne Tees studios on Wednesday of the broadcast week and spend a couple of days preparing. I can't honestly say that we rehearsed; well, not in the sense I was used to in the theatre anyway. It was useful for all of us to get a feel for the studio, the structure of the programme and where we needed to be at any given time. As it was live it would have been a disaster if we'd got lost and missed a cue. As silly as it sounds, getting lost wasn't entirely impossible. The dressing rooms were quite a way from Studio Five where the show was made.

I was yet to discover all this by the time the first programme went out. On the Friday afternoon on the day of broadcast I called Muriel again and wished her all the luck in the world. She was in an even worse state than the night before bless her. Just at that time I was still in excited mode and the fear hadn't quite grasped my brain stem to mangle my emotions. It would come though.

At 5.15 Channel 4 announcer Paul Coia (whom we had met and I'd quite fancied during a strange visit to Channel 4's HQ a few weeks earlier to meet with the head honcho Jeremy Isaacs) said, 'But now here on Channel 4 a programme that promises to be very different. A mixture of magazine features and music for everyone with a sense of fun. *The Tube* is live and guests tonight include Pete Townsend, The Jam and Sting. *The Tube* is presented by Jools Holland and Paula Yates. You're watching Channel 4 at 5.15.'

From the clock on the screen cameras flickered into life to a shivering queue of liggers outside the TTTV studios and then onto Jools who instantly proved that our show was about as far away from the starchy, established BBC as it was possible to be.

'Right! Pay very close attention indeed. Walk to your television set and turn it up. It's November the fifth… '

(Jools is handed a sparkler by a floor manager)

'… And we're going to do something now that's going to go down in the anals of television history. It's a live rock show, we've got an enormous firework display laid on *(waves sparkler)* at great expense, Channel 4 spare no expense whatsoever *(chucks sparkler to one side)*. This is now time for *The Tube*. You're going to see live bands, remember turn it up. *(Gestures at shivering crowd queuing.)* These people are going to go in there and we're going to have an absolutely insane time. From now on, you're watching… Fantastic… *Tube!*'

And then with a crash of thunder the main titles burst onto the screen with that theme tune that still has the power to strike both fear and pride in me even after all these years. What's weird about that is how much I hated it at the time. But in researching this and after watching the shows for the first time since they were broadcast I think it was way ahead of its time. It still sounds good even now.

The titles announced the featured bands already mentioned plus Heaven 17. Surprisingly (at least for me as I'd assumed that Paula would have had first shout after Jools) it then cut to Northern street poet Mark Miwurdz for a short bit of banter before punk band The Toy Dolls burst into their opening number 'She Goes To Fino's'. The lead singer of their band was a guy called Michael 'Olga' Algar, one of palest, whitest and skinniest guys I have ever seen. He was so thin that looking side on he disappeared. The microphone stand blotted him out. But what he lost in bulk he sure made up for with energy.

They only played about a minute of their bouncy number before the cameras cut to my Muriel in the 'Green Room'. As always she looked stunning with fabulous spikey blonde hair and huge hooped earrings which Tyne Tees could have broadcast to London with (and maybe did?). Although it sounds faintly ludicrous to say this now, her beautiful broad Scottish accent was an utter breath of fresh air and a total departure from the naff BBC southern voices, which seemed up until then to have only been broken by Jimmy Savile's Leeds brogue and Kid Jenson's transatlantic drawl. She gave a bit of background stuff about the Toy Dolls and then returned for them to finish their number from the foyer area. It was good to see the crowd there just being themselves and not being herded around like sheep with smiles stapled on their faces like we were used to seeing up until the night on shows like *Top Of The Pops*. The liggers here were all cool looking and full of Newcastle pride (like we often were in the pub afterwards).

Mark Miwurdz's actual surname is 'Hurst', which wasn't particularly streetwise and hence his wise adoption of something with a 'Z' in it. He was a really lovely guy who I had a bit of a soft spot for. Offstage this quietly spoken and incredibly intelligent ginger-haired lad was someone I utterly adored. I loved his rapier wit and clever use of language. Oddly, although we were very friendly with each other I didn't keep in touch with him after I left the show. I think like so many other friendships which could have been, the differences in our private lives were such that it just wasn't to be. For the record though Mark, I wish to record just how much I admired and liked you as a person and an artist. Top man!

Muriel told me she was not happy at all with her Paul Weller interview, a view I was more than happy to disagree with. The point was that it wasn't staged or scripted. Despite her nervousness he seemed relaxed and comfortable. Well, he did from what I saw anyway. He was certainly clear about what *The Tube* could bring to music TV, perhaps being amongst the first to realise that this was a sea change from the usual slick and smarmy presenting style at Aunty Beeb. Sure it was rough round the edges and a bit haphazard, but right from the very first minute it was honest, truly different and very down to earth. When the cameras cut to Paula Yates for the first time she was clearly very pregnant and wearing the most fabulous blush pink frock which made her look like an enormous puffed meringue. I'll record my thoughts on Paula later, but for the moment I am back in my shitty flat in Queens Park North West London watching the programme I was to be a small part of for the next two and half years unfold. The narrative of the magazine section on the show was pretty 'matter of fact' and almost flat in relative terms. Paula followed up Weller's fashion look with a piece about Mod magazines, throwing over to Jools interviewing three guys from a self-made street publication called *Shapes Of Things*. There was a glorious innocence about it all along with a clear feeling that at last the fans had an outlet that established radio and television would never have offered them. The other thing which became quickly apparent was that both interviewers and interviewees of all sorts realised they didn't have to agree, concede or play ball; for the first time they could say (almost) anything they wanted to, including disagreeing with the presenters' views. Contemporary viewers will no doubt find this somewhat baffling as nowadays nobody is backward at coming forward, but in 1982 this presentation style was truly revolutionary. It's worth saying also that at no point did the production team or the directors attempt to influence or steer us to present in any set way. They were quite happy to leave us to our own devices, whether it worked or not. That was a bold decision, but in retrospect it is one of the key elements that gave *The Tube* its feel and ambiance. Yes, OK we cocked up a lot. But what the hell?

Episode one continued with a feature on a black dance company from Birmingham called Dance D'Afrique, then segued neatly into Duran Duran's video of 'Rio' which was filmed in Antigua, creating that astonishingly luxurious image they became known for. As I watched the video end I saw from the superimposed titles that they were to be talking live on the programme the following week. Shit! This was to be my first show, and Duran Duran would be there, live (as opposed to being there dead). I could not have realised that just a few days later I would be in the band's tour bus with Paula as it arrived for their gig at Newcastle City Hall. It may seem strange but we rarely ever discovered in advance who was to be on the show until we arrived up at Tyne Tees for the shows we were to present.

Paula's first interview with Sting was preceded by an excerpt from his film *Brimstone & Treacle*, bit different from The Police the fans knew of. Her overt and very sexual interviewing style was apparent from the get go as she alluded to him trying to squeeze his body parts into his jeans. In the first couple of minutes she'd managed to secrete her foot in his leg area and then offered to poke him if he 'got lippy'. You have to hand it to her, you wouldn't have heard that on BBC2 after the watershed let alone at 5.45pm barely out of *The Magic Roundabout*'s timeslot. The audience loved it, especially when she mentioned him showing his bare bum in the film. She flirted and fidgeted and blushed through questions about sex on his kitchen table and Newcastle's 'spunky atmosphere'. I have to be honest that as I watched it I squirmed with embarrassment, preconditioned as I was to having everything slickly shoved in front of my eyes on other shows of its ilk.

If Paula looked fabulous preggers live in the Newcastle studio, then in the filmed segment about LA she showcased her unique fashion and style with even more stunning outfits. In one slightly chilling segment whilst interviewing Gary Numan, he comments following news reports of 25 itinerant farmworkers having been murdered recently that 'for every crook who wants a gun there are 5 million there they can go and get. It's too late for America'. In light of mass killings that now seem endemic in the US, those comments from 36 years ago now seem sadly prescient. Paula and Jools interviewed William Shatner, Pamela Bellwood from *Dynasty*, and Frank Zappa's daughter Moon Unit. I remember wondering if I would ever get to go to somewhere fabulous on the show, Sri Lanka with the Durans perhaps? Jamaica with Chris Blackwell and maybe Grace Jones? In reality the farthest I ever got was Sunningdale just the other side of Heathrow Airport. Still, you can't have everything can you?

After Heaven 17 performed live in the studio, Jools interviewed Pete Townsend who disappointed me with his (probably wildly accurate) summation of how crap the band thought playing at Woodstock was. I'd always revered that ill-fated festival for its music and its place in rock and social history, and yet here was the PT dissing it like mad. Even worse was that what he said sort of rang true. It probably was a very self-congratulatory affair. Clearly The Who didn't like the politics of the whole thing, although had I interviewed him I would have asked him why they'd even agreed to play it in the first place. Half a million hippies in a field seemed about as far away from the ethos of a Mod band as it was possible to get. I can only assume it was for the money. Though I wonder if they ever got that? It's even more ironic that the band's performance was one of those which eventually cemented Woodstock as one of, if not THE greatest rock festivals of all time.

What struck me about Jools' interviewing style was just how unafraid he was to ask questions that the establishment would never have countenanced. Things like, 'I saw on *Newsnight* the other night, film of you at Shea Stadium, it struck me… you'd had enough of it all, playing live and stuff, and also had enough of Americans.' Bold stuff that. I feel. You see. I admired him greatly for it too. However it never occurred to me to even try and emulate this in any way.

Even before my first show I knew that whatever I was to do it had to be true to my personality and nobody else's.

Show one continued by showcasing some new and unsigned bands from around the country, including a Glasgow outfit called 'Set The Tone', whose lead singer appeared to have a marrow down the front of his light grey trackie bottoms. I was transfixed, as I imagine a lot of viewers were. I don't think it did him or them much good though as they came and went fairly rapidly despite the exposure (or maybe lack of it).

Finally on came The Jam for their very final televised set together. I was thrilled that Muriel got the task of introducing them. You go girl! They played and made history I suppose. I wasn't ever a lover of their stuff personally. It was a sound I never quite got. But each to their own eh?

And so ended the first show. I sat back on the falling to bits sofa and tried to take in what I'd just seen. I've been putting off saying this for far too long so now it's finally time to admit what I felt and what I did.

cues dramatic horror film like music sting

It may surprise you to hear that I thought the show was a mess and wondered what on earth I was a going to do. What seemed amateurish and cack-handed to me then was almost certainly because, like most people, I was simply too infused with the status quo to realise what Paul, Malcolm and the whole team at Tyne Tees were trying to do. As bonkers as it sounds I decided to phone the studio and tell them what I thought of it. I even considered pulling out as I just couldn't see how I would fit in with what I'd seen. I was just 24, with no experience of television work and used only to being scripted and directed with weeks of rehearsal time. For the first time I realised that I would truly be on my own and I wasn't sure I would be able to handle it. The phone rang at Tyne Tees and I asked to be put through to the control room to speak to co-producer Paul Corley. When he answered I could hear celebration, jubilation and partying noises in the background. Clearly they were triumphant. This completely wrong-footed me and I stumbled into our conversation completely out of sync with how they were all clearly feeling. 'What did you think of the show?', said Paul. 'Err... Well... I've not seen anything like it before,' I mumbled with slightly less than two molecules of conviction. 'It'll be great, we're all over the moon about it and we're all looking forward to seeing you up here with us next week,' he said before we quickly concluded and I rang off.

Silence.

Oh fuck.

What was I going to do?

What was it they'd seen that I hadn't? For the first time the reality of what it was I was going to have to do hit home. I honestly hadn't really thought about it up until then. It had somehow seemed unreal. The auditions were fun, but I was used to all that mullarky. Now the light at the end of the tunnel seemed like the lights of an approaching train on the same track (every train driver's nightmare). I realised I'd never really met Paula, that at the very least Duran Duran would be on the show and that somehow I had to wangle 3 days off work to get up there to do the bloody thing.

Remembering that I'd managed to spin London Transport some old yarn to get the time off, it was now painfully apparent that somebody there was actually going to see what I was actually doing. I wandered around for the next four days in a sort of daze. Then on Wednesday 10th November 1982 I snuck off to King's Cross and got the train up to Newcastle. It was right nice sitting in First Class with a fully paid up ticket too. My goodness golly gosh I felt like an economy film star. They even served a hot breakfast. Yes! They did! With fried eggs and everything!

Was there no end to this luxury?

As it happened there was, because a few hours later I arrived back in the Toon. This time I was staying up in Gosforth at the Gosforth Park Hotel. It was a much more exclusive type of a place, and the same gaff that all the bands and celebs were put up in. I discovered that Jools Holland was in the next room to me. As I'd met him previously it seemed like a good opportunity to get to know him a bit better. He seemed an amiable sort of a bloke. Very down to earth, South London and matter of fact. We didn't really have a great deal in common. I can be painfully shy meeting new people and even having discovered that Jools liked Marc Bolan's music wasn't really enough to fire things up. Actors and musicians have never traditionally demonstrated the greatest of synergies, not because they don't like or respect each other, but mainly I suppose because their worlds are so different. Surprisingly so even in stage musicals and shows, where the beers for the band are rarely ever shared with the gin for the actors.

When I arrived at the studios I was welcomed by associate producers Lesley Oakden and Jeff Brown and a rather strict looking woman called Averil Peacock who was apparently a 'programme co-ordinator' (whatever that meant). I don't recall ever being taken around the building but I suppose I must have been because it was an absolute rabbit warren of corridors and staircases. The production office had two main sections – one as a sort of general milling around area with some armchairs and a coffee table in the middle and a load of smaller individual offices off of it, some full of equipment and the others full of the person whose office it was. The other section was a large meeting room with a huge table in it at the front of the building overlooking City Road, the pub over the road with the sombre River Tyne flowing in a silky grey sludge behind that.

I seem to recall that the front room and office which adjoined it was very much Averil's patch. She was kindly but firm, a bit like one of your favourite teachers, but one you wouldn't want to cross. She dealt with all the admin, expenses, contracts, travel, hotels, and all the stuff you don't realise you need until you need it.

Meanwhile I was still trying to figure out who I was going to be on this programme. Would I present like my hero Kenny Everett? Would I be camp? Would I be butch? Would I be cultured? Would I be rough? Would I be serious? (I soon dumped that idea). Would I be… Oh for fuck's sake I didn't know! I didn't even know who I was.

I was introduced to the show's incredibly talented research team. These were the people who, from what I can gather, were at the very heart of the show's content. They were the ones who had the connections, who scouted for bands and for magazine content and who looked after us presenters, feeding us with background info and support. Chris Phipps, Lesley Oakden, Jeff Brown, Chris Cowey and my favourite of all Nigel Sheldrick. I fancied Nigel like crazy and was probably pretty obvious about it. But he was totally professional and never once took advantage – however much I wished he had.

I also got to know the production team and many of the technicians, some of whom I am still in touch with today. Wise actors quickly learn the value of appreciating the backstage and technical people as they hold the key to so much in a production. I had a natural affinity with their down-to-earth nature and actually preferred being with them to being in front of the cameras. As the series went on I struggled increasingly to relate with the 'star' elements and felt little urge to establish this in myself. Actors don't really have to do this and I certainly wasn't comfortable with creating a television persona of my own. If I ever managed to find out who I was then that would be it as far as I was concerned. Clearly I wasn't playing a part, as I had no character or script, and the direction we had was mainly just where you had to be, who you were talking to and how much time you had to do it.

We held our first production meeting and it was there that I met Paula Yates properly for the first time. It was very much a kind of 'sounding out'. As ever she looked utterly fabulous in a brilliant yellow and black striped outfit so figure hugging that I could read the washing instructions. I asked her how she'd managed to get her hair so bleached white and looking so fabulous when mine ended up looking and feeling like upholstery stuffing? We swapped hair conditioning and make-up tips. On discovering that I was gay (at least I assume that's what it was as she clearly wasn't going to get a shag out of me) she warmed somewhat and later that evening we shared a cab back to the hotel.

I learned that day that I would be interviewing Andy Summers from The Police. He wasn't someone I was terribly familiar with and that made the prospect slightly easier. He'd been booked to talk about a new project of his with multi-instrumentalist and ex King Crimson band member Robert Fripp. Also on the show would be a new band called Strange Days, American band The Go Gos, and heroes of mine Yazoo, with Alison Moyet and Vince Clarke. Duran Duran would headline the whole show. The magazine section would also feature interviews with ex-Animals and War frontman and local hero Eric Burdon, as well as (for reasons not entirely clear to me other than the fact he lived up the road) local sports hero and Olympic runner Steve Cram. It seemed an interesting selection, even if the only bands on the show I genuinely liked were Yazoo and the Durans. I don't 'DO' sport in any way, so wasn't enthused by the idea of even talking to Mr Cram, let alone interviewing him. I had no idea what to say or ask him. Well, what do you ask a runner? 'What's it like to run?', 'How do you train?', 'What was it like winning a medal?', all of which are about as interesting as cable ducting. My little bit with him was to be mercifully short as I was to introduce him into the show in the foyer area prior to the more in-depth probing he was going to get with Paula later on. It was somewhat comforting when Paula told me she hadn't got a clue what to talk to him about either. 'Ask him how big his knob is then,' I helpfully advised. 'Even better, he can show us!' she squealed in delight. You know there were times when it was just as well we were pre-watershed. God knows what would have happened had we been a late-night show.

The following day we met round the table with the production team and talked our way through the running order. These came printed on bright yellow paper and contained detailed timings for each segment of the show, who was presenting each bit, the cameras and locations and which band or guest was on at what time and location. Still with me? Good! I used the running order to start scribbling link and interview words as a sort of script, not being at all confident to just hoof it. This was live TV and I only had one opportunity to deliver the goods or look like a twat. Oddly enough, looking like a twat was something I had every confidence in delivering. I was desperate to have at least something scripted as a fallback. At least that's what I had convinced myself I needed. I was too nervous to ask anyone about this. I felt like I ought to just 'know what to do'. The production team seemed quite happy for us to manage it in whatever way we wanted. I couldn't make my mind up whether this was supreme confidence or utter madness. It sure as hell meant it would be unique. Ace researcher Chris Phipps came to me and said that Andy Summers was insisting on having 15 minutes to talk about his new album and that he wanted especially to focus on the LP cover artwork. This was about 10 minutes longer than anyone in the magazine section was ever likely to get, no matter who they were. He then gave me a copy of the album sleeve and the first seeds of panic crept into my brain store. It was a plain cream colour square with a small black and white drawing of two heads in the middle. I'd never be able to fill 5 minutes talking about that. I knew that we'd be playing a bit of their music video before the interview and I vainly hoped that it might inspire me to ask something interesting. We concluded the planning meeting and then I was taken round the studio and shown my locations for each link. I was a lot happier with this bit as 'blocking' moves on stage was a familiar activity.

After the day's studio planning and production meetings we were taken back to the hotel by 'Noda Taxis' to prepare for the big day. Prior to that though was something more gripping. We had an invite from the Durans to go to their gig that night at Newcastle City Hall. Paula and I met up with the band in the foyer of the hotel and we duly clambered aboard their tour bus. We laughed and giggled like a couple of teenage schoolgirls. I seem to recall her having something of a soft spot for tall bass guitarist John Taylor. At least I think that's who it was. The band had a load of Taylors in it (John, Roger and Andy) and Paula was excitedly over all of them both in the hotel and on the tour bus. They were a warm, friendly bunch, with no airs or graces. Drummer Roger Taylor and bassist John in particular were very sweet to me, which meant a lot considering I was a complete nobody. As we approached the venue their tour manager stood up and gave all of us an unexpectedly forceful lecture.

'Get in line to exit as soon as the bus stops. When the doors open you run fast for the stage door. Do NOT stop, do NOT hesitate until you are inside and the door has closed behind you!'

I thought this was funny at first, until we drew up outside the stage door and I saw hundreds of screaming, baying girls clamouring against a few valiant policemen and a couple of stagehands. From the look of them they would have torn us to shreds. It was terrifying. The bus shuddered to a stop and the doors opened. 'Go! Go! GO!!' yelled the tour manager as one by one we flew across the few metres of pathway towards the stage door. The agitated crowd of pubescent fans surged towards each person as they exited the coach regardless of who they were with blood curdling screams. I wondered what on earth they were yelling at me for? But in reality it didn't seem to matter who left the bus, everyone seemed to be fair game. Once inside the stage door it calmed down and we laughed it off. Well, they did. I was still in shock for about 10 minutes afterwards. A cup of tea and a lie-down would have been nice. Up in the band's dressing room was a large table with drinks and snacks, bowls of fruit all that type of affair. Some of the group were plastering on make-up in gloriously be-bulbed mirrors, whilst others slummocked about on the sofas. I noticed that as Simon Le Bon was pulling on his brown leather jeans he was stuffing rolled up socks down the front. Bit naughty I thought, but then leather is pretty unforgiving and has a tendency to sag where you don't want it to. The gays know how to deal with bulge enhancement of course, but it was a novelty to see a straight man doing it.

Paula and I went to the side of the stage as the band went on to a tumultuous welcome, then we decided that we wanted to see the show from the audience rather than side of stage, so we crept out the side and went to the very back of the hall together. We danced, frugged and sang along together ignored by the crowd who were all fixated at the stage rather than us two up the back. The guys put on a great show and a good time was had by all.

Weirdly I don't remember how we got back afterwards. I suppose it must have been on the tour bus, though that part is a blur. I must have gone to bed with 'Rio' ringing in my ear holes.

As Friday November 12th dawned I made my way to the studios for final meetings and rehearsals. One minute my mind was a whirl of trying to remember rehearsed links and wording, as well as questions for Lord Summers, then the next thinking 'oh bollocks to it, just go with the flow and see what happens'. Once again the researchers, production team and floor managers worked their magic in not only calming me down but making it all fun. Stage manager Colin Rowell always made me laugh and with his band of merry lads helped me find my way around when I didn't know what the hell I was supposed to be doing (which was most of the time). We didn't use talkback earpieces on that first show and the handheld radio microphones we used had a small on/off switch on the bottom which needed careful attention as it could easily be activated without realising. Despite how obvious all this was, even the great and the good got caught out at some time or another.

Just before we went on air Chris Phipps came to my dressing room and told me that Andy Summers had thrown a wobbly about having his interview time cut down. This was just what I needed as I was nervous enough as it was. In a sense though it only served to bolster my 'what the fuck?' attitude to it. There wasn't anything I could do and I just hoped that he would realise this was an editorial decision and not mine.

I got myself into position for the start of the show. I felt sick to the pit of my stomach as the gallery production team wished everyone good luck and the show started with Jools outside the *Tube* entrance at Tyne Tees TV, whereupon his handheld radio mic promptly crackled and failed during his intro speech. Then with a crash of thunder the programme titles exploded onto the screen with that twiddly theme I disliked so much. Floor manager Christine Llewellyn stood in front of me and gave me the countdown for my first ever live TV appearance. My hair was bleached to buggery and I had somehow managed to squeeze myself into a pair of jeans so tight they left little to the imagination. I managed not to trip over anything whilst clumsily introducing myself and then unsigned band Strange Days, all in an odd, yobby sort of a voice which wasn't me at all. Where the hell did that came from? After The Maisonettes warbled their way through their first hit 'Heartache Avenue' I did runner Steve Cram in the foyer area. That sounds vaguely rude, but it was all above board and very non-flirty I assure you. He may have been blond and good-looking, but he also wore a shirt, tie and a woolly jumper, so on aesthetic grounds we were miles apart. I linked into a bit of video of The Animals' 'House Of The Rising Sun' (one of my all time most loathed records funnily enough), which in turn segued into Alison Moyet (though introduced as her nickname 'Alf') and Eric Burdon duetting the same number with Jools on the piano. Their version was much better than the original I thought. Already the programme was establishing a feel quite unlike anything else I had seen on TV. You never saw Noel Edmunds, Tony Blackburn or Jimmy Savile tinkling their ivories on *Top Of The Pops* – thank Christ.

Alison was one of the nicest people I met whilst doing the show. As I was to find out, there was a huge difference in the way some stars interacted with gobshite nobodies like me, and it wasn't always the ones who had a reputation for being difficult who proved to be so in real life either. At this time she was with Vince Clarke in the electronic band Yazoo. Whilst researching the shows I did for the first time since they were made it occurred to me that some of the acts and personalities who appeared were a complete blank to me. As much as I recalled how lovely Alison was I don't remember even speaking to Vince. Similarly I remember nothing whatsoever about Belinda Carlisle or the Go-Gos beyond their rehearsal on the main stage that afternoon.

We came out of an ad break to Paula's interview with Steve Cram, which started in true *Tube* style with her mic switched off. It was good to see the others ballsing things up as much as I did. After interviewing Duran Duran, during which Simon Le Bon used the term 'bloody knackered', the show's first of many pre-watershed verbal outrages, it was time for my interview with Andy Summers.

I had relocated to the Green Room sofas for this bit. We shook hands and he gave me a classic 'Who's this twat?' look. Although I'd been told he'd had a strop earlier all seemed calm to me as we went through the interview. Looking back on it after all these years it doesn't seem to be quite as bad as I had imagined it was. Andy's explanation of the album title and the artwork by New York pop artist Jimmy Rizzi now strike me as really interesting. Back then all I could think about was getting to the end of my three minutes without him suddenly going off into one on live TV. It's taken me over 36 years to conjure up enough courage to watch that first interview again and now I have I'm not sure why I'd got so worked up about it. Having said that on reviewing so many of our shows it's clear that many established stars did not quite know how to react to interview and presentation styles in this open, offbeat and somewhat chaotic manner. The best of them went with the flow and enjoyed it, but plenty didn't, as we were all to find out as the show progressed.

Yazoo played a wonderful set of tracks from their album 'Upstairs at Eric's', with beautiful live versions of 'Situation', 'In My Room', 'The Other Side of Love', 'Midnight' and ending with a roaring performance of 'Don't Go'. I'd been watching from the side and bopping along with the rest of the audience.

I did my intro to The Go-Gos playing live in the studio but didn't stay to watch their set. I crept back to my dressing room to get my breath back. Somehow I'd managed to get through this first show without too much of a problem. And here, dear reader, is where writing this becomes tough. You would imagine that I'd recall exactly what happened after the show. But in fact it is a complete blank. I assume that we must have celebrated in some way? That we would have partied into the night? That I'd have shimmied back to the Gosforth Park Hotel with the others... Or maybe I rushed back to Central Station and caught the next train back to London? In truth I have no memory of it whatsoever. It's deeply frustrating and if anyone out there has some form of magic device that would enable me to recall these memories like out of a Harry Potter film then please get in touch.

One thing I do recall is returning home to my dreary, threadbare council flat in Queen's Park. I also recall being on the Bakerloo Line home when a group of girls sitting opposite recognised me and did that thing where they'll make you aware they're talking about you but won't actually say anything. It was very unnerving and I was totally unprepared for it. I hadn't actually considered being recognised at all, probably because I didn't think any great numbers would have watched the show. Even more bizarre is that when I got home and eventually back on the trains in London that same weekend, nobody said anything. I'd told my driver Jerry that I didn't want to talk about it and to my enormous relief nobody did. For the next three weeks until my next programme I managed to live out train tube life just as I had done prior to TV *Tube*. My flat mates had recorded the programme on the VHS recorder we had rented, but the tape remained unwatched by me as I couldn't face going through the stress of those links again. They stayed unplayed until I decided to discard boxfulls of videos which had moved house with me multiple times and I knew I would never look at again. On seeing the *Tube* tapes amongst the piles of *Carry On* films, sci-fi movies and off-air recordings of *The Avengers* I was within a hair's breadth of dumping the whole lot once and for all. But after more than 30 years of them never having been rebroadcast and with my Marc Bolan feature the only one I had wanted to keep and see again, I decided to keep them and ask a friend to digitally transfer them for me just in case I ever wanted to look at them again. Despite the adverts those TDK Video Tapes were certainly not going to 'last a lifetime' and their guarantee as such was by now worthless. And thus I disposed of about four large boxes of VHS tapes at the local dump, saving only my *Tube* tapes and some off-air recordings of Manhattan Cable which I'd forgotten about and which contained the UK's first ever appearance of RuPaul. I used some of the early transfers to illustrate a brief history of my experiences on the show and found myself watching performances for the very first time since they were broadcast. It was a very bizarre experience to see myself again after all that time.

In the three intervening weeks from my first show to the second, I was able to watch the other guest presenters do their stuff; on programme 3 it was Nick Laird-Clowes, 4 was Michelle Cremona and show 5 went back to Muriel again. Although Nick and Michelle were both as all over the place as I was, Muriel quickly established herself as a real tour de force. I mean she actually looked and sounded like she knew what she was doing, whereas the rest of us fluffed and bumbled along like shop assistants delivering an address to the United Nations. Michelle was probably the most confident of us apart from Muriel, whereas Nick delivered his bits in a curious transatlantic, enthusiastic without being drug-fuelled (I assume), *Top Of The Pops* accent. I was still trying to figure out why I had tried to sound like a dustman from Maidstone. It made me cringe, but I didn't know how to get out of it. It was a relief to go back to being my old self again on the radio making the Gaywaves programme with Phil. I was terrified that Channel 4 would find out that I was involved with pirate radio programmes, so didn't mention it on radio air and forbade Phil from doing so either. This created three areas of my life that were all in conflict with each other – the trains, the telly and the wireless. It could be that it was this which caused me so much personal angst and has left me not wanting to face raking up all this stuff again after so long.

Get on with it you twit. Ed

The guest list on the next show I did was much more up my passage so to speak. I caught the train up to Newcastle on Wednesday December 8th 1982 to prepare for programme 6. By this time my full head of bleached white hair had mostly grown out. I couldn't face the third degree scalp burns of a full blond job again, so I asked the potty Australian woman Denise who cut my hair to leave a sort of flat Mohican stripe of white down the middle with the rest of it my natural dark brown. I looked like I'd been run over by a road lining paint machine.

After getting comfy again up in Gosforth at the hotel I felt much better going back to the City Road studios as I'd been looking forward to seeing Nigel again. Being the professional he was he kept his distance. I had suspected that he had a boyfriend anyway, but was too shy to ask. His colleagues Lesley and Michael knew how much I fancied him but they too helped keep everything very businesslike. On the Thursday afternoon we had our usual production meeting, although this time Paula had seemed a bit more withdrawn and distant. The magazine section of the show was to feature music video production and technology. The music section had some truly awesome guests on it: rappers Laurel & Hardy, Grandmaster Flash & The Furious Five, George Clinton, Wall of Voodoo and Soft Cell, with a filmed feature on the Rolling Stones.

During the Thursday afternoon whilst Soft Cell were rehearsing in the studio I got talking to their manager Stevo. He was something of a controversial figure and I never quite got the dynamic between him and the band he was there 'managing'. Marc Almond and Dave Ball didn't appear to want anything to do with him. My friend Colin Bell who was running London Records back in London at the time and who had responsibility for Cell's label 'Some Bizarre' had already told me of Stevo's reputation for being somewhat silly, awkward and aggressively childish with his bands. I didn't get the feeling there was much love lost between anyone on the record label side of the business and the band's management. I like people who challenge authority and the status quo. I had grown up on that and it matched my rebellious political activism back in London. Thatcher's Britain was a bitterly cruel and divisive place to live in. What with her right wing ravings and nutcase US President Ronald Reagan seemingly about to nuke us all into oblivion the art world rebelled with the same great passion it always did when ignorance challenges society. Stevo's 'couldn't give a fuck' attitude may have upset those in authority (and probably made for a deeply frustrating time for anyone who had to deal with him) but his impish humour made me laugh. This might explain why I didn't get to talk very much with either Marc or Dave for their entire visit. What brief words Marc and I exchanged seemed to me rather cold, aloof and distant, whilst Dave was... err... well, I'm not even sure where he was outside of the stage appearance. They kept themselves very much to themselves.

Stevo certainly didn't though; he had me in hysterics telling me how much he loved pissing off the record company execs and their legal staff by insisting that they put stupid things into his contracts. 'This one cunt pissed me right off,' he lovingly related, 'so I told him I wanted two pounds of jelly babies delivered every week on the same day at the same time. You ever fail to deliver and I'll see you in fuckin' court!' London Records' boss Colin Bell, who was a good friend of mine, told me Stevo had driven their contracts people crazy with his messing about, but actually I think he found it as amusing as I did. Fair enough, it wasn't very professional, but the music industry was still so up itself at that time. People like Stevo just didn't give a shit what the establishment thought, it was all about getting the best deal for him and having some laughs on the stiffs he had to deal with along the way. I don't know what Marc Almond really thought of him, but having been a great lover of Marc's music from those early times right up to the present day it's always disappointed me that even now there's still a blank there. Back then he was very non-committal about his sexuality. Perhaps he felt he wanted to keep away from any overt association with the gay world or maybe even had been advised that way? Who can say? Well, he could I suppose. In any case it wasn't until his eventual work with, of all people, my old friend Jimi Somerville, that his preferences ever really broke through the public rumour mill.

Following the cock-ups we made during the first few shows, the production team decided to try hooking us up with 'talkback', a wired-up radio earpiece through which the directors in the control gallery could talk to you and give presenters cues into and out of links and any other info which they felt necessary. Apart from the discomfort of having a wire fed underneath your clothes to the back of your head and then into one ear, there is no way of separating the feed to each person. We heard everything for everybody. Cues direct to you are given by name, but we all struggled to cope with what was right in front of us let alone having voices yabbering away in one earhole whilst doing it. As chaotic as it all was the talkback didn't help, and although my bits went OK it somehow didn't feel right. The producers and director obviously agreed, because after trying it for a few programmes it was eventually dropped and we went back to having floor managers in front of us giving us manual counts on their fingers or sometimes running into a piece of video, film or cut to another part of the studio by rolling off our scripted word.

During the show I interviewed producer Tosh Ryan who had made a wonderful video with Graham Fellows, better known at the time for his eponymous hit 'Jilted John', for an unreleased number called 'How Are You?'. The researchers had been raving about this all week and at the production meeting I begged them to show the whole thing as I'd loved it so much. We cut back slightly on the interview time in order to squeeze in the rest of the song. Whilst viewing the recordings of this show for the first time during the research period for this book I tweeted some stills of the show and Graham, bless him, contacted me to ask if he could have a copy of it as he'd never seen it! I was dead chuffed to be able to send him a copy a mere thirty-six years after it was broadcast. Job done! To this day I believe Graham Fellows wrote the greatest rock lyric of all time in the 'Jilted John' record from 1978. 'I was so upset that I cried all the way to the chip shop', utterly brilliant!

Meanwhile Jools did an interview with someone who only identified themselves as 'Q' with an eye and a mouth split between two TV screens. From a band of video artists called Question Mark Videos in London they predicted that 'holophonic sound would eventually render live tours obsolete'. They were curiously right in their prediction as both Elvis Presley and Roy Orbison have been projected as holographs in shows in recent years.

In the live performance section whilst Grandmaster Flash did a superb set, the real spine tingle of the night for me was an appearance by Funk giant George Clinton. As one of my idols I had spent some time talking with him that afternoon after his rehearsal. A fascinating, sweetly spoken, gloriously eccentric man who exuded love and peace from every orifice. The soft voice and calm demeanour shattered once he stormed onto the stage to perform his masterpiece 'Loopzilla' in a skin-tight red shimmering spandex cat suit, platform boots so high his head practically scraped the studio rigging above him and a screaming long blond wig. It was one of those moments that I will always treasure having been there for. Utterly fabulous!

The show concluded with me introducing a live performance by Soft Cell. When Marc came on stage he looked really grumpy and bad tempered, probably because their technical rehearsal hadn't gone very well. Their set consisted of songs from their 1982 album ' The Art Of Falling Apart' (actually my favourite of everything they ever recorded), starting with epic track 'Martin'. Whilst this was going on I was standing next to stage manager Colin Rowell who kept saying to me that the way Marc was holding the microphone was putting a stress on the connecting wire. Sure enough it went even more pear-shaped when during their second number 'Where The Heart Is' the mic started flickering and cutting out. 'That's him fucking about with that cable!' Colin said as he rushed about with his sound crew to get a standby replacement. Marc was absolutely fuming by this time and at one point I almost thought he would storm off. They finished their set with a truly blistering performance of the album's title track 'The Art Of Falling Apart'. As the end titles scrolled on screen and they reached the climax of the number Marc suddenly threw the offending mic to the floor and flounced off leaving Dave Ball there to finish off the track on stage alone. It was a real angst-filled performance and despite the technical hitches it stands up even now as a great live set. This to me was what *The Tube* did really well. That night's show had some truly awesome performances of the type that you just didn't see anywhere else on TV. Sure it was rough round the edges, sure it had its tech faults but it was honest and very, very live. I actually enjoyed watching this one back for the first time and it gave me a curious sense of having been a part of something I had up until now simply blanked from my memory.

A couple of weeks later we all assembled up in Newcastle for the Christmas Eve show. This time although I caught the train up to Newcastle the Southerners were all to fly back on the last British Airways shuttle to Heathrow. Not something I was looking forward to as I didn't like flying and had worked myself up into a state worrying about it.

At the production meeting we discovered that it was to be a fancy dress edition. Hmmmm… Not something I was wildly enthusiastic about, but what the hell. At the time I was totally in adoration of Mari Wilson with her superb Beehive image and music, so in a moment of complete madness I decided to dress up as her for the show. It was the first and only time I was ever to drag up. It really wasn't my scene at all, butch thing that I am.

As usual we were all staying at the Gosforth Park Hotel, but this time all the supporting presenters were there: Muriel, Michelle, Nick Laird-Clowes and me. It was one of the rare occasions that we all appeared together. With just the one night up there before the show Muriel and I took advantage to have a catch up over dinner and a few drinkie poos, though having learned the lesson from our earlier experience we resisted the temptation to get shit faced. It was a joy to be back with her again. We had been in regular touch by letter, postcards and telephone calls (how archaic does that sound now?) and so looked forward to working together. At that time it didn't occur to us that the show could only have one male/female pairing and that was obviously Jools and Paula. But that didn't stop us planning the fun we thought we would have and the ideas we took on to the production meeting on the Thursday. Muriel wasn't enormously thrilled at my impersonation of Mari Wilson, but as she was going as the Christmas Tree Fairy I didn't think she had much of an argument quite frankly. It was good to meet the Depeche Mode guys, who seemed very down to earth and grounded. I had something of a pointless crush on Andy Fletcher, who had glorious red hair and was several feet taller than me. With my usual poker face I hid my adoration quite well I thought. As working class (I assume) Essex boys they were easy to chat with and good fun to be around. Their rehearsal was terrific and another one I wish there was a surviving recording of.

On the day of the show I had a field day with the women in make-up. My friend Wincey Willis, who did the local weather on Tyne Tees TV before she became a much loved part of the thrilling TV chase show *Treasure Hunt*, was there egging me on whilst I had my eyebrows blotted out with mortician's wax and a huge high wig fitted. 'You look fab darling, it suits you!' she lied. I looked ridiculous, but quite enjoyed mincing around the studios like some grotesque transvestite without any class, style or an act. I don't think Jools approved though. This mincing about wasn't up his alley at all and I recall him looking at me as though I was a walking advert for anthrax. I was really disappointed that he ducked out of dressing up completely, the spoilsport. He could have made an effort I thought?

On the show playing live that night were DooWop band The Bouncing Czechs, R&B groups Imagination and Sylvia & The Sapphires, electronica gods to be Depeche Mode, Alison Moyet, a filmed feature on Gary Numan in LA, and Brian Johnson from AC/DC live in the pub over the road from the studio. Incidentally, that pub (which I understand was demolished years ago) was really popular with TTTV staff and the bands that visited. I found it sparse and a bit on the rough side, so I didn't go in there unless I absolutely had to. It's weird how these things only occurred to me after so long. Jools was always holding court in there as I think they had a piano. He is an incredibly talented pianist and his frenetic and colourful boogie woogie keyboard trilling would enthrall and excite all those who like that kind of thing, as I'm sure it still does. Musically it wasn't my cup of tea though and that probably explains why we didn't really socialise much outside of the studios. Jools was a man's man; beer, booze and birds. Whilst I don't ever recall any real negativity between me and him, we clearly came from very different worlds, as happens.

That evening as the show started I was mortified when Jools introduced me as one of their 'bi presenters'. Damned cheek. Nothing bi about me thank you very much. The audience in the lobby area physically backed away from me as Jools and I worked our way through the crowd doing vox pops. I can't say I blame them to be honest. I looked like a jumble sale on legs. Whilst the make-up ladies had done a grand job, the rag bag outfit they'd cobbled together for me from wardrobe was a curious mixture of Hylda Baker and Old Mother Riley. Poor Mari Wilson must have been watching through her hands. Sorry Mari!

The magazine section of the show featured a very curious act called 'Foffo Spearjig', the self-styled 'Hardest Man in the Universe'. Visually he looked like a typical tall, balding, moustached gay guy who'd just been chucked out of a fetish club. In this appearance he was even wearing a pair of cut-down denim shorts which made him look like Leonard, Catherine Tate's camp sidekick to Derek Faye. His act appeared to consist mainly of threatening anyone in the vicinity whilst shouting about how 'hard' he was (but not in the gay fetish sense you understand!).

Muriel had (thank goodness) been given the job of being insulted by him outside the studio. As your man leapt off the vehicle and rushed around swinging a fake ball and chain he yelled 'Starin' at me are ya, ya skinny nowt, skinny nowt!', directly at a strategically located Muriel. At which point she whipped out a fake bottle and smashed it over his head with incredible force. Even Jools was visibly shocked at the strength and speed with which she clonked his head, and he didn't sound at all convinced when he announced that Foffo would be appearing again later in the show. I was convinced she'd actually knocked him out. Alas though, she hadn't and he recovered to appear in a curiously unfunny sketch where he pretended to be a 'hard' Father Christmas. Very odd.

Back then I wasn't a fan of AC/DC's music, but in recent years I've come to love their albums. I'd probably have been too scared to talk with Brian Johnston who appeared playing pool in the pub and being interviewed by Jools, but by Jove how fabulous it was to see the band playing 'Back In Black' live on film. Great stuff. Back then it was another world though, and one me and my poofy friends shrank away from. Much more to my taste was Alison Moyet, back on the show again this time without Vince and singing solo a truly spine-tingling version of Billie Holiday's 'God Bless The Child'.

It was fun to spend some time with all of the other presenters and we bopped along to two great live sets from Depeche Mode ('See You', 'Tora Tora', 'Leave In Silence' and 'Meaning of Love') and Imagination (with a youthful Sinitta on backing vocals). By the time the show finished I was desperate to dump the drag and get back to my jeans and a T-shirt. We would have a mad dash back to Newcastle Airport to catch the last BA flight back to Heathrow. I was going home to my family in Tunbridge Wells and as Paula was returning to the home she lived in at the time with Bob Geldof in Westerham we decided to share a cab, dropping her off at their huge place and then me carrying on to our little council house further south. I'd been fretting about that flight for the entire time I'd been up there and had got myself into a right tizzy over it. My lovely researcher Nigel Sheldrick, who was also flying back with us, comforted me and promised to hold my hand on take-off (the bit I was dreading the most). As it happened that flight would indeed turn out to be one of the most memorable I ever took, but for good reasons, not bad. As soon as the show finished we said our goodbyes to the crew and locals at the studio and jumped into our cabs for the airport. On the plane that night were Sylvia & The Sapphires, Depeche Mode, Imagination, Alison Moyet, Jools, Paula and a huge number of PAs, band managers and crew. The champagne flowed and even as the small 727 taxied on the runway the interior was alive with singing and festive frivolity. The cabin crew joined in as we shouted requests to the various bands on the plane. But of all those wonderful performances the ones that stick in my mind the most were Alison's. 'Ali! Ali! Do "Respect"!!' I shouted. And to the cheers and clapping of everyone – *Tube* people and other travellers alike – she blasted out the Aretha Franklin classic, with a chorus of just about everyone on the plane (including the pilots) to the point where you couldn't hear the engines. It was magical. What a voice.

When we landed at Heathrow Nigel gave me a big hug and wished me a Merry Christmas. Pissed as most of us were by this time Paula and I found our car home and settled in the back seat together. She could be very, very sweet and loving at times. Obviously tired and still very pregnant, she kicked off her shoes and snuggled up to me. We talked and laughed about some of the shitty clubs we were fond of in town, the mutual friends we had and the fashions we loved and that's how we spent the whole journey. When we reached Westerham Bob was there to meet her. She gave me a big kiss and wished me a Happy Christmas before disappearing into the house. That was probably the closest that Paula and I ever got. As time went by she seemed to me to become most erratic. One minute she would be all over you like your bestie, the next she'd sweep past and totally ignore you. That wasn't something I liked from anyone, regardless of who they were and as a result of that our working relationship was never quite the same. I also noticed that she was radically different whenever Bob was present at the studios. He seemed nice enough and always approachable and friendly, and she almost regressed whenever he was there like a giggling love-struck teenager. On her own though she was a firebrand and had a wicked temper and attitude. Definitely yin and yang. For the record I never saw her take drugs or for that matter even talk about it. Just as in previous years I became an observer of sorts. I knew what was going on and where and with who, but it all washed past me. It's intriguing to wonder what might have happened had I not been grounded by the day job that I was still doing back in London. I wasn't going to give that up on the basis of just doing *The Tube*. I wasn't a natural presenter and knew this couldn't be my future direction. I missed the stage and acting and began to wonder what effect the TV work might have on getting cast in drama roles. I still had to consider the fact that I needed my Equity card to do this and that I'd stopped accruing the valuable weeks of employment I needed to get my full membership. It hadn't occurred to me at the time that this TV work might contribute to that.

When I got indoors my mother hugged me and assured me that I had done a fabulous job on the show. She always said that even though I knew I was rubbish as a presenter. 'You were the best one on there, better than all the others,' she'd say. Bless her. That's what mums do. I am so lucky that I had unerring support through all of this time from my parents. Meanwhile back in London I just carried on working on the trains and nobody batted an eyelid. It was quite bizarre. One minute live national TV and the next shouting 'Mind the doors' at Baker Street. Perhaps even more bizarre is that I was still recording Gaywaves articles, sketches and content with Phil, but it never occurred to either of us to mention what I'd been doing the rest of the time. Now it seems to me to have been something of a missed opportunity, but as I mentioned earlier, I was concerned that this mixture of legal and illegal broadcasting would not do my career chances much good if it got out. On reflection I think Phil may have been a bit irritated by my mainstream activities. If he'd had the chance he'd have used the opportunity much more aggressively than I did. To me it was just a job and it wasn't the sort of medium that could be exploited in the way Phil would have. Make no mistake I was as passionate as ever politically, but *The Tube* was not the mechanism to express this beyond me just being me. I was just a very small and insignificant cog in a much bigger media machine than Phil was ever party to. How he would have loved the multitude of broadcast opportunities we enjoy now. It breaks my heart that he's not here to carry on the fight.

On the 16th of January 1983 Muriel, Nick, Michelle and I went to the *Daily Mirror* offices at Holborn in central London for an interview with journalist Margarette Driscoll and photo shoot. The pictures they took there were some of the nicest of any I have for the entire time I worked on the programme. I treasure them to this day as they really captured us in the full flush of our eighties style and fashion. I think Muriel and Michelle in particular looked stunning in those photos. These have become probably my most treasured artefacts from that time and I have very happy memories of that whole day together, maybe as this was without Jools and Paula. As such it felt like this was our small moment of time in the spotlight.

On 3rd of February 1983 I flew up to Newcastle again. I had conquered my fear of flying somewhat and was brave enough to do the trip on my own this time. I would still occasionally revert to the train, but the flights were so much quicker and I didn't need to take so much time off. That night at the Gosforth Park Hotel Paula, Jools and I decided to have dinner together in their main restaurant. As we arrived the snotty maitre d' stopped Jools and me and told us we could not go in without a shirt and tie. After remonstrating with him a while and veering dangerously towards the expression 'Don't you know who I am?', Paula stepped in and with an astonishing display of expert diplomacy said 'Boys, go and find a tie. We will be back shortly. Hold the table if you please.' Jools and I looked slightly baffled at each other, then Paula said quietly to us 'Jools, you have loads of ties. Find one for Gary and meet me down here in 10 minutes. I promise you we'll get our own back on that fuckwit.' With that she laughed and swept away. I went up to Jools's room and sure enough he found me a tie (he always had a sharp selection of suits and was rarely ever a jeans and T kind of guy), which I then tied in a rudimentary knot round my neck. Of course it looked ridiculous, but it fitted the bill from a technical if not sartorial perspective.

When we reconvened in the corridor leading to the restaurant Paula had changed into a truly stunning white outfit with a tight skirt and a huge fluffy white stole round her upper half and neck. She looked sensational and would have given both Marilyn Monroe and Jayne Mansfield a run for their money. Having complied with their stupid dress code the twat on the door grudgingly showed us to our table, which was a large circular affair raised above the lower levels with a prominent view over the entire room. Jools and I sat down as our waiter came over and Paula gestured for him to take her stole. As she slipped it off her shoulders she revealed a completely see through pastel chintzy top and no bra. Her gloriously huge titties stood out like two enormous fleshy mounds with a cherry on top of each one. Jools and I fell about. 'That will teach that stuck up bastard to tell my friends what to wear!' she said, posing and pouting for the entire restaurant who gawped and choked on their gourmet tucker. Although Paula and I drifted apart I loved her for doing that. Bless you Paula, thank you for giving me one of the best laughs of my life.

That week we had The Gap Band, Yarborough & Peoples, Aztec Camera and Paul Young – all playing live in the studio, with features on Orchestral Manouevres In The Dark and Tears For Fears. The magazine section at the start of the programme featured interviews in LA with William Shatner as the second Star Trek film, *Wrath of Khan*, was then in production. The theme of the show was space and computer games, with Sinclair ZX Spectrums, Commodore 64s, Atari and BBC Model B and Acorns all the rage. For some reason all of us on the programme seemed to have a troubled time with our links and interviews. I had decided to try and become more incisive in my interviewing technique and to challenge whatsoever poor sod got lumbered being interviewed by me. After totally ballsing up a link into Bowie's new video of 'Boys Keep Swinging' I interviewed a bloke called Paul Lowesby. He was a promoter who was planning a huge festival happening type of thing at the NEC in Birmingham to celebrate the arrival of the apocryphal year 1984. The cost of the tickets was to be… Yes, you've guessed it £19.84, which back then was a sod of a lot of money, especially for a show with no announced acts or format. I tried my best to be all cutting and critical but it just didn't work. It's not in my nature to talk in that way with people and I really struggled to give him a hard time, which is a shame actually as I don't think the festival ever actually happened in the end. My scepticism appeared to have been well placed.

Elsewhere Jools and Paula both fluffed their links and Paula had a truly toe curling time interviewing Tears For Fears. This turned out to be one of those 'look through your hands' moments that the programme managed to do quite well. Both lead band members Curt Smith and Roland Orzabal came across as surly and uncommunicative, like they really didn't want to be there. On looking back at interviews like this (they weren't the only ones who were hard work) I have wondered if it wasn't just a misplaced attempt to look cool, hip and groovy? Remember this show was unique, no other pop music programme had ever had such a relaxed and informal style, hampered only by that early, pre-watershed schedule timing, which presented restrictions on language and content that were a real challenge for the programme makers and those of us at the sharp end. Paula really, really tried to make the interview work, to engage them and to bring them into the spirit of the show, but they just refused to play ball. By this time I was starting to take notice of who the good people were and which of the artists I felt were not worth the bother. After all, everyone experiences this in all walks of life and the arts is certainly no exception. Paula and Jools had more exposure to the arseholes side of the business than I ever did and they eventually learned how to deal with it without ending up looking crapped upon. Sadly I never managed that.

Just about the only good bit of this show was Paul Young's live set, which was awesome. Paul had stunned everyone at rehearsals that afternoon and his performance with backing singers 'The Fabulous Wealthy Tarts' and superb band (including ace bass guitarist Pino Palladino) brought just about all the staff at the studio out to watch. This was equalled on the live broadcast as they delivered a truly epic set including numbers 'SEX' and 'Love Of The Common People'. As much as Tears for Fears were difficult, Paul was a delight; warm, friendly and just lovely to be with. *The Tube* really helped make his career soar and I know everyone on the show was pleased that he reached the heights he did. So well deserved.

This was also the show where The Gap Band did 'Oops Upside Your Head' and the whole audience lined up sitting on the floor doing that rowing formation dance which drove everyone nuts in discos and clubs all over the country. I wash my hands of any responsibility for that though. Paula turned her nose up at it and that was good enough for me.

The Tube producers were always on the lookout to try new things and the show broadcast on February 25th 1983 was split between the studio in Newcastle and a live outside broadcast from the Camden Palace club in North London. I think of all the programmes I did this one sticks in my mind as the one which could have gone even more seriously pear-shaped than it actually did. I was within a gnat's whisker of beating Jools to uttering the word 'fuck' on live TV. In fact I don't think anyone at Tyne Tees or Channel 4 knows just how close I was to it. The Camden Palace was the haunt of Paula's old friend Steve Strange who had recently taken over as club host there. I probably did get introduced to Steve at some point there but if I did it must have been quick and I remember nothing about either him or it. Oddly, whilst I was never part of the Blitz group which Boy George et al infused themselves into, I felt I had nothing in common with any of the Camden Palace and Visage set people either. Whilst George and his closest friends were quite happy to come along to the smaller (and I think more edgy) clubs, Steve Strange was definitely mainstream and operated on a much bigger and more commercial scale. This was not popular with the political gays and those who liked the more extreme music clubs like The Carved Red Lion in Islington, where the 'Hipper Than Shit' guys really pushed the boat out with their eclectic and sometimes truly bizarre choices.

Whilst Paula and I were outstationed at the Palace OB in North London, Jools and Michelle presented back in the studio in Newcastle. During rehearsals that afternoon I became a bit concerned that some of the links I was to do later on in the show from a balcony area left me a bit on my own. With no floor manager easily visible it was going to be risky when the place had packed out. Paula was heavily pregnant at this time and certainly couldn't do with getting any undue hassle, so she quite rightly positioned downstairs in a location of relative safety. My first task was to interview Abby James the guy who operated the computerised lighting system. How gripping is that? I tried to make it sound vaguely interesting, but lighting displays on TV don't really work. After giving him and the system a huge build-up, the piddly-looking laser graphics and swirling light balls were distinctly underwhelming. I didn't see what all the fuss about personally. I thought the lighting was better at the Embassy Club than in there, but hey ho.

This show also featured a filmed item about the famous Gold Mine Club on Canvey Island in Essex. Run by DJ Chris Hill the club was one of the first big Essex soul boy dance venues; very straight and laddy. Paula and I had been out there to film the club and to interview those involved. When we arrived the weather was bloody awful. Canvey itself is flat, desolate and full of oil refineries. In fact the air there smells of crude oil, amongst other things. The production crew was led by lovely Michael Metcalf who was always a joy to be with. When we got there the only place we could find to stay was a shitty pub with a B&B upstairs. The crew had gone out filming in a small airplane to get some external shots to illustrate the beauty of the location from on high, however the weather closed in and the flying conditions got so bad that Michael and the cameraman press-ganged into going up on the plane began to feel sick. Michael told me they weren't really getting any usable shots of the club, so worrying that they might never make it back to the airfield Michael said to the cameraman 'Fuck it, just film the coastline. Nobody will ever know the difference, and let's get off this bloody thing!'

We gathered together in the shitty pub and over lunch planned what filming we would do in the club that night. Paula was to interview Chris Hill and I was to do the vox pops with the clubbers. Unfortunately for me the pub food gave me horrendous food poisoning and I spent the rest of the day ejecting what I'd eaten through every orifice. By the time we came to film the club that evening I was still feeling like the bottom of a handbag and with my stomach in knots I begged Michael to let me off so I could crawl away and die quietly in a corner somewhere. 'Tell you what,' he said 'just pop down for 5 minutes and bop around a bit, we'll film that just so we know you were there and then you can creep back upstairs to die in your room. Don't worry, I'll come and check on you later.' Bless his heart, our Michael did look after me. I duly did my bit and then rushed off quick as soon as they had the shot. I felt ill for almost 2 days afterwards. In Paula's interview with Chris Hill he referred to the place as being 'at the end of the world and that there's nowhere else to go once you get out here', and that 'there's also the element of danger here as we're right next to the petro-chemical plant which could explode at any moment'. The last statement was exactly how my stomach was feeling. I've never been so glad to get out of a place in my entire life as I was off that bloody island.

This feature segued into a live interview with me stuck amongst the crowd and no visible floor manager to give me a count. The interview was with an outfit called 'Soul On Sound' who produced a soul music magazine sold in cassette format. The three guys involved included one blond-haired guy who I thought was bloody gorgeous. However as always my protection mechanism came into play and I carefully disguised my youthful lusting by going extra yobby in the interview. God how I hated my voice in this. Instead of finding the real me I was actually becoming more common with every show. It surely wouldn't be long before I started trailing my knuckles along the ground. The crowd there was by this point starting to get... err... lively? Although my link back to Jools in Newcastle worked this time, it was to be all downhill from that point onwards.

Although it seems weird to think of this now, Jools did an item on live record mixing with effects being created by playing the same disc on two turntables, supplemented with a huge reel-to-reel tape machine. The segment linked new soul funk artist David Joseph's club hit 'You Can't Hide Your Love' live mixed in Newcastle to me introducing him singing the track live on stage at the Palace. The soul jazz funk track wasn't a natural vibe for the Camden Palace crowd and Joseph struggled to get much reaction from them. The crowd just stood like statues through his whole performance as they were really there for a rare live set from their hero and fashion muse Steve Strange. I'd liked the record a lot and had tried talking with him during rehearsals. I think as he and his entourage felt the vibe just wasn't there he came across as somewhat cold and unfriendly. Fair enough I suppose, but I did at least try to make him feel welcome even if I got little back in return.

By this time I had relocated onto an upper level of the club and just then it wasn't too full. Unfortunately for me the outside broadcast presenter's worst nightmare was about to occur. I'd been given a really long list of clubbing events in London to read out with the cameras shooting me from a fair distance away on another area of the upper balcony. A group of inebriates had moved in behind me and decided they were going to get their moment on live TV by stroking my face and making wanker hand signs in front of me as I ploughed my way through the link. Although I kept my cool through most of it, inside I was seething as I'd been concerned about this happening earlier in rehearsals and I felt if the live show was now getting stuff they might regret before the watershed then that was their own fault. My irritation forced me to turn around and ask whoever was there to keep away, although in my head I was so tempted to tell them to Fuck Off! The memory of this event has played on my mind all these years. For the purposes of writing this I watched the event for the first time ever and saw that from the gallery in Newcastle they had come in close for a headshot in an attempt to block out the interlopers. In fact I think I did a bloody good job at handling this in the circumstances. The producers though never knew just how close I was to losing my rag and decking the bloke behind me. I wonder what Jools would have done? I suspect he may well have uttered the forbidden word had it it been him there instead of me.

After that debacle my pleas to be moved somewhere less risky were granted and I relocated to a quiet area for a piece into a filmed feature on Jools' band Squeeze. Sadly they didn't link out of my words into the VT and I stood there looking like a prune for about 7 to 8 seconds until the fade finally rescued me. I hated it when that happened. I wasn't as good as Jools was at managing those cock-ups. We all had these moments and nobody was immune from it however. It was just one of those quirks which gave the show its earthy and edgy feel.

The show culminated with two great live sets from Visage in London and The Eurythmics in Newcastle. I have never been so glad to finish a show as I was that one. For years afterwards the feeling I had up on that balcony never left me. Actors are usually protected from that sort of hassle on stage and I really wasn't equipped to deal with this at all. To this day I don't know how I coped. It probably sounds like a drama queen overreaction, but inside my head I died that night. All these years later I can now see a different side to it and the show I had feared watching again for so long didn't actually seem that bad after all. I had created a demon which didn't really exist.

Weirdly Paula and me hardly spoke through this programme. She was going through one of her 'don't come near me' times and blanked me as she was prone to do. She spent most of her time draped round Steve Strange and really didn't want to know anyone else. This was classic Paula, one minute your BFF and next walking past you as though you were invisible. I really didn't like this and had no time for that sort of diva behaviour. At the time I just put it down to her advanced pregnancy and perhaps the effects of that, but actually I think I knew it was something more fundamental. The real Paula was starting to push through and we drifted apart as friends more or less from that point onwards. And so we drifted into March 1983 and I appeared on all three programmes leading up to the end of the first series. I flew up to Newcastle again on Thursday March 3rd 1983 to prepare for the show the following day. In between production and script meetings, blocking in the studio and general prep work on the items that were featured I was spending more time with the production team and other people around the Tyne Tees Studios. In particular lovely Wincey Willis. She was such fun to be with and spending time with her always cheered me up and gave me the confidence that I so lacked. Living this curious double existence was taking its toll on my temperament and sometimes I really struggled to focus and keep myself together. My work down on the underground in London was run of the mill and regular. My colleagues there had got used to my escapades by this time and the TV stuff was almost never mentioned. It was very strange.

The show of Friday March 4th 1983 was designated a 'new band special' and featured both magazine items and live studio sets from unsigned outfits Jimmy Gaynor, Fatal Charm, The Sign, No's 28 and Campfabulous (by far and away the best of all the bands on the show), all of whom disappeared into obscurity like I eventually did. Right at the start of this broadcast the producers must have had collective heart failure almost as soon as Paula started her live studio interview with music producer Martin Rushent (of Human League and Altered Images fame) and Kate Garner out of fashion band Haysi Fantayzee. He'd also produced Shirley Bassey and when Paula asked him what the difference was between Claire Grogan and Bassey he said 'Shirley Bassey had bigger tits'. Once again the pre-watershed curse of *The Tube* had struck. I know 'tits' isn't exactly the rudest of terms, but back in those days even 'fart', 'bum' and 'knickers' was enough to enrage the permanently offended and provoke jams on the Channel 4 complaints switchboards. Rushent and Garner were there to pass comment on the various new bands that played live on the show. Garner didn't appear to like anything or anybody and had the personality and attitude of a boutique shop assistant who'd wandered in by accident. And I'm sorry my dears, but that ghastly scraggy chewed up Croydon-dreadlock hairdon't of hers turned my stomach. To me this was everything about the mixture of fashion and music I didn't like. Trying to get anything of interest from her was painful and Paula really had to work hard to get anything coherent. Sometimes you can take 'cool' too far and it just becomes 'cold'.

My main task on this show was to interview the band Kajagoogoo, who had just become a huge chart success with their hits 'Too Shy' and 'Ooh To Be Ah'. At the time of this show they were still in their original formation with lead singer Limahl. I was plonked in their dressing room and after posing the usual questions about breaking big and how did you get your band name, I was to present them with a cake baked by one of their adoring fans. Even better was dragging the adoring fans who baked it in to meet their heroes. Dressing room interviews could be potentially hazardous as within the safety of the four walls bands were inclined to let rip without warning. This could be dangerous on a show like ours. I had no such worries with this band though. I found them sweet, good fun and certainly no prospect of a careless profanity slipping in with them. Their live set at the end of the show was really terrific. Musically they were a really tight band, at times even sounding like a more funky U2. Look, I know that sounds somewhat unlikely, but be honest, how many times did you ever hear them play truly live or hear anything other than their major chart hits? The great strength of the show was that it gave all bands an opportunity to go beyond what people heard on the radio or saw on *Top Of The Pops.*

I made a fleeting appearance on the following week's show of March 11th 1983, co-hosted by Muriel, in a previously filmed interview with two blokes from a rock band tour merchandise promotion company. I've no idea when I did this filming or even where it was, although I assume it was probably in London somewhere. Such is the nature of presenting; it's very much come and go. Proverbially I came and I went. And so we approached the last show in series one on March 18th 1983. For this programme all the presenters were present for the only time in the show's history. It was nice to finally see Mike Everitt make an appearance. He was the guy who should have joined us as one of the original co-presenters but was prevented by his day job company from appearing. I adored him and was so pleased he made it onto the show, even if it was to be his only full presenting appearance. He did a great job interviewing Bono and really didn't shy away from provocative questioning, despite the usual wankery and pretentiousness from the greatest living Irishman. Mike was a very sweet guy whom I never forgot. He'd have done a much better job than I ever did had he been given the chance. Meanwhile we celebrated the end of the show with epic live studio performances from Big Country, The Undertones and U2. Big Country's live set was one of the best *The Tube* ever broadcast. Stuart Adamson's lead guitar and vocal performance that night was sublime and his untimely death in 2001 was so terribly sad. He was another of the really beautiful people I recall with great fondness. It was great to be back with my pal Muriel again. I had really missed working with her and as usual there was much mucking about and fun in general as we interviewed the presenters of *Switch,* the show that was to replace *The Tube* the following week and during the show's summer break. For some bizarre reason I'd decided to start the interview by snogging Yvonne French, the co-presenter of *Switch*. I can't imagine what possessed me to do that to the poor woman, but I've never received a summons so I guess she must have agreed to it. I shouldn't think it fooled anyone though. If I'd been true to myself I would have swapped places and tried for a kiss with the blond bit she was to work with, except that he was Uber-straight and a bit of a lad. He even dared to slag off The Tube saying its interviews section was boring. Hmmmm, that would do him no good. His show only ran for 1 series and was never renewed.

*does wet finger in air swipe type manoeuvre**

Editors note: Don't get bitter. It's unbecoming. Get on with it.

Just after the last show was broadcast and the *Daily Mirror* article appeared I received a phone call from BBC producer Peter Estall. He asked me if I would be interested to guest on the Radio 4 *Midweek* programme. Well, why not? I wasn't an avid listener of the programme. In fact I'd never listened to it before. It was presented by ex *Game For A Laugh* and sometime TV quizmaster Henry Kelly and radio journalist Libby Purves. When I arrived for the broadcast, which was live from BBC Broadcasting House in central London, Peter welcomed me like an old friend, which was slightly unsettling as I'd never met him before. I was duly introduced to the other guests on the show whose names and occupations I instantly forgot, apart from actor Norman Painting, who played Phil Archer on the long-running Radio 4 daily serial *The Archers*. Neither Henry Kelly nor Libby Purves were my cup of tea though; too starchy and formal for a rough old 'H dropper' from High Brooms like me. When they got round to my interview bit they predictably majored on the strange combination of my working on the trains and then on live TV. This was the first indication I had that actually what I was doing in presenting the TV show was potentially going to damage my acting career. Not once did they ask me anything about my thespionic endeavours, although even if they had I wasn't sure I could have told them about the Royal Court or Gay Sweatshop shows, and I sure as hell couldn't have said anything about Gaywaves! In an odd sort of a way I felt professionally cornered. It didn't help matters that after the show whilst having drinkie-poos on the roof terrace at BH, Peter Estall asked me if I would like to return as a guest presenter on the programme. You can just imagine the faces of Kelly and Purves on hearing that news. Somewhat swept along with the glamour of it all I agreed. Norman Painting meanwhile tried to chat me up, bless him. He was a sweet man and a few days later I received a letter from him telling me how witty and talented he thought I was. I can't imagine what possessed him to say that as I thought I'd come across as a gobby little twerp, but hey ho. Remember I was still trying to find my voice and personality as a presenter, and struggling with it. I always found accepting compliments tough. When people do this I feel an almost instant desire to deny or reject it. I've watched others soak up praise and then build their careers by riding the waves of publicity whether good or bad. I just couldn't do this, and it may well have been that which would eventually influence my decision to revert back to theatre and leave the presenting to those better able to manage it. Meanwhile I pocketed the forty quid fee for the guest appearance (few ever got rich by doing BBC interviews) and agreed the fifty-five pound pay packet to do the guest presenter spot on the 6th April 1983. When I turned up for that second time Kelly and Purves were distinctly frosty and patronising to me (although Peter was as lovely as ever). It was quite absurd for either of them to have perceived me as anything more than a slight annoyance to put up with for a while as I clearly had no talent as an interviewer whatsoever. It was debatable whether I was even Radio 1 material let alone Radio 4. I was to interview young actor Todd Carty, who at that time was appearing on the BBC children's soap *Grange Hill*. He was nice enough, but the interview sat uncomfortably alongside scientists who had discovered cures for every known disease and arty sounding women authors discussing feminist activism at the US airbase at Greenham Common. Whilst I stayed in touch with Peter for many years after that I didn't want to do any more highbrow stuff. I felt it best to stay rough.

As a result of the *Midweek* programme the *London Evening Standard* decided to do an article and came to take pics of me on the trains at Neasden depot with the embarrassing strap line 'A Tube Ticket to Success for Gary'. The article had two photographs of me, one posing with a hat I never wore on the back of a Jubilee line train at Neasden to illustrate my tedious train job, and the other a truly incongruous picture of me at the BBC with Henry Kelly. In that one I'm not sure who looked more embarrassed by the whole thing, me or him. I notice that Ms. Purves managed to steer well clear of that photo shoot. It's quite possible that Kelly only agreed to it at gunpoint. But hey ho, it goes down in the scrapbook as one of my more unusual endeavours.

Though my workmates laughed it off with me it was to be the last time I would ever let any publicity go anywhere near that side of my life. From then onwards I kept it all totally separate, and ever since then I have led an almost perfect double working life. As far as presenting went I much preferred doing radio. Gaywaves was still being made and broadcast and I even did a couple of recorded features for Radio 1 on the *Saturday Live* programme, one feature on the Marc Bolan fan club, and their other on so called 'Indie-Pop', where I got to interview Monsoon/Sheila Chandra record producer Steve Coe. He was a bit of a hero of mine as I loved the Indian crossover music he championed as part of the Mobile Suit Corporation production outfit. Monsoon had had three massive chart hits with 'Ever So Lonely', 'Shakti' and a cover of The Beatles' 'Tomorrow Never Knows'. Lead singer of the band Sheila Chandra (who co-incidentally had also appeared in *Grange Hill*) had one of the most beautiful voices I have ever heard and it is terribly tragic that in recent years she has reportedly suffered from 'burning mouth syndrome', which makes singing, speaking and other emotions intensely painful for her. Coe, a huge imposing but gently spoken man, was delightful. I only wish that the music they made was more widely appreciated, as it strikes me to have been largely forgotten whenever 80s musical retrospectives are broadcast.

During the summer months of 1983 *The Tube* was replaced by a programme called *Switch*, which I thought was rather good. It was presented by Yvonne French and Graham Fletcher-Cook, who Muriel and I had interviewed on our last show of the series. I don't remember a great deal about it except that it seemed less frenetic and a bit more polished than *The Tube*. However, there's precious little information, clips or otherwise on the internet about it now, so I'm guessing that it wasn't considered a hit in the same way our show was, and anyway it only ran for one series.

Away from the hubbub of the TV I had let my stage career drop almost completely. It was all I could do to keep with working on the trains and flitting up and down between London and Newcastle. In the summer of 1983 I had met one of the great loves of my life, Michael. He was one of the few people I have ever met who could put up with my mood swings and mercurial personality. When things get too much for me to handle I need people around me who can bring me back to earth from the mind trips my strange brain takes me on. How I ever coped with doing live television I will never know. It wasn't made any easier by the fact that I was now having a terrible time back at the flat in Queen's Park. I was clashing terribly with my flatmate Peter and I had reached the stage where I just didn't want to be there. Michael and I spent more and more time together and I only went back to the flat when I absolutely had to. We would be together for the next six years and I'm happy to say that we have remained close friends ever since. Despite the fact that as a staunch left-winger (not a euphemism) he hated the relative extravagance of the TV life I was leading, Michael was my rock through all those years. I honestly don't know what I would have done without him. I was desperately insecure and convinced that I was crap at presenting. He persuaded me to carry on with it despite my reservations. I agreed to do the summer special edition of the programme in June of 1983. It was to be the longest ever live music TV broadcast up until that time and was to be called *The Midsummer Night's Tube*. I didn't have an agent at the time and agreed my fee of £250 for the five-hour live special. I have never really cared that much about money and as that sort of fee was a lot more than I ever earned on stage it seemed fair enough to me. As we prepared for the event Paula, Jools, Mark Miwurdz, Muriel and I filmed some promotional spots for 'Look Ahead on 4', a sort of naff Channel 4 week ahead on TV show. We did our bits at, of all places, the London Transport Museum in Covent Garden, whilst sat sitting in some of the beautiful vintage underground train carriages they have there. It's no doubt a sign of the way my strange mind works that all I see when looking at it now is the show's host making a complete balls up of pretending to drive a train and then after fucking it up boasting that it was 'simple when you know how', (which he clearly didn't). I'm not sure that we did this filming on the same day as I have no recollection of meeting up with any of my fellow presenters that day. Muriel and I were very close and I suppose that we must have got together during her visit. Yet why don't I have any memory of it? Watching the grainy VHS recording made of it by my mother I appear to have a strange hairdo that makes my head look like someone on a bicycle ran over it. I am pleased to say that this aberration was dealt with by the time I flew up to Newcastle on Wednesday June 22nd 1983.

The five-hour marathon midsummer broadcast was a real game-changer and involved a truly massive amount of production preparation. So much so that Thames Television came up and filmed us doing it. This 20 minute curiosity made for ITV Schools Programming proved to have some historical value as it contains aerial film taken during rehearsals of the entire Tyne Tees Television studio lot with surrounding buildings and roads, none of which are there any more. Apart from the myriad production meeting shots of us genuinely discussing what was going to be in the show, what we had to say and where we would be saying it, there were heartwarming bits where *The Tube* backroom boys had probably their only screen time explaining what it was they did. This pleases me because dear reader, as you already know, I was very fond of them all; more fond of them than I was my fellow artistes (Muriel and Mark excepted).

The show was to have live performances from Shalamar and Culture Club (who were at their highest popularity peak at the time) with features on David Bowie, U2, The Tubes, Duran Duran and Malcolm McLaren. Live guests included, of all people and much to my utter joy, Barry Humphries who was slated to appear both as dribbling, sex mad drunkard Australian Cultural Attaché to the Court of St. James, Sir Les Patterson, and also Dame Edna Everage. It is odd that during this show I was probably at my most relaxed and happy with what I was doing. Yet it also marked the distinct end to any real friendship with Paula. On the day of the show one of the researchers came to me and asked me if I minded sharing a dressing room with Muriel? Of course I didn't mind that if she didn't and at the time I didn't think anything of it. We were hardly in there anyway as we were flitting about in the studio and busy with whatever it was we were supposed to be doing around the building. Pieces to camera happened quite literally all over the studios, from the entrance 'Tube' and lobby to the Green Room, dressing rooms, the scene dock and Studio 5. I hadn't bumped into Muriel for a wee while so I went looking for her to ask if she minded me dumping my bag of old rags and crap in her dressing room. As I did so it struck me as rather odd that I'd been asked about this as my dressing room was one of the smaller ones which was of little use to man or beast. As I passed the guy who'd asked me about moving I asked him why? 'Oh, because Boy George has said he wanted a dressing room on his own away from the rest of the band,' he said. Knowing George as I did I knew this was highly unlikely. George was always with the rest of the band and for something like this I just couldn't imagine him demanding to be on his own. So when I saw him a few minutes later and we were chatting I asked him. 'Did you really ask them for a dressing room on your own?' He laughed with that glorious happy face of his and said 'No darling of course not.' In true gossip style when I later mentioned this to one of my crew confidantes they told me that Paula and Jools had supposedly objected to Muriel and I having separate dressing rooms. Although it seems trivial now (and probably untrue anyway) this really pissed me off on the night. If it wasn't for the fact that we were so busy I would have brooded over it. But hey ho, things to do, stars to introduce and all that.

As we approached the late afternoon I took the opportunity to meet up again with Barry Humphries in his (much larger individual) dressing room.

This wasn't the first time I had either met or spoken with him. Way back in the mid 70s I had been at his 'Housewife Superstar' show at the Apollo Theatre in London's West End and as an adoring fan had had my photo taken with him at the Stage Door. Some years later after the showing of a BBC documentary I had naively but sincerely believed that he really lived at The Dorchester Hotel in the Oliver Messel Suite. So I phoned the hotel and asked if I could speak to him. I can't for the life of me think what was going through my mind, as I don't have any stalker tendencies I assure you. I was at that time living in Neasden in the very early days of my Underground employment, frustrated by having to park my stage career and reinvigorated by seeing Humphries perform. At that time I was auditioning for almost anything and even went for a singing engagement at Dover Court Holiday Park in Essex, where classic BBC TV comedy *Hi De Hi* was filmed. I can only imagine I was filled with some sort of weird bravado. Maybe Philip urged me on? He was always telling me I should pester and push for work and, sweetheart that he was, he used to give my confidence the urges it needed. In any case one evening whilst I was sitting at home waiting to hear if I'd got the job the phone rang and my housemates called me down. 'Oh, who is it?' I rattily replied, expecting it to be yet another rejection. 'He says it's Barry Humphries!' said Wayne, coincidentally my Australian housemate. 'Very funny, why on earth would he be calling me?' I said, grabbing the phone receiver. 'Hello? Who is it?' 'It's Barry Humphries, I understand you wanted to ask me some questions?'

Slightly stunned silence.

'Oh, err… yes, sorry,' I mumbled incoherently. We then had a short and rather confused conversation during which time I managed to string a few rambling sentences together before we parted company. Fast-forward now a few years and here I am sitting in his dressing room in Newcastle chatting away and laughing like we were old mates. He utterly fascinated me. I don't think I have ever met, in my entire life, anyone more obviously stimulated by the world around him than this most enigmatic of performers.

As we talked and talked he made himself up as Sir Les Patterson. Although the 625 line UHF television picture was incapable of showing such detail, he painstakingly drew on every single line and bloodshot vein on his face to indicate the hard drinking of the character. As the visage took shape he would contort his face invoking every one of Les's grotesque expressions, then adding whatever was needed to emphasise it even more. Sir Les was to be accompanied by an actress who'd been hired to be his on-screen girlfriend. 'Wait till you see her face, when the dribble starts flowing,' he laughed whilst pulling yet another Patterson gurn in the mirror, 'The poor girl is absolutely terrified and keeps backing away from me.' 'Won't that be a problem?' I said. 'Oh no, it adds to the fun of it when I grab her closer, you watch!' How we laughed.

When we went down to rehearsals the woman they'd hired, who had enormous titties and was wearing an incredibly tight and low-cut top, clearly had never heard of Sir Les Patterson and I can only assume had been very poorly briefed by her agent as to what to expect. 'This is my personal secretary Meg,' drawled Les with dribble flying everywhere and the enormous prosthetic knob in his trousers appearing to move about with a life all of its own. During the live show Paula, who clearly got the gist of it all, played up to him perfectly, but 'Meg' struggled and can be seen barely able to stand within camera shot.

Technically the show was an absolute triumph. Even the airborne shots taken from a helicopter they'd hired worked well with barely a flicker. There were multiple shooting locations and the gallery, floor managers and techies really had their work cut out flitting about from so many places in and out of the studios. It was lovely to see George again. We laughed about the Carved Red Lion football incident I mentioned earlier and one of our mutual friends, a charmingly named guy called 'Fat Tony' with whom I'd had a brief fling before meeting Michael. It was all very pally.

For some reason I have believed that my links were mostly awful and that I fluffed up multiple times. But watching this for the first time in thirty-five years I saw that actually I didn't balls up a single link and even managed to sound like I knew what I was doing. Working with Muriel again was an absolute dream and we had such fun together. I barely interacted with either Jools or Paula during the show. All of us just got on with what we had to do and that was that. Paula was mostly all over Geoffrey Daniels from Shalamar, who she fancied (without success from what I gather) and had been fawning over ever since they arrived. Muriel and I did a feature on Malcolm McLaren's latest obsession 'Double Dutch', the American double rope skipping craze which came out of the ghettos of NYC and was currently giving him a chart run with a themed song. When we were introduced to him I was looking forward to talking about the early days of punk and the times I had spent down at the shop in King's Road. However we were all so rushed that I never got the chance to reminisce with him. Instead we wedged up close together in the main studio whilst his skipping girls flicked and jumped around below us. Sadly this interview sticks in my mind not because of the music or the fashion, but because of McLaren's appalling bad breath. Every time he opened his mouth a sickly sweet, warm aroma of rotting meat through yellowing teeth assaulted my nostrils. It was almost more than I could bear. He seemed nice enough as a person, and was an easy and interesting guy to talk with, but my dear, that breath?!? Yikes.

I'd been introduced to handsome singer and ex-swimmer (?) Nick Heywood, who was the latest teenage girls' heartthrob and whom most gay men would have killed for too. But he came across as one of the 'one-syllable, I'm a star' brigade and not interested in conversing with nobodies like me. Whereas Claire Grogan from the band Altered Images, who were also chart busting at the time, was really lovely. This was something I learned very quickly during my time on the show, that there really wasn't any rhyme or reason behind who was fab and who was a twat. They could be megastars or newbies, it made no difference, in fact no different to anyone any of us might meet anywhere. And of course why should it be any other way?

At some point during the evening Barry Humphries had undertaken a truly awesome lightning change from Sir Les Patterson into his more famous alter ego Dame Edna Everage. During a walk through the audience segment with Jools where liggers had been given gladioli to wave about in her honour, Edna made her usual witty brag about being 'in touch and close to her adoring public', and then unwisely invited the audience to 'touch me if you'd wish', at which point the crowd surged forward and started grabbing at her whilst using the gladioli stems (which were sharp and lethal) as poking instruments. Being the utter professional that he is, he sailed through it without batting an eyelid, despite almost losing his wig at one point from an overenthusiastic flower wielding youth. Humphries also delivered the best line of the entire evening thusly:

Jools: *Are you enjoying any of the bands particularly that we're having on at the moment?*
Dame Edna: *No, but I'm having a lovely time all the same.*

Classic.

People often think of Frankie Goes To Hollywood as being one of the more risqué bands to appear on the show, but to me the winners of that accolade were The Tubes. On the five-hour special (well after the watershed) we showed a recorded live set from them during which they displayed incredible scenes of leather-fuelled sadomasochism on stage. Scantily clad women and a gimp mask wearing leather man appeared to be shagging ET whilst playing their opus 'White Punks On Dope'! I kid you not. There was no way this could ever have been broadcast at *The Tube*'s normal early-evening slot. It remains now probably one of my all-time favourite performances from all the shows I worked on.

Following other superb live sets from African band King Sunny Ade and The Truth, Muriel and I did another of our rare links together during which for some reason I decided to camp about in. Not like me I hear you say? Normally I positively exude butch, dear. But it was so great to be with her again that I forgot where I was and started to be myself. During the course of that wee link and during all my over-the-topness I called her a 'silly cow'. Given Mu's predilection for feminism and contemporary politics I can't believe I actually said that (in jest of course!). But say it I did. Forgive me Mandy, I meant not what I did! It was during this programme that I realised just how good we could have been as a pair of co-presenters. It was only when working with Muriel that I felt comfortable and at ease with what I was doing. She'll hate me for saying that but it's true. All that time I spent sodding about roughing up my language and realising even as I was speaking that whoever this person was, it wasn't me. At last I seemed to have found my true voice and what I wanted to project. It was especially important for me to come to this realisation, because all my political life and work with Philip on Gaywaves, my time with Gay Sweatshop and the Royal Court had all been about coming out, fighting oppression and being true to oneself. Even at the Underground I didn't take any prisoners. I was out and proud there and didn't give two shits what anyone else thought. And believe me I had fights there too. But the bigots soon realised that I was no pansy pushover and I earned respect for my resolve. Here on national TV though I was head on with an establishment that I didn't trust and didn't feel comfortable with. The majority of people I met and worked with there were absolutely fine with it all, but one or two made me nervous and that was enough to put me out of sync with who I was.

As the long show drew to a close almost 5 hours after we'd kicked off it fell to Dame Edna and Jools to say an official goodbye to Paula before the night's events concluded with a live set from soul dance outfit Shalamar. Of course there may have been nothing in that farewell just being with Jools, but wouldn't you have thought Muriel and I should have been there too? Not that I was that bothered to be honest. At that time I was glad to see the back of Paula and her weird mood swings and attitude. I know that sounds bitchy (perish the thought), but professionally I genuinely respected her without reservation.

Presenting TV, especially live, is much tougher than most people realise. She and Jools were naturals at it and although at the start we were pretty much all as shaky as each other, they had time to work at it and hone their craft. They were both also intimately connected with the music business one way or another, whereas most of the rest of us (with the sole exception of co-presenter and musician Nick Laird-Clowes, whose presentation style had begun to sound like Peter Powell on acid) were just proverbial passers by. Muriel was clearly Yang to their Yin as she had a gravitas none of the rest of us had. It served her well and of course she would go on to co-present *The Tube* for the rest of its days and launch a well-earned successful alternative career from her museum beginnings.

I was a bit of an oddity, and that's putting it mildly. I had managed to hide my nervous twitch, anxieties and fraught dislike of crowds very well, although watching back some of these shows during the research for this book it was almost amusing that I could see it all there, in my eyes and just now and again in my body language.

The summer of 1983 came and went. I went along to the Gay Pride March with Michael and Philip and the rest of my gang as usual. That was the first year it was renamed 'Lesbian and Gay Pride' (remember there was no active Bi, Transgender or Queer recognition back then). The effect of HIV/AIDS was beginning to reverberate through the community and the Tory government of the day was in no mood to recognise this as a world health issue, instead feeding the monstrous proposition that this was in some way a 'Gay plague'. The TV adverts of the day were scary invocations of gravestones, death and despair with the rather ironic tagline 'Don't Die Of Ignorance'. All that coupled with a voiceover by, of all people, John Hurt (who had so sensitively played gay legend Quentin Crisp in the acclaimed TV play *The Naked Civil Servant*) in full scary voice mode made for a pretty depressing time. Yet somehow it all washed over me. I certainly didn't modify any of my personality to creep away and hide again as the government's corporate messages would have had us do.

Meanwhile my old friend from Tyne Tees TV Wincey Willis had joined the new ITV breakfast TV station 'TV-am' down in London. I enjoyed mincing over to Egg Cup House at Camden Lock in North London whenever I could to have coffee and a bitch with her and her friend there, presenter Jeni Barnett. They were great fun to be with although I don't think they realise that they were inadvertently responsible for the end of my TV career on the *The Tube* a year later at the end of June in 1984. But that's for later. You'll have to contain yourselves a wee while before I get to that bit.

I received a call in the late summer of 1983 to say that we'd been given another series and that they'd like me to continue appearing on it, albeit with a slightly revised emphasis on bigger magazine articles and fewer regular supporting presenter roles. It was then I learned that the new partner for Jools was to be fellow actor Leslie Ash. I was overjoyed at this news as I instinctively knew she would be easier to get along with than Paula was. We both came from the same type of theatrical background and had similar approaches to work. Apart from having had a starring role in The Who's rock opera thingy type film *Quadrophenia*, she was also unconnected directly with music in the way that Jools and Paula had been. At the time of series two she was dating actor Rowan Atkinson.

I signed the contract with Tyne Tees to appear in the forthcoming series on September 30th 1983, with the series itself kicking off on Friday October 28th 1983. Somehow I managed to wangle the time off from working on the trains in London, and just like before nobody batted an eyelid. The second series had its launch party at a bar in St Christopher's Place, a really trendy affluent area in the West End of London, just off Oxford Street and round the back of Selfridges. As I arrived in the sound of a solo musician was blasting out and bouncing off the wall of the surrounding buildings. This was singer songwriter and left-wing activist Billy Bragg, who at that time was performing under the name of 'Spy Vs. Spy'. He played electric guitar amped up to two massive speakers protruding from his shoulders. He was utterly superb and mesmerising to watch. The bar where the launch took place was much smaller than the Rock Garden where we'd launched the first series, but all the usual gang were there minus fellow co-presenters Michelle, Nick and Mike. Jools and Leslie were to be the main presenters with Muriel and myself as back up. From time to time others were also drafted in to assist including punk rock journalist Tony Fletcher and even French and Saunders, reprising their earlier appearances as Jools obsessed fans Janice & Carol. I didn't actually appear on the second series until Programme 5 on Friday November 25th 1983. But what a show that was to be.

In the autumn of '83 I had somehow managed to get myself invited to appear on BBC Radio London's Friday night show 'Track Record' presented by resident DJ Malcolm Laycock. I think it must have started out with another guest interview spot, but for some reason or other it ended up being a regular appearance. Even though I was still writing and recording sketches with Phil for Gaywaves I discovered it was alarmingly easy to get into the second of the two studios at Radio London and use it to record my sketches and jingles. Phil's flat was always a fun place to be but it could be a mite distracting as we spent half our time there laughing and messing about. I got to know most of the BBC crowd there very well, many of whom knew BBC John (remember him?). There also seemed to be a fairly sizeable gay contingent there, although being the BBC it was all terribly closeted. God knows what they must have thought of my screaming about and campery though. Malcolm was wonderfully open and embracing and I managed to somehow get him to broadcast my comedy sketches, most of which were under the title 'Two minutes Thirty Second Theatre'. These were potted film or play spoofs, some of which were quite near the knuckle for the BBC. I used to turn up in the early evening of a Friday night with a script I'd hastily written and armed with my music and sound effects records nip into the free studio to record. I liked the immediacy of the thing and have always preferred to work that way. The more I sit and ponder over something the less I am likely ever to either finish or be happy with it. Of the surviving tapes I still have, only a few of my rough cuts remain. These were diabolically shortened spoofs of things like *Under Milk Wood*, *Gone With The Wind*, *Cinderella* and *Brief Encounter* – all heavily influenced by my heroes of yore 'Round The Horne', 'Monty Python' and Kenny Everett. After editing the tapes with help and guidance from BBC Children's TV producer Paul Smith, and BBC DJs Guy Hornsby and Mike Grey I'd have them loaded onto a cartridge and ready for broadcast at some point on Malcolm's show later that night. He was very brave because he always did this without having heard them beforehand. Not that I would ever have compromised him in any way by slipping in anything too rude or suggestive, but listening to the rough rehearsal tapes I still have they were fairly outrageous for their time, especially given that the mainstream broadcasting establishment was in general meltdown over any form of lesbian and gay politics, fuelled on by that witch Thatcher and her bigoted government.

At the time veteran radio broadcaster and personality Tony Blackburn was also working there and had a regular afternoon programme. Radio London must have seemed a bit of a comedown for him really as in his peak he'd been the presenter of the Radio 1 Breakfast Show and a major BBC celebrity. As is common in our profession the highs can just as easily be followed by lows and that was where he seemed to be just then. His ebullient, over-the-top style of broadcasting wasn't fashionable at all in those years of Comic Strip alternative comedy and right-on anti-Thatcher politics. It didn't help to be honest that he was so unfriendly and up himself to us whippersnappers. I don't think he liked me very much either and I imagine he would have loathed what we were doing on *The Tube*. I often used to see him in the Radio London offices and he was one of the few who didn't mix or join in our banter. So much so that we used to enjoy deliberately calling the office direct phone line when we knew he was the only one there and when he answered ask to speak to somebody else – all the while failing to register who he was. This must have been unbearable for him, especially when we'd say, 'Who is this speaking?', and play up to not knowing who he was, despite the fact that he had one of the most distinctive voices in British broadcasting. This must have infuriated him. I know it must seem childish and disrespectful now, and it's not something I'm terribly proud of, but at the time we thought it was hilarious. If he'd been a bit nicer it wouldn't have occurred to us. Oh well, I don't suppose he's remotely bothered about that now, if he even remembers any of it. His career has stayed the course whereas we are all forgotten-about nobodies again.

After a while the show seemed to attract more and more weekly visitors, all of whom were welcomed with open arms by Malcolm. The champagne flowed and it did get very boozy, smoky (?!) and 'lively'. The regular Laycock show gang consisted of him, me and my partner Michael, 'Producer' Gary Rae who did the weekly 'Gig Guide', Stopwatch Roy (who did all the data logging of music played) and his friend Alex, Clive Bull manning the phones and record plugger Ian Goddard – along with whoever else happened to be wandering by at the time. One night Alex had brought along a leather queen friend of his who proceeded to get extremely drunk and whilst wandering around looking for the bogs took the opportunity to proposition a gentleman who happened to cross him in the corridor. Unfortunately for him (and us) it turned out to be the Station Manager. Needless to say he was not amused and Laycock was duly summonsed to explain himself. He must have got away with it though as his listening figures were quite good and Stopwatch Roy tells me that the show had a cult following by the time we had expanded it into the 'zoo' format. This style of broadcasting with a main presenter and then a 'posse' of other contributors had been started by Radio 1's Steve Wright a couple of years earlier back in 1981 and later built on most notably by Chris Evans, with whom my friend Ian Goddard would go on to become a close friend (but you'll have to read the Evans autobiography for the low-down on that). I think we can safely say that our show was the first late night zoo format programme, which was probably just as well as sometimes the guests were even more drunk than we were (incredibly). The worst guest we ever had on in that regard was sometime Public Image Ltd musician and punk lurker Jah Wobble. He turned up at the studios so rat-arsed that he could barely string a sentence together. To his credit Malcolm attempted to interview him but after only about 30 seconds decided that the chances of a stray 'fuck' or 'cunt' going out live from the transmitter was not worth his meagre BBC salary being put at risk. So he made furious gestures to Stopwatch Roy and the gang to 'get him out of here'. His mic was cut and Wobble was unceremoniously booted out of the studio before he had a chance to get the station taken off air. Shame really as I've always been a big Wobble fan. We had a lot more in common than either of us realised because he also in his time, unbelievably, had been a London Underground train driver like me. Maybe if I'd interviewed him about that the tediosity would have sobered him up? It could go down in history as the shortest interview ever, although Malcolm's place in the broadcasting cavalcade of fame might have been even more assured had he allowed Wobble the chance to really wobble.

Radio London was a very strange place to be. It had the atmosphere of a little-known broadcasting backwater. It was like discovering studios nobody ever realised were actually there. Even weirder was that after about 6pm security was non-existent. The front desk used to go home and we used to let guests and visitors in and out by the back door. Roy made me laugh at our recent reunion (first time we'd seen each other in over thirty-five years) by reminding me of the time Phil Lynott from rock band Thin Lizzie turned up to be interviewed with two women in tow. He obviously came to the front doors of the building and then discovered it was all closed. When one of his entourage called on the phone to find out what was going on he was told rather unceremoniously to 'go round to the back door' where Gary Rae let them in. The two women he had with him were obviously twins, though none of us could figure out which one he was shagging. I suppose it's possible he could have been doing both of them, but one doesn't like to ask that type of question does one?

After every Friday night programme we would inevitably go out clubbing somewhere. The venue of choice was usually a rather tatty gay disco bar called The Euston Tavern, which I believe was another of those ubiquitous Tricky Dicky Discos I wrote of earlier. Malcolm used to run competitions in the programme and, as the show had a BBC budget of nothing, offer prizes of a night out there. This used to baffle me because no mention was ever made that this was a gay venue, and it only cost 50p to get in anyway. Hardly *The Wheel of Fortune* was it? Christ knows what the competition winners must have thought when they turned up to enjoy their prize, especially if they were straight. Nobody seemed to care though, least of all Malcolm. I don't recall it ever causing a problem though. Now I come to think of it the show's regular entourage of guests seemed to grow ever bigger as a result of competition winners who somehow stayed on and became part of the furniture. Astonishingly nobody other than Malcolm and Clive, who were both BBC staff, actually got paid – not even Roy and Gary who both saw to the show's admin and production for no money whatsoever. Extraordinary and vaguely shameful now I think back on it.

By this time I was tiring of mainstream clubs, but Malcolm, Roy, Alex and the others often went on to mega-club 'Heaven' after that to party away until the small hours. Roy tells tales of glorious excess there with shirtless Kenny Everett riding around on equally shirtless Freddie Mercury's back like a jockey, sex going on round every corner and every table looking like it needed a good 'dusting'. That type of hedonism just didn't appeal to me though, which is a shame for you as a reader because if I had been this book would have been a bloody sight more interesting to read than it probably is. Well done for sticking with it so far though. The prize for this is a night out at The Euston Tavern. See you there.

I loved the glorious freedom of radio broadcasting. In later years I would go on to work more in local radio myself, although it was never as much fun as those Laycock programmes. It's also strange thinking back now that I never invited Phil to come along. This is probably because he would have gone really over the top on the politics side and I preferred to keep that hard side of our friendship apart from the mainstream TV and radio work I was doing by then. Having said that I was and still am immensely proud of the pioneering work Phil and I did to bring an outlet for lesbian and gay politics to broadcast media. Somehow the rather seditious nature of it all on pirate radio validated it as fight back against the establishment. None of my mainstream broadcast contacts ever knew about all this other stuff I'd been doing. Ha bloody ha.

Back at Tyne Tees TV, I had been regularly pestering the producers to do a special item on my hero Marc Bolan. Perhaps as a sop to shut me up they finally agreed and sometime in early October 1983 I discovered that they'd managed to get ex-Beatle drummer Ringo Starr to agree to an interview. This was a real scoop as Beatle members rarely ever gave interviews – especially Ringo. But on discovering that the article was to be about his old friend Marc he had agreed to meet us. In addition to this there would be an interview on film with music producer legend Tony Visconti. Although the feature itself didn't air until programme five of series two, filming for the feature took place a couple of months before that. The first piece we did was with Ringo. I met the film crew and location director at Heathrow airport one hot and sunny late September afternoon and we jumped into a black cab which took us all the way out to Ringo's house just outside Ascot. The charge on the clock was flying round like the clappers as we belted down the motorway and by the time we arrived I was bloody glad it wasn't me that was paying. Still, this was TV man, money was no object (apparently).

Whilst we were squashed together in the cab the director said to me in that glorious Newcastle accent, 'Look Gary, gettin' Ringo to talk has been a real scoop. It's great that we'll get the Bolan stories, but we really need to get him onto Beatles stuff as that'll be the money shot. So, whatever you do, somehow we need you to steer it that way.' I duly nodded my head and agreed vigorously with him, whilst having absolutely no intention of doing that whatsoever. It had irritated me as I knew that the only reason Ringo had agree to do this was precisely because it was about Marc and not him or the Fab Four.

The cab drew up outside the enormous fancy wrought-iron gates of Tittenhurst Park, which Starr had bought off previous owner and fellow Beatle John Lennon. The place was guarded like Fort Knox and we were met by security guards with a pack of dogs that were hungrily eyeing us up for lunch. As they strained at their leashes and we walked up to the front door we were met by the man himself. It's worth me recording that he was one of those people who in an absolute instant you could tell was one of the proverbial 'nice guys'. Smiling, warm, friendly and totally down to earth he shook hands with me, put his arm round my shoulder and led us into the house chatting away like we'd known each other for years. Although the interview was to be filmed out in the garden where the fantasy sections in the T.Rex film of 'Born To Boogie' were filmed back in 1972, he told me he had a few things he thought I'd be interested in first while the crew got set up. With that he led me downstairs into the very studio where eleven years earlier he had filmed Marc playing 'Children of The Revolution', with Elton John on the piano and himself on drums. The original instruments were all still there and visually the studio didn't look like it had changed very much from what you can see in the film. 'Have a go on the drums if you like,' he said as I began regretting that I hadn't brought a camera with me. After an impromptu percussion lesson, during which time it became hilariously apparent that I played the drums about as well as he could have driven a train, he saw that I'd spotted the large free-standing, life-size black and white cut-out of Marc which had also featured in the film 'Born To Boogie'. 'I've kept that all these years mainly because after we finished filming with it Marc wrote a message on it to my son Zak.' Sure enough there, in black pen, was a sweet little message handwritten by Bolan. I guess Ringo could see how in awe I was of this. It was the first time I had ever seen anything of my hero's up so close, and I think he was genuinely touched by my reaction to it. 'You know what would be really cool? If when we are doing the interview we could have the Marc figure moving in behind you in camera shot just like in the original film?' 'Good idea, that would look great. OK, let's do it. It hasn't been outside this studio since we made the film. I just hope the stand at the back doesn't break off as it's a bit fragile now,' he said. Whilst the Bolan was carried up the stairs and out into the garden we carried on talking and went up into the huge white room overlooking the garden. I recognised it from the film of Lennon playing piano in the Imagine film, with Yoko standing statuesquely by his side. As we looked out onto the garden I came clean. 'You know what they want me to do don't you?' He laughed. 'Oh I guessed that,' he said. 'Well, I'm not going to do it,' I said. 'This is about Marc, and I know that was why you agreed to do this.' 'Yep, you know I really loved the guy. He could be a pain in the neck sometimes but we had a blast making the movie. I understood the pressures he was going through only too well. But despite everything we had a lot of fun together. He was great company, and I really miss him.'

We walked out into the garden and Ringo sat on a bench for the interview, which was actually one of the easiest I ever had to do. The closest I ever got to mentioning the Beatles was when I asked him what it was like for him being on the other side of the fan adoration during the filming sequences at Wembley Empire Pool all those years back in '72? He said that the biggest problem they had was in dealing with the noise from screaming fans, something that the Beatles had had to deal with constantly, but that during the filming of 'Born To Boogie' it was the technicalities of getting the soundtrack mix right without losing the excitement of the performance which was his biggest concern. And with that he only alluded once more to his own band in summarising Marc's legacy:

I think a lot of his music, like a lot of ours, holds up today. And his music had a certain attitude with the words and he did have a definite sound, and he was the sound. I mean he could have played with anyone but it was Marc's guitar and his vocal that gave it something that remains.

Ironically my direct question comparing his experiences with Marc didn't make the final cut! All that badgering for nothing. I think though that the director was pleased with what he got that day because there was a real rapport and Ringo was so easy to work with. I'd be a liar if I hadn't secretly hoped that he would give me the Marc cut-out as a memento, especially when he said that now Zak had grown up and moved on he didn't really know what to do with it. But actually I think he kept it because he genuinely liked having it there. At least, that's what I've chosen to think.

We said our goodbyes and jumped back into our taxi for the drive back to Heathrow, with one of my biggest ever interviews safely in the can. How I would love to see the whole thing unedited. I have no pics or film of me and Ringo together. I am just a disembodied voice in the final version, but it's something I'm really proud of nonetheless.

I wish I could say the same about the next interview I did for the feature. If I was in awe of Ringo then meeting legendary music producer Tony Visconti was a close second. Visconti had been close to Marc throughout his formative superstar years and produced all of the main Tyrannosaurus Rex and subsequent T.Rex singles and albums. During the same time he was also producing work with Marc's friend and chart rival David Bowie. I was to meet Tony and interview him at his office somewhere off the Edgware Road near Maida Vale in North West London. Unbeknownst to the director and film crew I was feeling really unwell that day. With no smartphones or Google Maps back then it was down to finding your way around with the paperback map book *AtoZ of London*. Fat lot of use it seemed to be though as I was buggered if I could find the bloody place. This made me more and more agitated as I hate being late for anything. The later it got the more pissed off I became. When I finally found the place I was about 15 minutes late. The director was not amused and that made me even more confused. To cap it all Visconti was cold, unfriendly and hard to talk with. Maybe he was having an off day too? Hey, it happens. Compared to what I'd just done with Ringo this time it was like trying to squeeze blood out of a bloody stone. With every fibre of my body I felt that he hated me. Every question I asked I felt he responded to as though I was some kind of an idiot. 'It's often been said that Marc could only play about seven chords. Is that true?' I asked him. There was a pause. 'That's all you need,' he said.

Whilst researching this book I watched the interview back again and it was very strange to compare the negative emotion and feeling I so distinctly recall that day with the edited interview which doesn't give any of this away on screen. Although he appears somewhat reserved there is little sign of the smugness and patronising feeling that I perceived at the time. What I didn't know until after we had parted and I had returned back to my shitty flat, was that I was actually suffering from a form of viral meningitis. As a result I was laid low for just over three weeks recovering. None of it was helped by my inability to cope with stress that day and my muddle head and bad temper. It was one of the few times when it very nearly got the better of me. When the filmed interviews were broadcast as part of the 15 minute Bolan feature I saw what a wonderful job the directors and editors had done with it all and it really is one of the things I am most proud of having done during my two and a half years on the programme.

On the day of the broadcast I arrived up in Newcastle to discover that I was to be joined by veteran BBC broadcaster John Peel, who had been a personal friend of Bolan's for years and who had brought up some of Marc's hand written poetry to show and read out. Not only that but the researchers told me they had one big surprise: they had found Mickey Finn (Marc's percussionist partner in the band T.Rex) and that he had agreed to come up and do a live interview. I could barely believe this. Nothing had been heard of Mickey in years after his somewhat acrimonious split with Marc a couple of years before he was killed in the car crash at Barnes Common in West London. Researcher Chris Phipps took me to one side during the afternoon of transmission for a quiet chat. 'We have a problem,' he said. 'Mickey is not very… err… with it. He is paranoid about his ex-wife or partner or someone finding out where he is and is very nervous about anyone seeing him on TV. But on the other hand he really wants to do the interview and is pleased that Marc is finally getting some recognition again.'

'Okayyyyyyy,' I tentatively drawled. 'So what else then?' 'Unfortunately we aren't sure if we can sober him up enough in time for the broadcast,' said Chris. 'He has a bit of a drug problem and isn't very coherent right now. It's probably best that you don't meet him just yet as we are not sure he's in a fit state to interact with anyone.'

This wasn't very helpful as I had no time to meet and greet and talk about what we would be talking about. With live TV it is perilous to do everything cold as you never know what might actually come out. As a result I didn't get to meet Mickey before the actual live interview. Peel's bit went well. He'd brought along some little books of handwritten poetry, thoughts and jottings by the great man himself in somewhat tatty little notebooks which, according to Peel, looked that way because his children still read them. Particularly sweet was this little musing:

'Ills are merely one's bed feeling neglected and making you snuggle in for a cuddle'

Furious waving from the floor manager forced me to cut him off early before he had a chance to read anything else from Marc's little book, which on reflection I should not have done. The gallery cut to amazing filmed footage of Marc I had never seen before, together with my interviews with Tony and Ringo. Then it was over to me and Mickey Finn. I had barely five mins to talk with him before we went live but despite the earlier stern warnings he was coherent (just about) if a bit breathless. He'd decided to wear this great big brown floppy hat, in which he had stuck his studio security pass into the headband. The trouble with that was that it covered most of his face. The floor manager was giving me signs to try and get him to lose the hat and turn to face the cameras. This was not going to be easy I thought, without spooking him, especially given his somewhat fragile state. I let the discussion go on regardless of the hat droop as he seemed genuinely emotional talking about his old friend and music partner after so long. Right at the very end in an act of mild desperation I reached over and whipped it off suggesting that we put his fee for the show into it. He almost panicked but then eased back and seemed to enjoy the moment despite it. I felt terrible doing it, but was only obeying orders. I am so pleased I got the chance to meet him. He'd been part of my childhood music obsession and it was comforting to discover he was one of the nice guys too. Over the years since this show was broadcast I have been heartened by the numbers of people who have told me just how much this Bolan feature had meant to them. It was the first time anything had been shown on mainstream media about him in the five years or so since he'd died. I am so pleased that it was worth it and glad it worked out so well.

With the Bolan feature done and dusted, I could relax and enjoy the rest of the show, which concluded with me introducing The Style Council playing live in the final set of the show. Not a band I was a fan of personally, but you can't like everything can you? I was more amused by the fact that the programme got some complaints from the easily outraged when Dawn French took out a Tampax box for Paul Young to sign. OUTRAGE! Someone dared to mention a tampon on national live TV before the watershed! Was there no end to the depravity of this filthy Channel?

I was back up at Tyne Tees on December 1st 1983 although I didn't appear on the live show of the following night. The reason it sticks in my mind is because the show featured a live performance and interview with the late, great John Waters protégé, Queen Of Trash and movie legend Divine. I had been pestering the producers to feature him because his cult film status had recently been transmogrificated into the Gay club scene in the form of dance music. I knew the boss of Proto Records, Barry Evangeli, quite well at the time and Divine had just signed to his label. I was so excited that finally we would get to see this great artiste perform live and a first for British (and quite possibly worldwide) TV. Div was over to promote his new single 'Shake It Up' and also to record some new music with producer Pete Waterman, who at that time was also working out of Proto Records. I can only assume that it was during this time that I recorded my interview with The Weather Girls, which would be broadcast as a rare recorded segment in the *Tube* show of February 17th 1984. I can't think of any other reason why I would have been there. More of them later, but for now back to Divine. The night before the show I'd been out clubbing at Rockshots in Newcastle with Divine, his manager Bernard Jay, Muriel, Barry E, Nigel, Leslie and Michael from the production team. Whilst the gang partied hard I went and sat with Div who was quietly sitting alone in his beautiful pure white kaftan on a long couch. He was a kind, gentle and softly spoken man and polar opposite to his over-the-top stage character. As we talked we dreamt up a plan to make the interview on the programme something that people watching wouldn't forget in a while. I had naturally assumed that they would give the interview to me. Why else would I be up there? 'How about I say something that will outrage you and then you beat me up on live TV?' I said. 'Ooh yes, that sounds like fuuuuuun,' he drawled in that glorious Baltimore accent of his. And so we worked on the idea that I would challenge his status as the trashiest person alive by comparing him to some of the girls I'd gone to school with and who were trashier than he could ever have been. Outraged in the same way that Grace Jones was when she walloped Russell Harty on his TV show, Div would go one better and we would have a mega scrap. We figured it would be outrageous, not too risky and still suitable for our early evening time slot. I might have been brave but I wasn't stupid. I knew it was a real risk the producers were taking having a drag queen perform on the programme as it was. All this planning and scheming helped make the night fly by. He came across to me as a desperately lonely man. Every now and then I'd notice him gazing into the dancing crowd and seeming miles away from what was going on around him. It made me more determined than ever to do the best possible interview and for his performance on the show to give him his first major chart breakthrough in the UK.

Well, at the production meeting the next day I was mortified when they allocated the Divine interview to Muriel. Whilst the rest of the show was predominantly concerned with the usual mainstream stuff of the day, The Pretenders, Culture Club, Bowie and Icicle Works, a small item had ben slotted in to cover the burgeoning Gay dance scene known as 'HiNRG'. As the show's resident poof and the world's first out gay TV presenter I naturally expected that at least some of this item would fall to me? For goodness' sake, they even showed Miquel Brown's video of 'So Many Men', and it doesn't get much camper than that. I'd spent most of the afternoon of December 2nd having a ball with Martha Wash and Izora Armstead, The Weather Girls, and then on to record what would probably be one of my best interviews of my entire time on the show. As a consequence of this I was somewhat out of sight and out of mind for the purposes of the live show that night. I watched Divine in rehearsal and had been laughing with Nigel, Leslie and Michael as we supposed what the crowd would make of this towering mound of quivering flesh descending amongst them 'Shaking It Up'. But the sad fact is that I think word of what Div and I had planned to do had I been interviewing him had got to the producers (or equivalent high up execs) who must have been mortified at what such antics might have resulted in. As a result it was allocated to dear Muriel instead, who in truth didn't really want to do it as drag culture didn't sit comfortably with her politics.

Jools introduced the 'Boystown' and 'HiNRG' section of the programme in an oddly offhand way, which gave me the impression he didn't approve. This may be doing him an injustice, so I hope he'll forgive that observation, but you have to remember just how off mainstream gay culture still was back then. The status quo media outlets steered well clear of it unless it was to peddle sensationalism, morbidity or outrage. For sure Boy George, Jimi and the Bronski Beaters helped break this political log jam, but even George wasn't overtly Gay as such at the time. And remember, this show went out at half past five of an afternoon; there could be kiddies watching! This could also be the reason that my Weather Girls interview was taped and not broadcast live? Just to be on the safe side eh? The scourge of political correctness was rife back then and even in those early days it was even being used to kill off any aspiration that the LG community might have had of breaking through into the mainstream.

Back in the studio the show was going out live as usual and I stood to one side in the Green Room and watched whilst Muriel sat with Div out of drag, dressed very conservatively and informally in a beige sweater. To my horror Muriel went for the very angle I was desperately hoping she wouldn't – the political side. She even started by referring to him simply as a 'female impersonator'. I was almost in tears with the frustration of it. As the interview progressed the terms grotesque, taking the rise out of women and dressing up were put to him as my jaw dropped in abject horror. This was a legendary figure being faced for quite possibly the first time with an interview covering aspects I am pretty sure he'd never dreamed would be raised. After all, he (and many others) had been treated as pariahs in the US for years and I doubt the politics of it all were even considered at the time. True to himself though he remained calm, cool, gentle and quiet throughout and completely unfazed by it all. There's one very telling moment in that interview when, just after Muriel had referred to his character as grotesque, Div fires straight back with the line, 'Actually I always thought it was glamorous,' And of course that's exactly what he was – the very epitome of Hollywood Glamour: a legend and a star.

I was really cross with Muriel for a while for taking that angle with it, even though as interviews go it was good and true to the probing style of the show. But I love her so I couldn't be cross forever. Anyway, I blamed the producers. Had they given it to me I'd really have had a ball and they would have had a piece of television that would have put them on the front pages (albeit possibly for the wrong reasons).

But back to the great man; later in the show and with a great flourish out burst the Trash Queen herself from behind rows of shimmering gold and silver strips at the top of a staircase down towards the astonished crowd of pubescent girls gathered there below. *'Your loving drives me crayyyyyyzeeee, Shake it Up!'* growled Div, wearing a figure-hugging fluorescent lime-green dress and huge peroxide blonde wig. As he wobbled and gyrated, thrusting his hips forward every time he sang 'Shake it UP, UP, Let's shake it UP!' the crowd visibly backed away in shock. We danced and sang along behind the scenes and laughed our heads off watching the faces of the mortified girls in the front row, who'd clearly never seen anything like this before. It was one of those great moments I shall always treasure. I met up again with him in London some weeks afterwards during the recording sessions for Proto during which he recorded what was to become one of his biggest UK chart hits 'You Think You're A Man', co-written and produced by Barry and Pete Waterman, who also mixed it for its

12" release. That was to be the last time I ever saw Div. Although he went on to become a huge mainstream star with films like *Lust In The Dust* and the original *Hairspray*, he wasn't able to enjoy the success he so richly deserved, passing away with heart disease in March of 1988 aged just 42. So sad.

This episode of *The Tube* was notable for a number of reasons, not least the points I just made. We had been given the rights to premier Michael Jackson's brand new video 'Thriller' and the producers had wanted to broadcast it in the main show. However Channel 4 got cold feet as the images were considered to be too shocking and gory for kiddiewinkies at that time of day (laughable as that seems now). Instead the video was given its own dedicated late night slot for its UK TV premier. It was introduced by Jools and Leslie and shown in its entirety for the first time. I wasn't an MJ fan to be honest. He always gave me the creeps, regardless of the 'Thriller' video, which I thought was laughable. But it is a great song and always good to hoik out of the record collection come Halloween every year. I only mention this because knowing that the video was to be given its first airing that day I had discussed it with Martha and Izora that afternoon. It was just as well that my interview with them was recorded because when I got them on stage we had an outrageous time. I asked them what they thought of Michael Jackson and if they'd seen the new 'Thriller' video? They said they hadn't and then when I told them that we couldn't show it at that time because in the film bits of him kept dropping off they roared with laughter! 'Mind you,' I said, 'from the look of him I'm not sure he had much down there to drop off.' More roars of laughter. For some reason we then started talking about his willy – I have no idea why. It was hilarious. I haven't ever had as much fun on an interview as we did then. It was a nice end to a strange day. During the afternoon I'd spent with them we had talked a lot about Sylvester with whom they had worked as his backing group Two Tons Of Fun, and whom I'd admired greatly for the gay rights activist I knew he was. Although the two great ladies were straight, they had a heartwarming empathy with the politics of gay rights as well as race, which was an ongoing struggle in the US. But they were warm, funny and an absolute joy to be with. I imagined how much fun it must have been to have been on those tours in the US with Sylvester back in the glory days of Disco. Sylvester himself was still making great dance records in '83 and would for another five glorious years, before HIV/AIDS would finally claim his life and rob the world of yet another beautiful star.

1983 was a year I was mostly glad to see the back of. Margaret Thatcher had been re-elected over Michael Foot's Labour leadership with an even bigger majority back in June of that year. Oddly enough my friend at the BBC Peter Estall had called me and asked if I would be interested in doing a rehearsal phone-in for a political radio news thing on Radio 4. I thought it might be a giggle so I agreed. The idea was that we would phone in with some sample questions to ask the politician panel and they could then get an indication of how best to respond. Most odd now I think back on it. I called in from my shitty council flat and ended up having my question put to someone who sounded suspiciously like the real Michael Foot. 'Everywhere I go I hear people saying that Labour hasn't got a chance of being elected. How is this overwhelming public attitude affecting your campaign?' I said, trying to sound like I knew what I was talking about. Whoever it was at the other end waffled on for a bit and I didn't really pay much attention as it wasn't a conversation, I was just posing a sample question. When the whoever it was had finished Peter came back on the line and thanked me. 'Here, was that really Michael Foot?' I asked him. 'I'm afraid I can't say, but thanks for that question. It certainly gave him something to think about – whoever it was.' I admired Michael Foot greatly. Subsequent to his election defeat I had devoured his autobiography which was utterly fascinating. He'd been consistently portrayed as a doddery, scruffy, confused old twat by both TV and red top news media of the day, and yet he was nothing of the sort. Highly intelligent and with deep conviction and principles, he suffered as many would from that time onwards from the image police. Tony Blair would eventually epitomise this by wresting power away from the Bagpuss-faced and dreary-looking John Major. But that my dears is another story entirely and not one I am going anywhere near (you'll be pleased to note).

As 1984 dawned the year was looking bleaker than ever in Britain. Thatcher's Tories were gearing up for confrontation with the Unions, which would devastate working class communities in the whole of the UK. My partner Michael was far more heavily into politics than I was back then, although mine had mainly revolved around Lesbian and Gay, Anti-Nazi League and Anti-Nuclear issues, all of these having strong cultural influences at the time. My dear friend Phil of course could be found in the thick of it all, through his subversive work on pirate radio with Gaywaves, to other activities funnelled through Gay Switchboard, Housman's bookshop and meeting rooms in King's Cross and of course dear old 'Gay's The Word' bookshop in Marchmont St, King's Cross (where it remains to this very day). Michael didn't really like the television media crowd and although he always supported me, he would make his feelings quite clear about what he considered to be 'the flagrant excess of the entertainment world'. We'd been out at a celebratory dinner for something or other thrown by *The Tube* programme-makers at fashionable West End restaurant L'Escargot when Michael had caught sight of the bill when it finally came round. There'd been about fifteen of us quaffing fabulous food and swilling gallons of booze to value of just under £5,000, which works out at about £333 a head. This was, even by today's standards, a phenomenal amount of money. With the hardships that were being meted out by the government of the day, Michael was outraged by this and never came with me to another event like that in all the years we were together. It's somewhat ironic that he would eventually go on to become a highly successful figure in the world of magazine advertising, and budgets which would have made what we did back in *Tube* days look like a charity shop collecting tin. Such is life. We were deeply in love and at last I thought I had found someone who would put up with my mood swings and oddball obsessions and frustrations. Things at the flat had gone from bad to worse and I was now desperate to escape the toxic atmosphere between me and my flatmate Peter. On February 3rd 1984 after seeing an advert in the *Evening Standard*, I went and saw a new development of studio apartments for sale down in Roehampton Vale in West London on the very edge of Wimbledon Common. Incredibly for Michael and me the daft sods not only allowed us to reserve the apartment for a measly hundred quid (with a bit of the money I had managed to save from the TV show) but arranged a 100% mortgage for us. I had never even conceived of actually owning a property in my life. Did people like me do that? I was a council house man through and through and for the past few years had lived in what can accurately be described as shitholes. Yet here we were about to get on the property ladder buying a flat for the mind-numbing sum of £28,000!

The following week I was back up in Newcastle for the show of Friday 10th February '84 with a truly awesome collection of bands playing live – Kool & The Gang, Thompson Twins and one of my all time favourites Siouxsie & The Banshees. Once again French & Saunders acted as the Jools-obsessed joint hosts 'Janice' and 'Carol'. For some odd reason I was presenting a feature on the world's worst records, shamelessly nicked from my radio hero Kenny Everett, who had been doing the 'Bottom 30' regularly on London's Capital Radio. My version couldn't stretch to that so I just did the 'Bottom 10', and invited viewers to send in their nominations for the worst records they could find. 'Remember, we want your crap!' I heroically said at the end of the article just before ballsing up my link and making a complete prune of myself. Christine the floor manager had done the dirty on me by giving me a countdown to two seconds and then waving furiously to give me another ten. I'd finished as far as I was concerned and on realising the camera was still on me I once again deferred to being camp. What was that all about? It wouldn't have fooled anyone. As far as I was concerned I was fucking useless as a presenter and moments like that would play on my mind for years afterwards.

It wasn't just me though. Poor Leslie Ash also suffered from the same difficulties as I did presenting. We both came from a theatre and acting background and needed scripts and direction to feel comfortable. It wasn't just a case of improvised spontaneity, you really have to know what you're doing when presenting – and with knobs on if it's live. No second chances there. Even though she had more shows to do than I did, having replaced Paula as Jool's permanent on-screen partner, you can see the unease in her face in much the same way as mine. Sometimes her partner at that time, Rowan Atkinson, would come up to the studios in Newcastle to be with her. I recall him sitting quietly in a comfy chair in the middle of the production office while everyone buzzed around him in general chaos. He was staggeringly good-looking in the flesh and I recall wondering how (and why) it was that on screen he managed to contort himself into the characters he was becoming famed for on cult BBC comedy show *Not The Nine O'Clock News*. Although Leslie and I often chatted away quite happily I regret never having really spoken with Rowan. The impression I got was that he considered this very much Leslie's patch and that he didn't want to get involved in any way.

I'd been staying with some friends I'd made in Bensham on the south side of the Tyne instead of at the hotel in Gosforth by this time and had also decided to take the train again rather than fly. On the Saturday morning after the show I boarded the inter-city train back to London and discovered that I was sat across from Siouxsie, Budgie, Steve Severin and Robert Smith. For quite possibly the only time in my life I was completely star struck and although we politely nodded as I said hello, I couldn't think of anything to say to them. Normally I would have piled in and gabbled away quite happily unfazed by anything, but not this time. She'd been an icon of mine ever since I'd watched her in the background on live TV as the Sex Pistols had ripped into interviewer Bill Grundy in that now legendary interview where the 'fucks' and 'bastards' led to him being sacked. I had so wanted to talk about the band's early days, especially as you may recall I had joined the Underground at the same time as Audrey, who had roadied for them in their early days. I kept schtum though because, let's be honest, why would either she or any of the rest of them be even remotely interested in that? Hell, even I wasn't. I was boring myself even thinking of it. In retrospect I am glad I didn't make a prune of myself trying to muscle in on their conversations. It enabled me to keep Sioux as a musical icon in my own mind ever since. If my brain craves musical subversion and deep thrills I will put on their album 'Juju' and turn up the volume to earthquake level. This pleases me greatly. We respectfully nodded goodbye as we pulled into King's Cross and parted company. I realise that this is probably the least interesting story anyone has ever written about in any book that's ever been written. But so be it. Just consider this as one of the bottom bits on the roller coaster of my life.

As I mentioned earlier, during my time at Radio London I'd become very friendly with a record plugger called Ian Goddard who worked tirelessly for promotions company Oliver Smallman. Record pluggers were always hanging around shows like *The Tube* pushing their acts and pitching to the production teams, desperate to get their product exposure. *The Tube* was THE show to get on as far as they were concerned. Ian was one of the most tenacious promotions guys I ever came across, but he made me laugh. I had no sway on who appeared on the show at all much beyond making suggestions if I really felt it was worth it, such as Mari Wilson, Divine and the Bolan thing. Much as I loved being with Ian I am not sure any of his bands ever made it onto the show, although he was very friendly with Holly Johnson and the 'Frankie Goes To Hollywood' guys. I adored Holly. He was so handsome I could have eaten him all up. But of course I was the consummate professional so just as I always did, I kept myself to myself and said nothing. Ian was a really hard drinker and enjoyed going out with bands especially when they were staying in London where he was based. A favourite haunt of his was the Metropole Hotel in the Bayswater Road near Marble Arch. This was a popular place for rock groups to stay at and it had a fiersome reputation for drunken antics. Once again though I sat firmly on the outside looking in. When the Frankies stayed there during one of their trips to London, Ian, Michael and me had spent some time with Holly whilst the rest of the band got shitfaced. We didn't lob any televisions out of the window, shred bed linen or spray the rooms with Bolly. We lolled around on the sofas in the lobby, had intellectual conversations and told dirty jokes (well, Ian did). It was a happy time. Ian would become one of my closest friends in the few years that followed. He was a complicated character, gay but not very in any way (unless he fancied you). He could spar with the toughest in the music business and wasn't someone who would put up with any shit from anyone. He could be bloody irritating and yet incredibly lovable at the same time. Michael became especially fond of him and stayed in touch with him right up until his untimely death just a couple of years ago. The most fun times with him were during my spell working at BBC Radio London towards the end of my time on *The Tube*.

On February 17th 1984 my interview with the Weather Girls was finally broadcast. I was looking forward to seeing this as the taping had lasted for almost a quarter of an hour and I knew that when it went out it would be a mere fraction of this time. As the Weather Girls finished their astounding live rendition of 'It's Raining Men' I sashayed on the stage to the rapturous applause from the crowd. Izora had told me of her massive family of eleven children and the menagerie of pets they shared the house with – including a pet alligator, which she told me they had to get rid of when it 'grew too big and started to eat the kids'. Martha regaled stories of her operatic training, informing us that 'you have to sing from the diaphragm', whilst patting my tummy area as I said I didn't know where that was. All the stuff about Michael Jackson and his willy was of course cut out, though looking at the way it was edited it must have been a nightmare to cut, probably because we were laughing so much. At the end of the spot I had them presented with a Stotty cake (a local bread type delicacy from the area) brought in on a velvet cushion by one of the production team wearing a bowler hat. As I handed them each the oversized bap and I told them with great gusto to 'get stuck in' they both roared with laughter.

On March 12th the miners went on strike in what was to become one of the most bitter industrial disputes the country had seen since before the war. What with demonstrations taking place down at the American airbase in Greenham Common by a large group of women protesting at the deployment of Ronald Reagan's cruise missiles on UK soil, the political scene was not exactly one big happy party. Despite all the negativity that seemed to be seeping into every household like a sort of Tory 'Blob', there was still a vibrant arts, fashion and music scene. In the spirit of earlier forays into demonstration and protest seen in the 1960s, the 80s would see initiatives like 'Lesbians & Gays Support The Miners' and my old friend Jimi Somerville with his band Bronski Beat and others putting on benefits concerts like the now famous 'Pits & Perverts' event at Camden's Electric Ballroom. Far from being downbeat and negative these gigs and the attitude that fired them were loud, proud and vibrant. The London clubs of the time were still thriving and new alternative venues were springing up all the time. At the time of writing this I have been reading other accounts of the time which suggested that the HIV/AIDS crisis 'stopped the music' and inferences that the gay scene was all but sent into hiding. This is manifestly untrue. It is true that the scene changed, but then it always would have. The fight against Thatcher and the ignorance, fear and bigotry of the time invigorated communities to find ever more ways of surviving in the face of such assaults. We were not giving in and despite all the pain and strife we experienced, we carried on regardless.

Weirdly in the thick of all this Michael and I had moved into our own property mortgaged up to our arseholes almost as a sort of two fingers up to the powers that be. I was enjoying all sorts of weird and wonderful showbizzy events by this time. One of the most memorable being the launch party of Gay night at the new 'Hippodrome' club in London's West End on March 20th 1984. As Michael and I wandered in we were introduced to comedy actor legend Kenneth Williams. What on earth he was doing there I don't know as his diaries seem to indicate he hated dos like this. He flared his wondrous nostrils and smiled as he shook my hand. I was pleased to be able to tell him that I had seen him many times on the platform at Great Portland Street station where he would regularly visit to talk to the station staff on his journeys to and from his nearby home. When I was a Guard on the Metropolitan Line I would hang out of the back of the train as it went past him and wave enthusiastically as he cheerily waved back. 'I adore watching the trains fly by,' he told me, 'and the staff are a delight! Now, what on earth are you doing 'ere then?' I wished it had been the time or place to have chatted but it wasn't. It was incredibly hot, noisy and crowded. I got dragged away and our paths sadly never crossed again. Story of my life – fleeting encounters and ever the bystander. It seems. I was even present up in Newcastle when The Smiths made their first live TV appearance with classic performances of 'Hand In Glove' and 'This Charming Man'. Bizarrely this programme sticks in my mind more for the presence of US personality 'Thor' who, standing next to Leslie Ash, took an inordinately long time to blow up a hot water bottle until it exploded. Say what you like about *The Tube* but it wasn't scared to entertain with unusual acts.

The last time I ever saw Boy George live was at the launch of their Culture Club video release at some place off Oxford St on March 28th 1984. I'd had my invite and turned up even though I recall being in a foul mood for some reason. As the video of a live concert they'd filmed (I think in Japan?) played out on the blurry screen in the bar to the gaggle of pissed journalists and hangers on I remember wondering what on earth they'd done to the soundtrack. George sounded to me like he was singing flat through the whole thing. I knew he was a wonderful singer and that this painful racket wasn't at all representative of his abilities. All I could hear around me were people praising the performance and saying how fabulous and talented he was, none of which I had any argument with and yet were they hearing the same thing I was? He was out of tune, and painfully so! I can only assume because his monitoring earpiece on stage must have been malfunctioning when they filmed it. I couldn't fathom out why they chose this of all the possible performances they could have when there was something so obviously wrong with the way that sound had been recorded. It was clear I was in a party of one on this and I chose not to say anything. The only reason I am even writing about this here now is because this was the most blatant example I had yet come across of people playing up to a star. Nobody had the guts in the production stage to say, 'Hold fire here, this vocal isn't one of George's best, we should do another one'. Instead they sucked up to him and just pretended it wasn't happening. I hated it. And I hated them for doing it. I liked George and felt he deserved better from those around him. This was a side of the industry that I knew I couldn't handle. Sadly by that time, just like Jimi, George had moved onwards and upwards and both were now way out of my friendship group. I was sad to lose touch with Jimi as I was very fond of him and we had had such good times together. Whilst the theatre and stage side of the business also has its negatives I don't think we are as susceptible to fake flattery as ultimately one gets judged by one's performances by live audiences who are not so forgiving even with those they adore. Bad notices can hit an actor with far more regularity and surety than the music business seems to.

On Friday March 23rd 1984 I did my last ever weekly *Tube* show, with guests Danse Society, Bo Diddly, Reflex and The Questions playing live in the studio. Muriel did an epic interview with singing legend Scott Walker and I got saddled with a very strange interview with features editor and photographer of *I.D.* magazine Steve Dixon. When I met him prior to the show in the Green Room I took an instant dislike to him, which was probably mutual. I found him pretentious and aloof and so I decided I would do the interview in a more cutting and incisive manner. Big mistake for me. It wasn't in my nature to be like this and it showed. Whilst we chatted and he took pictures of the fashionistas in the assembled audience I berated him for the cost of the magazine and for its up-itself attitude. It was without doubt the worst interview I ever did, not because I fucked up technically or anything like that, but more because I felt bad about being negative. It pains me to say this but I'm just too nice. I am happiest when camping about and being funny ha ha – but Paxman or Humphries I am not. It was perhaps a relief to then get back to doing another feature on the world's worst records (part 2). This was much more like me and I found my feet again by taking the merciful P out of terrible records that our adoring viewers had sent in by the sackload after the previous item on this. And so, the Friday Tubes ended for me. I was to do just one more show – the *Midsummer Night's Tube* on June 29th 1984. But not before things took an uncomfortable turn for the worst and a meeting amongst friends which would actually spawn the end of my TV presenting roles once and for all.

When I received the contract details for the second *Midsummer Night's Tube* programme I was surprised to see that it had stayed the same as the previous year's fee, two hundred and fifty quid. I called the contracts guy up at Tyne Tees to query it and try and squeeze a bit more out of them. If anyone is under the impression that TV money is big money then they're mistaken. I didn't have an agent at the time to represent me, so had to barter on my own. I hate quibbling over money; it's something I am really not good at coping with. As you might imagine the contracts guy there was hardly a shrinking violet, and he gave me a really rough time. 'You're only doing this show as yourself, and it's not like an acting job or a performance,' he said, in a deeply patronising and unpleasant way. 'I understand that,' I said, 'but it is 5 hours of live entertainment network television and surely it must be worth more than that?'. He then told me they would raise the fee by twenty-five quid to two hundred and seventy-five and I was 'lucky to get that'. He was so unpleasant that I left it there and ended the call. If that's what agents had to deal with then it was clear I needed to get one because I knew I couldn't have coped with all that mullarky every time. That probably would have been the end of the matter, but for a chance remark that I made when I went down to see Wincey Willis at TVam the next day. I was sat there with her and Jeni Barnett yakking away and I mentioned how vile this bloke had been to me on the blower the previous day. I thought Wincey would know who he was as she had spent so many years up at Tyne Tees TV. 'How much have they offered to pay you then?' she asked. When I told her both she and Jeni almost spat out their tea in shock. 'You have to be joking!', said Jeni. 'They are taking the piss out of you and you can't let them get away with that!' I explained that he had told me that it was what it was because I was 'representing myself' and that only made the two of them laugh even more. 'That's all ANY presenter does,' Jeni said. 'Have you been in touch with Equity about it? Is it an Equity contract?' I explained that I was still working to try and get enough contract time in to apply for my union membership card and once again they both looked shocked. 'Call Equity now and go and get some advice, because you can't let them get away with doing this.' I changed the subject because I really didn't want to get wound up about it and I genuinely didn't know what to do. However, the thought that I might finally, after so many years of working for it, be able to get my full Equity membership was tantalising and exciting. I did after all have to consider my future career, and I didn't intend that that would involve being stuck on a bloody train until I was 65.

I went home and after pacing up and down talking to myself for half an hour, fired up by the way the TTTV contracts guy had spoken to me I called Equity. They put me through to the ITV co-ordinator and I explained the situation. 'Can you bring the contract round to us now and we will have a look at it for you. Did you realise that as a result of the work you have already done you have enough qualifying work days to get you Equity membership?' Of course this was news to me, but also a huge relief as with full membership I would be able to work on stage, radio and television without hindrance, with the going rates and with the right protections. I gathered together my papers and hotfooted to the Equity HQ in London's West End. When I got there and started to explain the situation to them I made it clear that the contracts guy had intimated that I had no right to ask for any more as I was 'representing myself' and appearing as such. I also told them that I was concerned that if they saw me as a troublemaker I would not get any more work with them in future. 'Leave it to us,' she said in a soothing, actorish type of a voice. 'I promise you we won't jeopardise anything and we will take a dim view if they penalise you in any way for coming to us. Now go home, you'll have your membership through by the end of the day.'

At this point I became nervous. I was way out of my comfort zone and wasn't sure I had done the right thing. Yet Wincey & Jeni had been so certain, the contracts guy had spoken to me like I was Oliver Twist asking for an extra bowl of gruel and Equity had given me assurances all would be well. Hmmmmm. When I got home the phone was ringing. I answered to hear a raging angry voice at the other end. It was producer Malcolm Gerrie and he was not a happy man. 'Do you realise what you've done, man?' he yelled. 'Why didn't you call me first? You've now put us into official dispute with Equity. All our contracts have been stopped until the union have checked and cleared them.' I was stunned and upset that Equity had done exactly what I'd asked them not to do. They had not been honest with me and explained what they were going to do. I tried to tell Malcolm this but I think he was too angry to listen to anything I said.

I didn't say anything about Wincey or Jeni as I didn't want to drag them into it. In my mind I was also thinking about that vile contracts man and that what I'd been offered wouldn't have paid for one meal at the restaurant where the bill had upset my Michael so much. It all became a mad and muddled, angry and aggressive mess and I went to pieces. With hindsight and after so many years I can understand Malcolm's frustration, if not his anger. The smooth running of the show had been put at risk by a gobby little poof in London who didn't understand the way things worked. And he was right, I didn't. But it was never my intention to cause upset or discord to anyone. I felt terrible. I called Equity back and told them how upset I was that they hadn't been honest with me about what they were going to do. But they were unapologetic. So at the end of that day I had managed to piss off both the TV company and the union I had worked so hard to become a part of and who I thought were there to help me. It was just as well that I could go and lose my brain pushing buttons on a train. Maybe that's what I was really cut out for? Perhaps this TV stuff was just all one big pretension on my part? I should do the sensible thing and keep out of entertainment? I called Lesley Oakden at Tyne Tees to explain what had happened as I felt I had to tell someone up there what had gone on. Bless her heart she calmed me down and assured me not to panic and that all would be OK in the end. It was scant comfort when my Equity membership card arrived through the post. I held it in my hand looking at it like it was some form of golden ticket, when in fact obtaining it had ironically cost me my TV presenting career. Whatever happened after that between Equity and Tyne Tees they must have sorted out because the show went ahead without any hitches. I had made up my mind though that the *Midsummer Night's Tube* would be my last. I am guessing that the producers had decided much the same. Although I had enjoyed some of the experience I was beginning to realise that if I got known for presenting I would be unlikely ever to be taken seriously as an actor again. I didn't have any affinity with musicians and whilst I loved the music I realised also that I didn't really want to see what went on behind the scenes. Meeting Mickey Finn had proved to me that there was a lot of truth in the cliché about meeting one's heroes. I missed working with scripts and with direction and had managed to convince myself that I was actually rubbish at what I'd done. I missed working with Muriel and was frustrated that I'd not be able to build this on-screen relationship as it wouldn't balance with the core presentation by

Jools and either Paula or Leslie. It was all rather negative, depressing and more than I could handle.

One of the things that cheered me up no end happened the week before I flew up to Newcastle for the 5 hour special. Through record plugger Ian I had got to know and become friendly with singer and ex-Tight Fit band singer Steve Grant. Steve was launching his solo career at the time and had signed to the HiNRG dance record label 'Record Shack'. This was the same label that had singer and acting legend Eartha Kitt as part of its new roster of star artistes. She was having major chart and club success with a succession of dance hits aimed squarely at the gay market, but fabulously achieving mainstream chart success too. I knew that Eartha had been booked on the *Midsummer Night's Tube* show to sing her new release 'I Love Men'. This pleased Ian because the Record Shack releases were more often than not pushed for media exposure through Oliver Smallman promotions. One morning not too long before I flew up to Newcastle for that final show something caught my eye at my local newsagents in *The Daily Mirror*. It was an article about Eartha Kitt and Steve Grant apparently being deeply in love, with Steve popping the question proposing marriage! Well there may have been lots of reasons why this story was utter tosh, and I won't go into that here, but quite apart from the age difference (she was old enough to be his grandmother) was their obvious height mismatch. She was tiny and under 5ft tall and he towered over almost everyone at about 7ft tall (an exaggeration, but you get the picture). Whereas Eartha was thin, wispy and looked like she'd snap if she got caught in a light breeze, he was a towering mass of ripped muscles and bulging biceps. I mean dear they were everywhere! He had pectorals in places I never knew existed. It was a ridiculous physical match if nothing else, and obviously a cynical plug by the record company to get as much publicity out of it as they could. One thing was for sure – I knew Steve didn't know anything about it. So I called him up. We chatted for a while and then I asked him if he'd seen the papers that morning? 'No, why?' he said. 'Go out and buy a *Daily Mirror* and then call me back,' I said, trying hard not to spoil the surprise I knew he was going to get. About 20 minutes later my phone rang. Surprisingly it was Steve. I think it is fair to report that he was in shock. 'Oh my god! What have they done?' he said as I offered to be his Best Man, run up a dress and organise the flowers. Ian Goddard thought it was hilarious. So to celebrate, me, Michael and him went out and got shitfaced that evening. Oh how we laughed. On the positive side I mentioned it all to the researchers and production team up in Newcastle and they agreed to invite Steve onto the show to be interviewed with Eartha about their forthcoming nuptials. Hey! Everybody wins!

A couple of days before the show I flew up to Newcastle to prepare for what was to be my final work on *The Tube* on Friday 29th June 1984. I went with a surprisingly positive and open mind, determined to enjoy myself and just be me regardless. What helped this was a number of my friends and people that I really liked were also to be on the show. Lovely Leslie Ash, Muriel co-presenting with me, Steve Grant (with Ian Goddard plugging all over the place behind him), Alison Moyet, Holly Johnson and FGTH and even Divine. Of all the shows I did, these last two were my favourites. It was as if I knew my time there would be ending and that it didn't really matter what I did as long as I had fun. The line-up on this special was spectacular to say the least. We had live sets from Howard Jones and his weird baldy man dancing about in chains, Culture Club in Japan, Bryan Ferry, Hall & Oates, Nona Hendryx, The Cramps, The Police, Echo & the Bunnymen and Blues legend B.B. King. We also had guest appearances from Nigel Planer as 'Neil' the hippy from the TV Series *The Young Ones* (which had just concluded with them all being televisually killed in a double decker bus going over a cliff), and Robbie Coltrane as an over-officious security man.

At the production meeting the day before the broadcast I was hearing rumours about the possibility of Eartha Kitt being 'difficult'. I had heard things like this before and knew that certain stars had reputations for ripping people's heads off. I wasn't in the least phased by this and when she arrived I decided that as I was going to have some fun with the interview between her and Steve I may as well go and meet her and get a feel for how tough she was likely to be. I was taken to her dressing room by one of our researchers and I was surprised to find that she was quite alone. I had somehow expected her to have been accompanied by an army of effusive dressers, hair people and hangers on. But no, it was just her. The researcher duly buggered off and left the two of us alone. And that is how I spent the rest of the afternoon. I sat with her talking for almost three hours, utterly transfixed by her wit, intelligence and library of stories. It was almost as if she had not actually sat and talked with anyone very much for a very long time. We laughed about the publicity story with her and Steve (who unsurprisingly in the circumstances didn't join us) and she told me how out of her comfort zone she was with the music she was now doing. Whilst she didn't actively dislike the dance stuff being written for her on Record Shack records, she was more at home with show songs and luscious orchestrations. I assured her, quite truthfully, that these latest records were winning her a whole new audience of adoring fans and that it would be a useful mechanism for bringing them to her vast body of other work. As she relaxed in the confidence that we had between each other we discussed what it had been like for her developing a career in 1940s and 50s America against the backdrop of horrific racism and prejudice so prevalent where she was born and raised amidst the cotton plantations of South Carolina. She'd had a tough home life, and she spoke at length of the difficult relationship she had with her mother. We compared experiences of growing up and managing societal issues, in her case with being a black woman and mine of being a gay man. The longer we talked the more vulnerable she came across to me. It seemed from what she told me that most of what she had had to fight for in her career and her personal life she had borne totally alone. There is great synergy between the internalised feeling and dialogue that gay people go through when they realise that this world is just not 'formatted' for us and the experiences she described. She told me how Europe had been a mental release from the oppression of America and how much she'd loved living and working in Paris and London. She laughed at my stories of nicking off to Paris for the weekend and staying in crappy one-star hotels along with the cockroaches, all for no money and just for the hell of it. It was a wonderful afternoon I will always treasure. There were times when I honestly felt like I just wanted to hug her and let her cry out all the pains and frustrations she'd been talking about. It was clear she was dreading the performance that night. But I reassured her and told her that I was looking forward to it and I knew for sure the young crowd would be too. 'They love and respect you more than you think,' I told her as she nervously paced up and down the room. I began to really resent those people who had told me she would be 'difficult'. They were wrong. This woman was a star and a legend. She had every right to be demanding. Good for her! 'Let's just have fun later,' I said, hugged her and gave her a peck on the cheek before leaving for the studio and the start of the show. Fate had a trick to play on that fun I promised as it happened…

As the show kicked off I celebrated my first link with a microphone fault as I introduced Alison Moyet (once again embarrassingly pronouncing the 'T' at the end – forgive me Ali!). After that though the show was a triumph. Muriel interviewed gorgeous Billy McKenzie from The Associates, who came on to do a live performance in place of Paul Young who was unfortunately sick at the time. 'What are you here for?' she said to him as he gazed around looking slightly the worse for wear and like he wasn't quite sure where he was. 'I'm here to get wrecked and then puke up in the bog,' he cheerfully (and probably quite accurately) replied.

It was nice to see one of the first showings of my old mate Jimi Somerville and Bronski Beat video for 'Smalltown Boy' – especially as Leslie introduced them as 'Camden Heroes'. This was important because Jimi had been active on the political scene in supporting the miners, including the 'Pits and Perverts' gig at the Electric Ballroom in Camden I spoke of earlier. I loved Leslie for mentioning that, bless her. Mind you, when I saw the video and that my old friends Colin and Cliff were in it I was miffed that he hadn't asked me! Back then I would have looked good in pair of swimming trunks – whereas now it would clear a Bank Holiday beachful in seconds.

Frankie did two live sets on the show, the first with stunning performances of Edwin Starr's 'War' and then their own current hit 'Two Tribes'. I stood at the back of the main stage where I had been the first time they played live on the show and grooved along with everyone else. This was a band at the very peak of their stardom and the confidence and quality just oozed out of every note. They absolutely killed it that night.

As we headed towards the end of the programme it was time for Eartha to do her number. She was to start 'I Love Men' at the top of the staircase and then descend to a camp set comprising a chaise longue with a backdrop of ostrich feathers. After she had sung her live vocal to a plain backing track she would be welcomed by yours truly, we would recline together on the soft furnishings and I would interview her bringing in Steve Grant as her intended lover at the end. To my horror (and to hers no doubt too), when the backing track started they had put the wrong one on. It was an extended vocal mix which she had never heard before and certainly not rehearsed for. There she was with a live mic and a vocal track instead of her live voice. As a result she was forced to mime, something I knew she had hated doing. Despite this embarrassing cock-up she carried on like the trouper she was and mouthed the lyrics as best she could, but visually this made it look like she was miming badly and probably didn't know what she was doing. I wanted the earth to swallow me up it was so toe-curling. She made up for some of the misplaced vocal by walking over to the adoring crowd and shaking their hands, laughing, smiling and brushing the mime away as much as she could. Meanwhile I was stood on the sidelines thinking, 'She is going to murder me when this is over,' and that there was no way I could rescue this even given that it wasn't my fault. As the number finished, I came on in a pair of ludicrously tight, pale blue lurex shorts which left absolutely nothing to the imagination. I don't think even she was expecting that and most of the time we were standing up together she was looking me up and down like I'd just minced out of a gay sauna. Despite all this I whipped up the crowd into a frenzy and they genuinely went wild for her. Whatever they'd thought about her badly mimed performance and my obscene camp outfit they obviously didn't care. I was desperate to get her to relax and to have the fun interview that we had discussed earlier, so I beckoned for her to sit with me on the padded bench. As we sat down I realised that we were below the heads of the crowd in front of us and I couldn't see the cameras. Although we had no talkback I was imagining the gallery going mad saying, 'For Christ's sake what's he sat down for? We can't see them!' However in all the confusion I just had to hope that someone somewhere was actually able to see us. At the outset I could see that she was understandably pissed off with what had happened and after my first question there was deathly silence as her eyes burned into me. It was that moment when she was deciding in her own mind whether to love the moment or go for the kill. Then I saw the glint in her eye, an almost imperceptible relaxation and a shadow of a smile. I knew from that moment onwards she would be fine. I beckoned Steve on to the stage and he sat next to us both, albeit about three feet higher than the pair of us. 'What's all this about you and Steve then?' I cheekily prompted. Steve sat there still in a state of disbelief I think, so Eartha decided to speak for the pair of them. 'Would you like me to tell you about it in case he does not want to?' she purred. 'Well, I think I am feeling... very strongly about him,' at which point Steve started flapping his hand in front of his face rather unconvincingly (forgive me Steve!). Sensing his discomfort I thought I'd better rescue him from any further questions down that road, so I asked her 'What's the difference between English men and German men?' 'Darling a maaan, is a maaaaan is a maaaaaaaan!' she purred back, laughing in that wonderful seductive way whilst deciding she was going to start picking at the hairs on my thighs. It was all quite outrageous and I think we finally did get the fun I had so wanted from it all – eventually. That was quite probably the last time that she and Steve ever actually saw each other, but the papers had had their story so it didn't really matter. I never got to be Best Man at their wedding. Isn't that sad?

Just before the final number of the night Muriel got to do yet another short interview with Divine. Damn and blast! That was the second time I'd missed out. Those producers really didn't trust me did they? This time Muriel didn't go down the politics route and it passed off without me getting hot under those obscene shimmery shorts. The show concluded with Holly and Frankie Goes

To Hollywood doing 'Relax', with backing singers Nona Hendryx, Divine and Eartha Kitt. It is not often you witness a combination like that. It was so much fun. I was dancing along with Steve just behind Divine at the back of the stage as the boys belted out the number bringing the five hour special to a fitting close. That, my dears, although I didn't know it for sure at the time, was my last ever *Tube*. I returned to London the following day after we'd partied the night away. I can't think of a better way to bow out than that.

I carried on with my BBC Radio London appearances meanwhile and on Friday 6th July 1984 I went, on Wincey's advice, to see theatrical agent Peter Charlesworth at his offices in Old Brompton Road, Earl's Court. He was (and still is) a highly influential theatrical and variety agent at the time with a considerable roster of showbiz personalities, including my all-time comedy hero Benny Hill. It was quite something to get an introduction to him. I had a big problem though. I didn't really want to do any more presenting. I wanted to go back to theatre and stage work, and yet as I had feared nearly all my work had been on radio and television with my theatre work having been heavily influenced by gay politics, and that was something which still wasn't acceptable to the mainstream. In truth I don't think he knew where to pitch me or what to do with me. Nothing came of that arrangement sadly, but it's something I have always regretted. If I had been a bit more focused upon what I really wanted to do it might have been different.

On August 16th that year I got a call to go up to Newcastle again. This was surprising as I had assumed that *The Tube* producers wouldn't touch me with a bargepole after the Equity incident. I duly turned up at the City Road studios and sat with the producers. They told me that Paula was returning for series three and that they were still open to working with me on any features that I had ideas for. Whilst I didn't definitely turn it down I really didn't relish the idea of working with Paula again and had decided that I would rather move on to something else. At which point they asked me if I would be interested in moving on to co-present the children's pop programme *Razzmatazz*? I duly screen-tested and although I wasn't overly enthusiastic at doing something so close to *The Tube* I thought it might possibly work out. That evening I met up with producer Royston Mayoh and we talked about the new series, which was being joined by a new young female presenter called Lisa Stansfield. He told me that they thought the combination would work well and I was pleased at the possibility of creating the strong on-screen partnership which had been denied to me and Muriel and which I had so wanted. Then he said something very strange. 'Of course, you would have to let us handle your PR.' At first I didn't quite get what he meant. Although I didn't have an agent still I hardly thought that a minor kids' TV show like that would ever need PR. 'Why's that?' I said. 'Well, bearing in mind it is a children's TV show... ' His words trailed off and hung in the air like frost-stiffened washing on a line.

Silence.

Then the penny dropped with almighty finality. It was clear that whilst they liked the idea of me doing the show, they were less than enthusiastic about me being openly gay. After all, this was a kids' TV show for goodness' sake. All a sign of the times I'm afraid. I don't blame Royston. He was very nice and I appreciated having been given the opportunity. But I told him that under no circumstances was I going back into the closet, that I knew who I was and that I was happy with that. I'd seen what weird things PR could do to people even without their knowledge – witness what they'd tried to do to Steve and Eartha for example.

We parted on good terms and I duly forgot about ever working up there again.

6

New York, Sydney & Neasden – 1985 onwards

On my return to London I felt a bit down. My friend BBC John had been working on a television station in Saudi Arabia and was earning more money than I had ever seen. On a visit back to London in September '84 he asked me if I had an American visa in my passport. 'What on earth would I need that for? I can't even afford to go to Bognor let alone America,' I cheerfully told him. 'You should get one anyway because it looks great in your passport,' he said enthusiastically. 'Just go to Grosvenor Square and you can apply and get one in a day.' For reasons I still can't quite fathom I did just that. It was September 18th 1984 when I duly appeared at the US Embassy and sure enough obtained my first US visa. As I came out of the Embassy I saw John waiting at the bottom of the stairs. 'Did you get it?' he said. 'Yep.' 'That's good because we are booked on the plane to New York at 3pm, get your knickers into gear we have to get to Heathrow to check in.'

'I can't go to fucking New York!' I cheerfully responded. 'Yes you can,' he said. 'Michael has packed your bags for you and I've cleared it all with him. He knows all about it and wants you to have a wonderful time.' 'But I haven't got any money, I can't go to America with no money.' 'I have,' he said reassuringly, 'and we are staying with a friend of mine on the Upper East Side.'

And with that we minced off to Heathrow Airport and within a couple of hours we were sat sitting on a Pan Am Jumbo Jet bound for JFK. This was my first ever long haul flight and the experience was surreal. The plane seemed to be full of orthodox Jewish men complaining about the food. One extremely large man sat opposite me had his Kosher meal tray slung down in front of him by a rather bored-looking Pan Am stewardess who clearly thought the job was beneath her. The ensuing verbal exchange was joyfully priceless. Forgive the crude phonetics.

'Vat de hell iss dis?' said the man in that fabulous deep New York accent, flicking the meal tray with his hand.

'It's your meal – eat it.'

'I ordered Kosher, I expect Kosher. Diss iss not Kosher!'

'Yes it is – eat it.'

'Vere is it from Kosher? It doesn't say Kosher, so I'm not eating it!'

'It says Kosher right there – look. *points at paper seal on side of tray* Now eat your meal. I'm busy.'

'Diss isn't Kosher, it's shit, dats vat diss is. Shit. Bloody Pan Am. I don't know why I'm flying in it.'

'EAT YOUR MEAL ALREADY!'

And so the extraordinary exchange went on. It was like a cabaret show at 35000 feet. I was entranced. None of the stuffiness of a British airline here. The cabin crew even did jokes in the safety demonstration by pretending the oxygen masks were puppets. Times change. I actually rather liked this. After all if anything happens when you're on a plane you're fucked aren't you? Might as well enjoy it. During the flight I'd asked John why on earth he had wanted me there. 'I didn't want to come on my own and you make me laugh,' he said kindly, not realising that this trip was to end much earlier than the week he had planned.

We arrived at JFK after 7 hours of listening to complaints about whether the food was Kosher enough and a seemingly endless loop of tinny Hall & Oates's 'Private Eye' on the plane's speakers. Fond of John as I was and appreciative of his generosity I was emotionally unprepared for such a trip. My mind was in turmoil at it all and I began to suffer anxiety. NYC in 1984 was not the free and easy vacation spot that people tend to think of it as nowadays. It was still a dodgy and potentially violent place to wander around. I was convinced we would be murdered just after passing through immigration. John, bless him, was used to my mood swings and like all my closest friends he knew instinctively when to back off and how to calm me. So he picked a yellow cab to take us into Manhattan, the interior of which was riddled with bullet holes. I cowered in the back seat as the maniac driving it weaved in and out of the impossible traffic like he was auditioning for a Luc Besson film. I am not good in cars and by the time we reached East

72nd and 3rd I had mentally made out my will and was trying to decide who to leave my records to. We piled out of the cab and John buzzed the intercom for his friend Michael with whom we were staying. From the tone of the response I was convinced that he didn't realise we were coming and even more convinced that he didn't know it wasn't just John. To my relief we ascended in the elevator and were welcomed with traditional New York hospitality. The flat was minuscule in size and it wasn't apparent to me where we were going to bivouac for the whole week. Not to worry though as I was allocated a sofa to sleep on. So that was alright then.

Probably.

John had lots planned for us. We would be seeing the new must-see film that everybody was raving about – *Ghostbusters*. Then there was the Broadway production of *La Cage Aux Folles*, which was also being raved about. But before any raving could actually take place we had to actually move about the city. I had convinced myself that the Subway was little more than a penitentiary on wheels and that we would be stabbed, shot, raped, pillaged and murdered by death whilst waiting for a train, with the same again once we were on it. So, in my brain-frazzled state of panic I made John get cabs everywhere, despite the fact that these were all so riddled with bullet holes that it was like sitting inside a colander.

I had another even bigger problem (I hope this isn't boring you?). Whilst I had removed all jewellery and dressed as inconspicuously as I could in dowdy shades of denim and grey, John was dressed up like fucking Joseph out of the Technicolor Dreamcoat. If he'd had an 8-foot floodlit sign on his back saying 'I AM A TOURIST – PLEASE MUG ME' with a big red arrow pointing downwards he couldn't have been more obvious. On the way down to 42nd St and the cinema he was wearing bright red shorts, an even brighter yellow T-shirt, a watch that probably cost the same as a small family car and clutching a black leather man bag which was quite obviously stuffed full of fresh hundred dollar bills. He seemed gloriously oblivious to it all but it was freaking me out.

By the time we left *Ghostbusters* it was dark and the whole of Times Square was lit up in all its tacky Technicolor glory. The throbbing sidewalks heaved with people avoiding each other's gazes. It somehow seemed quite right that it was also crawling with prostitutes, transvestites and drunks. These people didn't scare me as I'd always been in awe of them, and in any case I'd known so many in my early London days. I thought of them as social pioneers and marvelled at their bravery and chutzpah. Having said that I still didn't fancy getting slaughtered on 10th Avenue, so I still insisted that we got back, shut the door and moved a wardrobe in front of it until morning.

The following day my paranoia developed into healthy culture shock, which surprised even me when I realised it was happening. We ambled down Park Avenue on foot, window shopping and taking in the sheer size of everything. The awesome height of the buildings, the width of the streets which took half an hour to cross, steaming manholes and a serial killer in every darkened doorway gave me a sense of awe I hadn't experienced before. Here was I, little Gary from Tunbridge Wells, the eternal observer and rank outsider feeling completely and utterly insignificant and lost. I had grown to love London and considered myself an integral part of it. I was one of its cells being swished around its arteries and keeping its vulgar, trashy gay heart alive and beating. But here in Manhattan I felt like an invading organism. I didn't belong. Every person I met and passed in the street was a New York antibody and I was to be enveloped and destroyed before I had a chance to infect it with my Britishness.

That evening we sat through *La Cage Aux Folles* in the cheapest of seats so far up the back that we were practically in Pennsylvania. There were two women in front of us who talked and talked and talked and talked and talked all the way through it. Of course if we had been in London I'd have channelled my British outrage and told them to shut the fuck up. But this was NYC. If I'd done that I would have been shot to death with the revolvers they assuredly had in their Bloomingdales Big Brown Bags. It was ignorant behaviour, but I was assured quite accepted in the US. Whatever America was, it seemed to personify a brash and crass attitude which rendered its citizens incapable of any internal monologue. Whatever they thought they just said, no matter how insensitive, crude or inflammatory. I didn't enjoy the show and thought it was a travesty of the brilliant original French film which I had first seen in Paris and loved so much. This weird version seemed schmaltzy and soppy and desperate to present camp gay men as marrieds with all the social conventions that straight society had been hung up on since Queen Victoria decided to be not amused by anything except her own sexual excesses and peccadillos. I still hate it and have loathed its anthem 'I Am What I Am' ever since I first heard it sung there. To me it had about as much conviction as someone irritated at being given a parking ticket. This wasn't the gay utopia or acceptance we had fought for all those years. I didn't go through all that to end up in a bloody marriage! John wasn't overly impressed with it either but as he'd forked out $65 for each ticket he put on a brave face.

We'd been there for three days when I finally snapped. I couldn't bear it any more, was missing my Michael and just wanted to go home. I didn't like not having my own money there and having things done for me. I'm fiercely independent and if I was going to be murdered then I wanted to be on my own when it happened. I badgered poor John mercilessly and eventually he gave in and went off to try and get our return flights changed. Back in those days this was a major administrative exercise which involved hundreds, if not thousands of office workers sanctioning things and filling out 500 page forms in triplicate. He was sure to be gone for most of the day. He persuaded me to try venturing out on my own whilst he was out and had kindly given me some cash from his stash to enable this.

About 15 minutes after he'd gone I left the flat, went down onto the Subway and travelled to the only place I had ever wanted to see and experience in person: The Chelsea Hotel. On my own this was achievable. I blended in and quickly discovered that the same techniques of grabbing the bollocks of a city that I'd managed so well in London actually worked here too. I ducked and dived between every rapist and murderer with rare skill. I ignored the beggars and tarts like a natural. And finally there I was outside what was for me the most iconic hotel in the world. The place that so many artists, writers and musicians had either lived, been drunk at or been murdered in. From my literary heroes Dylan Thomas and William S Burroughs, to film legends Stanley Kubrick and so many of the Warhol factory starlets I had idolised: Viva, Sedgwick and Nico. Virtually all my music heroes had also lived there at one time or another: Edith Piaf, Jimi Hendrix, Joni Mitchell, Janis Joplin, Bette Midler and Alice Cooper amongst them. This was a temple for me. Experiencing places like this was my drug equivalent and I revelled in it. Sure Sid Vicious had killed girlfriend Nancy Spungen there in 1978, but in murder terms it all seemed rather appropriate for such an austere location. Why should anyone be surprised by that? Sometime Chelsea Hotel resident Quentin Crisp had said that *'I'd been told that I would be mugged and murdered on the streets when I got here, but I can honestly say that when I am not being mugged or murdered everyone I meet is my friend. New York is more like the movies than you ever imagined.'*

And of course he was right. It is.

Of course I didn't have a camera with me as that would have indicated to all and sundry that I was ripe for robbing. As I stood outside taking it all in I got talking to a young American woman who was obviously there for much the same reason as me. We laughed and chatted and shared our wonderment at this hotel of dreams.

'How long are you here for,' she said.

'I was supposed to be here for a week, but this place scares me so much that I just want to get home. My friend is changing our flight tickets as we speak and I should be flying back to London tonight,' I fessed up, rather embarrassed at how twatty it made me sound.

'Know how you feel. This place freaks me out too,' she replied.

'Really? Where are you from then?'

'Yonkers,' she said.

And at that point I began to wonder if I hadn't made a horrible mistake in leaving so early. My new found friend took a couple of snaps on her Kodak Instamatic 100 and left me alone again. I decided to venture inside the lobby and have a poke around. It was much smaller than I had imagined, but the walls were adorned with the most stunning artworks, most notably perhaps for sheer size apart from anything anything else was the Larry Rivers masterpiece 'Dutch Masters Silver', presented to the hotel management in lieu of rent some years earlier. Whilst I stood there I could see the hotel manager Stanley Bard, whom I had identified from having been glued to a recent BBC Arena documentary on the hotel, there in his office. With my new found bravery I asked if I could see him. 'Sure, just go right on in...' said the huge woman on the front desk. So I did. To my delight he welcomed me with open arms and was enthralled when I told him that the BBC programme had been a big success. He offered to show me around and spent over an hour with me regaling stories of the weird and famous residents in that glorious thick New York accent of his. 'Where are you staying right now?' he said. 'We've always got room here if you wanna come down and spend some time with us. Who knows? You may decide to stay a while?'

I suddenly felt as if the whole course of my life could well have changed at that very minute. At that very moment I could have taken this city as my home. I wanted it. Badly.

But then I realised that my misplaced, stupid paranoia meant I was soon to be flying out. I thanked Stanley and shook his hand warmly. 'You'll be back,' he said. And he was right. I would – but not for many years. 'Here, I have something for you,' he said and gave me a beautiful book of black and white photographs by Claudio Edinger, writing inside the front cover the following inscription:

'To Gary. Wishing you well & hoping you are able to spend some time with us in the near future. Stanley Bard'.

It remains to this day one of my most prized possessions.

I made my way back to the bus terminal where I had agreed to meet John and before I had a chance to tell him I had changed my mind he confirmed our seats on the TWA flight back to LHR that very night. To his credit John never once complained or gave me a rough time over this. I think he realised just how much I'd been spooked by the place. I told him of my Chelsea pilgrimage and he seemed pleased that he'd been the enabler of something I'd actually enjoyed.

The TWA flight back was every bit as bizarre as the Pan Am out. More unfunny safety demonstration jokes, which draws me to the sweeping conclusion that Americans are not interested unless they're entertained. Which could also explain some of their recent political choices and a concomitant validation of Quentin Crisp's epithet about it being *'more like the movies than you ever imagined'*. At least the movie in question wasn't an 'Airport' one, and we got back safely to Blighty in one piece.

On my return I got offered the opportunity for promotion to train driver and despite the fact that I wasn't remotely interested in that as a vocation, I needed the money. This time, without the pressure of having to hoik my carcass up to the studios in Newcastle, I actually went right through with it all and finally passed the driving exams on November 8th 1984 from which point I drove trains on the Metropolitan & Circle Lines, before transferring to the Central Line in 1985. As I promised earlier I would not dwell on this dreary side of my life save for three stories. You've been subjected to two vaguely amusing ones; I only wish that I could say the final one was too, but it isn't.

I had trained alongside a small group of other hopefuls including a very sweet guy from the same depot as me called Tim. He knew his stuff well and had always been a kind, gentle and friendly guy to work with there when we were both guards. Like me he had passed the exams with flying colours and we'd both then gone on to complete the final driver training requirements involving thrilling subjects such as rolling stock familiarisation, fault finding and road training (where train drivers learn the routes they'll be working over for track, signalling, communications and train handling).

Still awake?

After ploughing through all that guff, if you're successful you finally get certificated and authorised to drive trains alone as a fully fledged and qualified train driver. Tim and I both did all that and were enthusiastically looking forward to a much increased weekly pay packet. Tim had recently married and his wife was pregnant with their first child, so they really needed the money. All I had was a mortgage and several permanently maxed out credit cards, as is the case with all responsible gay men. Tim had his first day driving on his own on Tuesday 11th December, and mine was booked for that Friday 14th. That Tuesday I had the day off and was planning to go up to Wembley to meet with a friend for lunch. It was quite a schlep from Roehampton up to Wembley so I'd left home fairly early. It was a cold day with the promise of some blue skies later on once the sun had burnt off the thick, dense fog which was blanketing London. When I reached Baker Street I was irritated to discover that both the northbound Jubilee and Metropolitan Lines were suspended owing to an 'incident' at Kilburn. I didn't particularly think anything of it as we were always getting signal failures and the like, so I just swapped over to the Bakerloo Line and made my way north, getting a bus across to Wembley Park to complete my journey. As I walked through Wembley Park station I saw a couple of my colleagues on the concourse and asked them what had happened down at Kilburn.

'There's been a collision.'

'What?! Met or Jubilee?'

'Met.'

'Oh my god. Who was on it?'

'As a matter of fact we thought it was you, but then someone told us it was Tim.'

My blood froze.

'How is he? Is he OK?'

'No. He's dead.'

And with those three terrible words time froze. Even typing this thirty-five years later I am barely able to describe what hearing that did to me. All I could think of was my friend, my lovely friend. I had never lost anyone I was that close to before. We were only in our mid 20s. This isn't how things are supposed to be. For the first time ever I'd been faced with a finality I wasn't even remotely prepared for. Poor Tim had been killed on the very first day of driving a train on his own after he'd passed a red signal in the thick fog and then made a number of procedural errors which would prove to be fatal. I will not go into details; that isn't why I am writing this. It is significant to me and the way my mind deals with adversity and pressure. Whilst I seem to be unnerved and rattled at what most people would consider to be ridiculously insignificant things like dropping a spoon or walking into an untidy room, I have a curious capacity to steel up and compartmentalise extreme bad things like I'm packing away house contents for a move. When Tim died I didn't know what to do and this was unusual for me. I went back into the depot and found my trainer and mentor Terry. I told him I didn't think I wanted to do this anymore. It wasn't as if this was my career or vocation in any way. It was proof to me that I wasn't supposed to be there; that I belonged on stage doing what I had always wanted from my life and the only job that really meant anything to me. Despite the comfort, support and reassurance Terry gave to me things never really felt the same there after that. And that is why I am happy to leave it at that for the railways. No more. Breathe easy (or wake up, whichever is the more appropriate).

Meanwhile I began to get more involved with theatre through my local Equity branch at the Lyric Theatre in Hammersmith. With the friendship and encouragement of acclaimed actor Vivian Pickles I became a member of the Riverside Studios Actors & Writers Workshop, which has now become Actors Writers London (AWL). This wonderful group exists to promote the work of new writers by having their plays performed in rehearsed readings. I have now been doing this for over 35 years and I'm proud to say the group is still going strong. Most plays which we perform are still in the development stage. Some are accomplished enough to go forward into production quite rapidly, whilst others are a little more... err... difficult to imagine on stage, radio or TV in their current state.

One evening when the group still met at the old Riverside Studios on the banks of the Thames at Hammersmith, a play was being read called *Roses Of Picardy*. Thankfully I wasn't in it, and as usual I was sat with my wee posse of fellow actors Barbara Keogh, Jane Partridge, Joan Geary, Lewis Rae and Sarah Brown. The room we used there was very dimly lit by only a few meagre bare lightbulbs and it was at times very hard to see the scripts we were reading. This particular play had been going for what seemed like hours and was painfully dreary. Its author also seemed to have had his world wars muddled up. The action (such as it was) was set in the Second World War. As my mind drifted in and out I had started to wonder why he'd named it after a song which is more usually identified with the First World War? The play went on and on and on and on – a bit like this book – and eventually I was reduced to writing notes to Sarah who was sitting next to me.

'Can you imagine anyone ever having to learn all this?' I wrote on the programme, nudged her and passed it surreptitiously across my lap to hers.

A minute or two passed and I felt her nudge me and pass the paper and pencil back. I looked down to see she'd written:

'I don't think anyone will ever have to.'

At that point I started to laugh. I am not proud of this and would usually frown on such behaviour. But I couldn't help it. It felt like we'd been in there since before either World War and there was no sign this play was ever going to end. The more I tried to stifle my laughter the worse it got. I buried my head in my hands and bit my clenched fists so hard I almost drew blood. Then I felt Sarah and Barbara trembling as they also succumbed to stifled hysterics. Somehow, I managed to stop myself from bursting out aloud and after a few days the play ground to a halt and the cast stood up for their much justified applause and bows.

After the discussion the writer came up to me and said, 'I was very moved to see just how much the meaning of the play affected you. Thank you!'

He had obviously observed my physical contortions and assumed I'd been crying.

I am not usually vulnerable to corpsing on stage and it's something I generally frown on, but probably the worst case of this I ever suffered was also at AWL in a curious play I was in about an entire family who hadn't realised they were actually dead and were trying to go about their daily business as ghosts. Lewis Rae and I played the young lads of the family, with his character having apparently been riding around on the back of a motorbike. The plot was so odd that I daren't go into any more detail than that. I was charged with saying to him 'Where have you been?', to which his reply was, 'I've been taken up the A1,' at which point I looked straight into Lewis's eyes and we both collapsed into fits of uncontrollable laughter. To this very day if we are ever cast in a play together we have to take care not to look directly at each other as it can be dangerous.

Despite the fact that I found it very hard to get taken seriously as an actor after having done so much presenting work, I even auditioned at one point for a role in a *Dr Who* series. I duly went along to the old BBC Studios at the Shepherds Bush Theatre in West London (scene of so many of my childhood favourite TV shows such as *Crackerjack* and *The Generation Game*) to be interviewed by the producer and director. All seemed to be going well until one of them told me that in this series there would be a new assistant for the esteemed Doctor. 'Oh yes,' I said, 'and who is that then?'

'Bonnie Langford,' he proudly announced.

Overcome with incredulity at what seemed like a bizarre casting in my book, and without thinking of the consequences I laughed out loud and repeated 'BONNIE LANGFORD?!?!' whilst pulling a face that clearly indicated my utter bafflement at the choice.

I didn't get the part.

Bum.

I would have loved that too. My big mouth had let me down again.

In early '85 whilst over at the old Kensington Market, famed for its fashion wear and grooviness in general, I happened to stumble across my old friend Muriel getting out of a taxi. We had sadly drifted apart since I'd stopped appearing on the show and we'd barely spoken since the last *Midsummer Night's Tube*. Paula Yates was now back on the programme and she would be there until its demise in 1987. We hugged and exchanged pleasantries, like you do, but something was strangely missing. For some reason our old spark just wasn't there. On reflection it was probably nothing more than change. It happens doesn't it? There was no animosity or bad feeling but inside I felt curiously like someone she didn't want to be seen with. I'd be a liar if I said I wasn't disappointed, although I wasn't cross with her for it; I could never be that as I adored her so much. When I got home that evening with my new knife-edge, flat-top haircut which I could have cut paper with, my mind was truly in that overdrive mode I hated so much. I secretly blamed Paula for poisoning Muriel's mind against me and the programme makers for splitting us up, not letting us work together more and other ridiculous rubbish. All that had actually happened was that we'd moved on. It was really no more than I had done to some of my own close friends over the years.

My mainstream TV and radio work had even led to me becoming estranged from my dearest and closest friend Phil Cox. As time went by I saw less and less of him. After having spent some years living and working abroad in the 1990s I lost touch altogether. I was deeply saddened to discover only a few years ago that Phil had died sometime in the late 1990s. I still don't know the circumstances and have been unable to find anything more, even by using the wonders of the internet as a search tool. Phil isn't mentioned in any official or published histories of the gay rights movement in London. As a result of this his dedicated work and passion for justice and liberty is all but forgotten, lost in the muddle of a history that seems still to only focus upon a few famous and infamous figures. There were so many more activists all of whom deserve to have their place acknowledged and their stories told. In March 2009 I placed a tribute page to Phil on my website to give him a web presence. I was subsequently thrilled to learn that he'd left his entire sound archive of taped audio recordings to the British Library for posterity. I was even more moved to find that amongst the boxes of reel-to-reel tapes of old Gaywaves shows and other miscellaneous gay related radio and TV recordings were all my old sketches and interviews, and that he'd copyrighted them all to me. For him to have done this so long after we had made them and despite us not having seen each other for years is deeply moving to me.

How Phil's geekery would have loved the sheer scale and possibilities of this internet age. But he is not forgotten. That one small tribute page on my website, and now this book will ensure his part in the history of the British Gay movement is duly recorded and acknowledged, just as it should be. He was my dearest of friends and I loved him and miss him terribly even now. Sometimes being an atheist is a great comfort.

At this point I suppose I should tie up a few other loose ends before I bugger off and let you get on.

Record plugger Ian Goddard passed away a couple of years ago, although I rarely saw him after the 1980s drew to a close. The demon drink had sadly taken its toll over the years. Michael had kept in touch with him throughout his final months. It's good to know that he wasn't alone.

I am still in touch with my old school friends Sally, Carol, Jackie and Kristine, all of whom look and sound exactly the same to me now as they did when we left school back in 1974. They have the secret of eternal youth. If you want to find out how it's done then why not pop them a note through? I'm sure they won't mind sharing with you. In fact, I'm seeing them for lunch this weekend. Would you like to come? You're very welcome. The dialogue is likely to be somewhat crude though. It always is when we get together. Let me know and I'll make sure we have a bigger table up the pub.

You might recall that I said I'd close off the Dad 1 bit? We were finally reunited in Australia in 1996 after twenty-seven years. It was an uneasy experience for both of us. I had decided to stay in a hotel in the centre of Sydney rather than with any family members, as I really wasn't sure how it would all go. I had two half-brothers whom I'd never met. What if they were Westies or Bogans? (You might have to look that up if you're not an Aussie). I knew they were all heavily into sport, just as almost everyone in Dad 1's side of the family were. What would they do when they discovered I preferred the Eurovision Song Contest to Cricket?

Despite all this the most important thing as far as I was concerned was to try and clear my mind of the hurt and confusion that had devastated me as a child on losing the person I loved more than anyone else. After an oddly polite and formal reunion at the airport we went back to the family house in the Western suburbs of Sydney for a traditional Aussie barbie. Later that afternoon I asked if I could speak with him in private. We sat somewhat uncomfortably together at the kitchen table. 'Ask me anything you want son.' He actually called me 'son'. Nobody had ever done this before. 'I've waited all these years to ask you this,' I said nervously but resolute. 'Why did you leave me?'. It was the pin that pricked the proverbial balloon, and with that he broke down in front of me and wept. I had not realised just how tough that break-up had been for him too. At that precise moment everything I'd waited all those years to say to him seemed pointless. Here we were, two adult men, talking about something that had happened for whatever reason so long ago. I couldn't do this to him. So, I backed off and we left it there never to speak of it again. We saw each other many times in the years that followed and over the years I've become close to my Aussie family. My stepbrothers and their families are terrific fun and I relish the time we spend together. Dad passed away a few years ago at the age of 86.

Through the wonders of modern technology I am now back in touch with Muriel Gray, Michael Metcalf and Mark Miwurdz (Hurst) from *The Tube* and also with Roy, John, Gary and Alex from BBC Radio London. They have helped me to put a lot of these recollected memories into some context, although to be honest I doubt any of it is very profound. It was after all entertainment. If it hadn't been for the badgering of my friends in the Twitterverse I doubt I would ever have bothered writing this down either. So, let it be said that this is my story. And in the words of my comedy hero Frankie Howerd, 'If you like it, tell your friends. If you don't; keep your big mouth shut!'